Style Wise

Style Wise

A Practical Guide to Becoming a Fashion Stylist

Second Edition

SHANNON BURNS-TRAN
JENNY B. DAVIS

FAIRCHILD BOOKS

NEW YORK · LONDON · OXFORD · NEW DELHI · SYDNEY

FAIRCHILD BOOKS
Bloomsbury Publishing Inc
1385 Broadway, New York, NY 10018, USA
50 Bedford Square, London, WC1B 3DP, UK

BLOOMSBURY, FAIRCHILD BOOKS and the Fairchild Books logo are trademarks
of Bloomsbury Publishing Plc

First edition published in the United States of America 2013
This edition first published 2018
Reprinted 2019 (twice)

Cover design: Anna Perotti/By the Sky design
Cover image © Getty Images

Library of Congress Cataloging-in-Publication Data
Names: Burns-Tran, Shannon, author. | Davis, Jenny B., author.
Title: Style wise : a practical guide to becoming a fashion stylist.
Other titles: Stylewise
Description: Second edition / Shannon Burns-Tran, Jenny B. Davis. | New York : Fairchild Books,
an imprint of Bloomsbury Publishing, Inc., 2018. | Includes index.
Identifiers: LCCN 2017031034 | ISBN 9781501323768 (pbk.)
Subjects: LCSH: Fashion design—Vocational guidance. | Image consultants—Vocational guidance. |
Fashion—Vocational guidance. | Fashion designers. | Fashion photography.
Classification: LCC TT507 .B835 2018 | DDC 746.9/2023—dc23
LC record available at https://lccn.loc.gov/2017031034

ISBN: PB: 978-1-5013-2376-8
ePDF: 978-1-5013-2377-5
eBook: 978-1-5013-2378-2

Typeset by Lachina

To find out more about our authors and books visit www.fairchildbooks.com
and sign up for our newsletter.

Contents

Extended Contents

Chapter 8   Fashion Lexicon: Terms, Icons, History, and Inspiration 181

Chapter 9 Preparing for a Test Shoot 209

Preface

Style Wise: A Practical Guide to Becoming a Fashion Stylist offers a comprehensive approach to styling to help aspiring stylists understand what it takes to establish a career in styling. It not only answers questions that many students commonly ask about styling but also goes many steps further by addressing feedback received from fashion stylists with established careers. The result is a book that presents the variety of career options that styling encompasses, shows how to establish a career in styling, and lays out the base knowledge that stylists must have to work in the industry.

Style Wise is meant to be a resource for the aspiring stylist striving to build an inspired and relevant portfolio. It provides sources of inspiration, instruction, and information to help an aspiring stylist through his or her first gig, whether that's a test, an assisting job, a client appointment, or a position with a wardrobe department. The book also includes material about terminology, history, photography, product recommendations, and best business practices that a stylist can reference again and again throughout his or her career.

Even fashion students who do not plan to enter the fashion styling profession will find value in this book. Every chapter has specific, real-world information that includes professional resources for stylists and nonstylists alike, including important advice on such topics as professional etiquette with clients and on set, industry terms, clothing and accessory terms and categories, and social media branding and networking.

ORGANIZATION OF THE BOOK

Style Wise easily can be integrated into a styling-class curriculum. The organization of the book is based on years of teaching fashion styling to upper-level college students.

Part I: The Fashion Styling Profession

The first half of the book focuses on the different areas of the styling industry. It provides an overview of print styling for magazines, wardrobe styling for film, theater, and television, personal and celebrity styling, and other areas of styling that go beyond fashion. It covers the ins and outs of each area of the industry, from understanding the fashion season and sourcing to considering a freelance career versus a salaried job for a publication or studio.

Chapter 1, "Introduction to Fashion Styling," provides the reader with an overview of the profession of fashion styling, beginning with what stylists do, progressing through a survey of the main categories of fashion styling, and concluding with an examination of the skills and personality traits that stylists need to succeed.

Chapter 2, "Photo Styling," covers both professional information and personal tips for the freelance stylist working in both editorial and commercial areas of styling for magazines, catalogues, advertisements, and other types of traditional media. Chapter 3 takes a similar approach toward "Styling for the Entertainment Industry," exploring aspects of dressing actors and musicians on set and on stage. Chapter 4, "Image Consulting," explores styling clients on an individual basis, focusing primarily upon personal shopping and celebrity styling, while Chapter 5, "Careers in Styling," explores additional employment opportunities like runway styling and visual merchandising, along with styling props, food styling, and styling for digital media, including blogs and Instagram feeds.

Part II: Getting Established as a Fashion Stylist

The second half of the book delves into the details of exactly how to create a portfolio, establish a business, and get started as a freelance stylist. It covers everything from how to organize a photo shoot for the first time to resources for creating a personal website. This half of the book also provides sources of inspiration and prepares readers by taking them step-by-step through a shoot, from preparation and pulling to next-day returns, and it provides guidance in the basic requirements for setting up a business, managing a studio, networking, and booking jobs. It also includes valuable reference materials that a stylist can consult throughout his or her career.

Chapter 6, "Portfolio Building, Branding, and Networking," sets out guidelines for creating a stylist's personal brand, in person and online. In Chapter 7, "Business 101 for Freelance Stylists," includes essential information about what stylists need to know to establish themselves, including creating a business plan, setting up an office and an accounting system, and what agency representation entails. Aspiring and established stylists will appreciate the depth of resource material presented in Chapter 8, "Fashion Lexicon: Terms, Icons, History, and Inspiration," which covers basic fashion terms and design principles, biographies of fashion icons, and explanations and lists of myriad references ranging from movies and magazines to subcultures that stylists consider touchstones for fashion shoot inspiration. Aspiring stylists will get a step-by-step guide to fashion shoot production in Chapter 9, "Preparing for a Test Shoot," and will gain valuable insight into every aspect of being part of a professional fashion shoot team in the final chapter, "At the Shoot."

NEW TO THIS EDITION

Tables and Charts

Photo Illustration, etc.

Text Features

Tables and Charts

The text includes many tables and charts that summarize key information and resources. Each table has been carefully created for students to quickly and easily reference and continue to use after they have completed the styling course. Examples of this information include styling supply sources, garment style guides, important art movements, influential movies, and much more.

Photo Illustrations and Sample Documents

The book contains more than 150 full-color illustrations showing tools and techniques of the trade, stylists at work in each of the areas of styling, and sample documents used by both emerging and seasoned stylists at the top of their careers.

Quotes and Bios

Working stylists and other fashion professionals contribute their advice and experience throughout every chapter, lending a personal touch to the instructional materials.

Glossary

Comprising terms and concepts that students will encounter in real-world professional settings, the glossary defines each chapter's list of Key Terms (bolded in the chapter text). Becoming familiar with these terms will allow the student to hold an educated conversation and negotiate for future jobs.

Chapter Summaries and Reviews

Each chapter ends with a summary for students to review chapter content and a list of that chapter's Key Terms. It also includes teacher-friendly questions to further encourage students to engage with key concepts in the text. Instructors can use these chapter questions as weekly assignments with a consistent weekly grading weight or point value.

Learning Activities

Learning Activities at the end of each chapter provide numerous assignment and project ideas.

INSTRUCTOR'S RESOURCES

Instructor's Guide

The Instructor's Guide provides more assignments, projects, and class activities. It also provides grading rubrics for the assignments that clearly communicate expectations to students as well as answers to chapter-review questions and tests with answer keys. The tests are downloadable, as are the grading rubrics.

STUDENT RESOURCES

Style Wise **STUDIO**
- Study smarter with self-quizzes featuring scored results and personalized study tips
- Review concepts with flashcards of terms and definitions and image identification
- Access samples of documents, forms, and templates for all stages of planning a photo shoot, including a call sheet form, supply checklist, planning calendars, and more

A SOLID FOUNDATION FOR SUCCESSFUL CAREERS

After reading this book and engaging in the activities that *Style Wise* offers, students who are motivated and serious about styling should be more than adequately prepared to enter the styling industry and commence an exciting and successful career.

ACKNOWLEDGMENTS

From Jenny B. Davis
I'd like to thank my family for their support and encouragement through the revision of this manuscript. My daughters Ellie and Coco got dinner on the table every night while I worked, and my husband Steve kept my internet connected and my data backups current, despite my best efforts to blow away my files. My parents, Richard and Kathy, also helped with meals and encouragement, and my mother-in-law, Paula, handled many more school pickups than usual.

I am beyond grateful to have been able to spend the past decade as a professional photo shoot stylist, fashion editor, and fashion journalist, and I've worked with countless amazing people. Thanks specifically to Cameron Silver for always being a terrific interviewee and a welcoming face at every fashion show, to Teri Agins for being so generous with her time and advice, to the Ralph Lauren PR Team, and to the creative types who have taught me so much about making beautiful images over the years: hair and makeup artists Walter Fuentes, Rocio Vielma, and L. B. Rosser; art director Jeremy Cannon; photographers Ross Hailey, Samantha Jane Beatty, and Simon Lopez; and social media star Elizabeth Savetsky (@excessoriesexpert). A million thank-yous to professional coach and motivational guru Ellen Malloy, whose friendship and tough love taught me how to contain my commitments to make room for opportunity, and to the incredibly talented novelist Julie Lawson Timmer for believing that I had a book in me—and making me believe it, too. Finally, I am grateful to Dr. Lorynn Divita, one of the most talented, dedicated, and inspirational women I have ever met. Thank you, Dr. D—our next Duran Duran concert is my treat!

From the Publisher

Fairchild Books wishes to gratefully acknowledge and thank the reviewers who have contributed to this revision: Lisa Newell, Dominican University; Billi Arnett, Clark Atlanta University; Carmen Carter, El Centro College; Arcadia Maximo, Community College of San Francisco; and Carol J. Salusso, Washington State University. Additional thanks to Rachel Wood for her contribution to the interviews and quotes. Bloomsbury Publishing wishes to gratefully acknowledge and thank the editorial team involved in the publication of this book: Senior Acquisitions Editor: Amanda Breccia; Assistant Editor: Kiley Kudrna; Art Development Editor: Edie Weinberg; Photo Researcher: Rona Tuccillo; In-House Designer: Eleanor Rose; Production Manager: Claire Cooper; Project Manager: Chris Black.

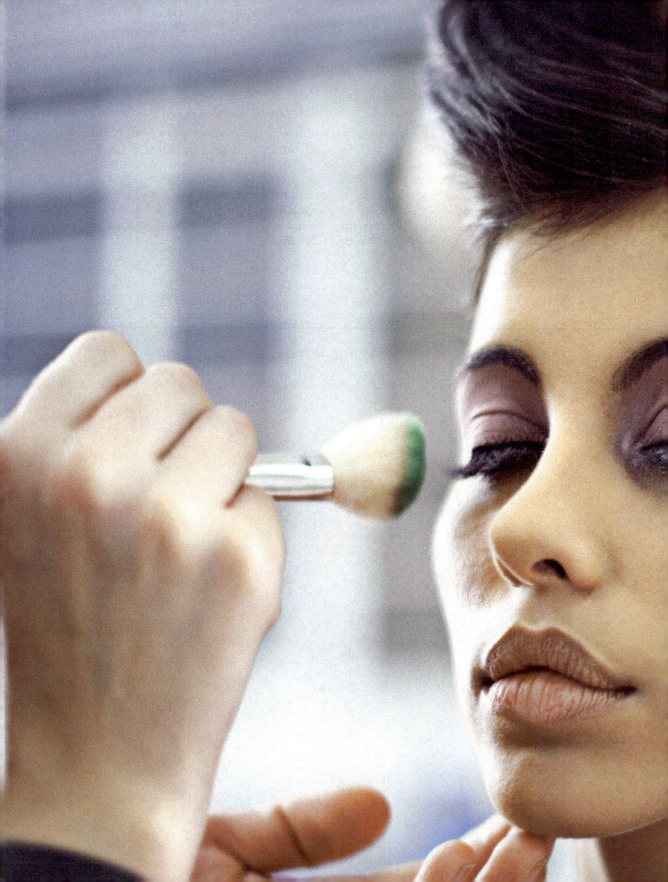

PART ONE

The Fashion Styling Profession

1 Introduction to Fashion Styling

CHAPTER TOPICS CALL SHEET

In this chapter you will learn:

- What is fashion styling?
- What fashion styling entails
- The three main specialties of fashion styling
- Diversifying into other areas of styling
- What it means to be freelance vs. salaried
- Personality traits that a stylist needs to succeed
- Ten how-to skills that a stylist must master
- How to spot trends

THE BASICS OF FASHION STYLING

In the broadest sense, **styling** means arranging things in a visually pleasing way. The items arranged can be clothes, furniture, food, or even a person's appearance, as in hair and makeup. Styling is a creative endeavor, and the person doing the styling—the stylist—must be artistically inclined, visually talented, and able to work as part of a team to create a stunning image.

Fashion styling is the process of orchestrating clothing and other fashion products to be photographed, filmed, presented, or worn. The **fashion stylist** is responsible for coordinating the clothing, accessories, and other fashion merchandise to create a specific outfit, image, or look. Fashion styling is an essential element of magazine photo shoots, runway shows, television shows, commercials, catalogues, Instagram posts, red carpet galas, movies, and music videos. Additionally, many regular people rely on fashion stylists to help keep their wardrobes current and to make sure they are appropriately dressed for business meetings, special events, and vacations.

Fashion styling doesn't involve designing clothing. It involves putting together existing pieces to make ensembles. There are three main subsets of fashion styling: print, entertainment industry, and image management.

To best serve their clients across all subsets of the business, fashion stylists need to stay on top of fashion trends and industry news. They must be well versed in what designers are showing on runways, what colors are on-trend, and what retailers have in stock.

A stylist must be able to identify the important **themes** arising in each season's most important fashion collections. A theme occurs when multiple designers show the same trend. There are always multiple themes each season. For example, athletic-inspired clothing is a popular theme that includes tracksuits, race-stripe detailing, and utilitarian embellishments such as clips and large zippers.

It's a stylist's job to determine the best way to incorporate a season's key themes into the styling work that he or she is doing for a client. A stylist working on a magazine feature might want to take the athletic-inspired theme to the extreme with a head-to-toe runway look. A stylist working to dress a celebrity for a luncheon, however, might only incorporate a touch of that theme—perhaps a striped purse with a large zipper, or designer tennis shoes—to bring a dash of current fashion to an otherwise classic look. (See Figure 1.1a–c.)

But understanding what's happening on the runways isn't enough. Fashion stylists also must possess a working knowledge of fashion history, street style, art, and culture to be able to put themes into context. This knowledge allows them to interpret themes and to forecast what's next.

Magazines, films, and artworks are essential viewing for designers and stylists alike. Often stylists are masters at piecing disparate elements together, drawing influences from fashion, photography, history, cinema, books, and art. All of these inspirations become part of a stylist's vocabulary of visual influences, as we'll explore more in Chapter 8.

[
"Getting a little fashion history under your belt can really help when a client is making references to a period of time, photographer or designer, this way you can help understand their vision and know what they're talking about."
—Chiara Solloa, stylist. "Interview: Life Lessons and Styling Advice with Celebrity Stylist, Chiara Solloa," Huffington Post, http:huffingtonpost.com/Christina-scribner/interview-life-lessons-an_b_5684939.html
]

Misconceptions About Styling

Many people new to styling envision it as a glamorous job filled with top models, hot celebrities, and expensive designer clothing. They might imagine a day spent putting together their favorite outfits from stocked rolling racks nestled in the corner of a sleek Manhattan studio, where techno music is pumping, a delicious buffet of sushi and mini cupcakes appears at lunchtime, and an army of assistants are hovering around, ready to rush to Starbucks whenever anyone craves a latte.

Unfortunately, this is not the reality for most stylists. A select few do work with the biggest names and have extensive budgets, but most stylists work with lesser-known people and adhere to tight spending caps on fashion as well as food. Often stylists work with everyday clothing instead of the newest looks. (See Figure 1.2.) They work long hours on their feet, and they do it wherever, however, and whenever they have to. That can mean a 4:30 a.m. call to beat the summer heat on an outdoor shoot, sewing a celebrity into her dress when her zipper breaks moments before the red carpet begins, or helping to lug heavy camera gear to a remote shoot location. Ask any fashion stylist if he or she has a war story, and you're sure to get an earful.

Figure 1.1a–c
Sometimes in one season multiple designers might show athletic-inspired looks on their runways. Each fashion season has multiple themes from many different designers.

Another common misconception is that stylists spend all their time doing creative, artistic things. Unfortunately, success in styling relies as much on business acumen as it does on creativity. A stylist must master a wide variety of nonglamorous tasks like recording earnings, keeping track of mileage and expenses, tracking incoming and outgoing packages, and filing taxes.

A stylist also must strive to cultivate and maintain **client** relationships at all times. A client is the business, company, or person who hires the stylist. The client can be anyone from a fashion magazine to a food company, from an office-supply manufacturer to a clothing manufacturer. Stylists also rely on professional relationships within retailers, design houses, showrooms, and public relations agencies to access merchandise for shoots. These contacts can be especially helpful if a shoot calls for exclusive or expensive items or a very short turnaround time.

This means that events like art openings and fashion shows are not fun opportunities to wear crazy outfits, drink free wine, and take selfies with friends. Rather, they are professional networking events where you must project a professional image in appearance and behavior. Every person you meet could help you land that next job, earn that next paycheck, and build up to an even bigger opportunity to further your career.

Figure 1.2
In this behind-the-scenes photo, the fashion stylist, makeup artist, and photographer are preparing to shoot the model.

"Let me tell you, working in fashion is not easy. In fact, it can be a total pain . . . ! People in the industry can be incredibly critical, even mean. Experiencing that didn't just toughen me up. It helped me to stay strong in my own opinions."
—Christian Siriano, fashion designer. Christian Siriano and Rennie Dyball, Fierce Style:
How to Be Your Most Fabulous Self (New York: Grand Central Publishing, 2009), 99.

WHAT FASHION STYLING ENTAILS

A fashion stylist's job is to help a creative team create an **effective image**, one that visually communicates the client's message and speaks to a target audience.

A typical creative team includes an art director, a photographer, a hair stylist, a makeup artist, and **talent**. The talent is the person in front of the camera lens. This might be a model, actor, or just an everyday person.

The fashion stylist's contribution to the team is to provide the fashion: basically, the clothing, shoes, and jewelry. While it sounds simple, it's not. The job of styling involves a decision-making process about what clothing and accessories are needed to create the image. The stylist must decide what items are needed to put together a complete look, and he or she also must be able to coordinate pattern and color in cohesive and creative ways. Then, the stylist must source everything while adhering to restrictions such as budgets and timelines. (See Figure 1.3.)

During the shoot, the stylist must ensure that all clothing and accessories are camera-ready. He or she must help dress and undress the model in every ensemble and monitor the clothing during the shoot so that each piece presents perfectly, whether it's on camera or in person, with no gaps, folds, wrinkles, or other problems. When the shoot wraps, the stylist must ensure that all items are returned in pristine condition and that all necessary information about the clothing is given to the proper person, if required. This is a time-consuming, detailed, and often stressful process, and stylists are hired for their expertise and efficiency in getting this job done.

THREE MAIN SPECIALTIES OF FASHION STYLING

There are many avenues to choose from within fashion styling. Overall, styling can be broken down into three general areas of specialty: *print*, *entertainment industry*, and *image management*. (See Figure 1.4.)

Print Styling

Print styling involves creating images used for selling or marketing purposes, including photographs for magazines, billboards, advertisements, brochures, catalogues, look books, ecommerce sites and commercially produced e-zines, blogs, and Instagram feeds. Any corporate client that creates sales or marketing materials can potentially hire a fashion stylist, from a medical supply company to the electric company to a bank.

There are two subsets of print styling: editorial and lifestyle. **Editorial styling** is the high-fashion styling seen in fashion magazines, and this tends to be more artistic and fashion-forward. **Lifestyle styl-ing** focuses on a more overtly commercial goal, like a department store advertisement, a website, or an advertisement where fashion is not what's being sold but the models hired to promote the product in the photo—maybe a car or a prescription drug—obviously need to be wearing clothes. Lifestyle styling is not always as creative as editorial styling; however, it often pays more.

Entertainment Industry Styling

Entertainment industry styling requires dressing professional performers who are being filmed or watched by the public, such as characters in movies and television shows, and musicians performing on stage or in videos. **Wardrobe styling** is fashion styling for television shows,

Figure 1.3
It is important for fashion stylists to have an eye for color. Sometimes this means putting some unexpected combinations together. Here pink, red, purple, green, and turquoise work together to create an attention-getting image.

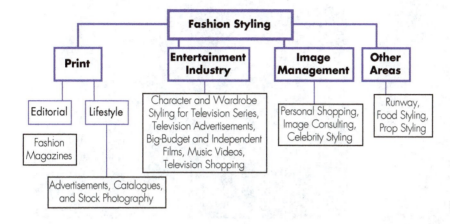

Figure 1.4
Styling can be broken down into three general areas of specialty—print, entertainment industry, and image management—as well as many other types of styling that go beyond fashion or what may be typically thought of as fashion.

movies, music videos, plays, music performances, or commercials. This styling entails dressing talent who move and talk as opposed to simply posing. Wardrobe stylists are not to be confused with costume designers. Unlike costume designers, they don't construct entire garments from scratch. Instead, they work with existing garments and accessories to create costumes and outfits for talent to wear while they're performing. (See Figure 1.5a–b.)

Image Management Styling

Image management is providing clothing and accessories to people who are wearing real clothes in the real world. It includes wardrobe consulting, personal shopping, and celebrity styling. Independent personal stylists and personal shoppers on the staff at a retailer often serve the same goal: to help their mostly high-net-worth clientele build and manage wardrobes, dress for events, and pack for trips.

This category also includes celebrity stylists, who are usually hired by movie studios to clothe talent for such events as red carpet appearances, press tours, and junkets. All fashion stylists who work with real people must master the art of dressing men and women of all shapes, sizes, and ethnicities. These stylists have a superior understanding of body shape, silhouette, construction, color, fabric, fit, and even how daylight and camera flashes affect clothing. They are often well versed in the customs, etiquette, and seasonal clothing requirements of popular destinations like Aspen or Saint Barths and popular events like Coachella and the Cannes Film Festival.

DIVERSIFYING INTO OTHER AREAS OF STYLING

Many stylists who work regularly in print and the entertainment industries diversify into other areas to keep their paychecks consistent. In smaller cities, the broader a stylist is, the more he or she might work.

Figure 1.5a–b
Stylists for characters in film or television often might not work with the newest or edgiest fashion; in fact, most television and film characters sport everyday looks.

Runway Styling

Runway styling, which is closely related to fashion styling, involves consulting with a design house on how to best present its collection. Often a designer needs an outside eye to help edit a collection to be presented during a fashion show to ensure that the looks coming down the runway communicate the designer's overall vision of the season. Runway stylists help refine head-to-toe looks, and they help designers coordinate accessories with clothing before they hit the runway. (See Figure 1.6.)

"As a fashion show producer, I hire stylists to make the designers lives easier. Stylists are key to the designer's vision. They help them with tasks like pairing accessories and shoes to rearranging the entire collection. The creativity and eye of a stylist are qualities that can't be taught."

—Adriana Marie, CEO and founder of fashion show production company AMCONYC (www.amconyc.com)

Food Styling

Food styling is the art of making food and beverages look appetizing in photographs or on film. The dishes and drinks that are shot for advertising campaigns and that appear in movies and commercials are not what they appear to be. Photography and filming can take a lot of time, and food doesn't look appetizing for long when it's sitting out, often under hot lights. It's a food stylist's job to know all the "tricks of the trade" to substitute, fake, and cheat ingredients to make everything look delicious. For example, a

Figure 1.6
Garments are steamed backstage before hitting the runway.

food stylist might use clear acrylic cubes in a drink instead of real ice cubes, flecking the outside of the glass with glycerin droplets to make the drink look cold. Pasta is often undercooked to make it look better on camera, and a scoop of mashed potatoes makes an excellent substitute for ice cream. Because food styling is so highly specialized, most fashion stylists don't do it. However, it can be helpful for a fashion stylist to know some of the basics in case a photo shoot includes any edible elements. (See Figures 1.7a and 1.7b.)

Prop Styling

Stylists who do **prop styling** and **set styling** work with objects to help create a setting for a shoot. They might work on the sets of television shows, films, commercials, home-catalogue shoots, and magazine shoots. These stylists work with draperies, furniture, and home accessories. (See Figure 1.8.) Their job is to make sure every item on a set is in place and in the proper condition. The background setting in a shot is as important as the foreground. Creating a believable setting is essential for films, commercials, and television shows alike. (See Figure 1.9.)

TOOLS OF THE TRADE THAT EVERY STYLIST MUST HAVE

Every fashion stylist must own a **styling kit** (or stylist kit). This is a portable case or bag filled with tools of the trade that a stylist uses to do the job, whether on the set and or in a styling studio, dressing room, or client's home. Every stylist is responsible for putting together his or her own kit and for keeping it stocked, clean, and organized. There is no "one-size-fits-all" kit; every fashion stylist's kit is different, depending on

Figure 1.7a
Food stylists work with food to make it look appetizing. In this shot the greens are painstakingly arranged on top of bacon and eggs. The food stylist selected the plate and added ground black pepper to further enhance the image.

Figure 1.7b
People love to post their meals on social media sites. Sometimes the plates are shown from above, before any food has been eaten. Here we see a meal midway, and a human touch as well!

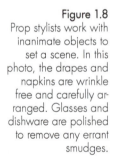

Figure 1.8
Prop stylists work with inanimate objects to set a scene. In this photo, the drapes and napkins are wrinkle free and carefully arranged. Glasses and dishware are polished to remove any errant smudges.

his or her experience and styling specialty. There are, however, some essentials that every kit will contain: pins, double-stick tape, masking tape, a small sewing kit, and a retagging gun to reattach garment tags. Also, most fashion stylists own a fabric steamer, a garment rack, and garment bags. Chapter 9 offers a more detailed list of styling kit essentials and essential equipment.

What It Means to Be Freelance vs. Salaried

Some stylists are salaried, while others are freelance. Salaried stylists work at their employer's office, whereas freelance stylists are self-employed and are responsible for finding their own jobs. Both types of jobs have their pros and cons.

Salaried Stylists

Salaried stylists often work for magazines or retailers as part of their full-time staff. A stylist on a magazine staff might be known as a *fashion editor*, while a stylist at a retailer may have the job title of *fashion director*. The pros of being salaried are steady paychecks, benefits, health insurance, paid vacation, and job longevity. Salaried stylists don't have the same lapses of time between jobs that freelance stylists do, and many of the expenses of fashion styling, like keeping a styling kit stocked or mailing merchandise back and forth, are paid for by the stylist's employer.

The cons are that you don't get to choose your jobs, there might be less variety in the day-to-day projects that you get to style, and you may not get to work with a wide variety of photographers, makeup artists, and talent. You also may be limited in what you can shoot and how expensive your merchandise can be. For example, if you work for a department store, you probably will be able to work only with merchandise that is sold in that department store. If you are on the staff at a magazine, you may be able to work only on fashion stories and shoots that appeal to that magazine's target audience, like middle-class moms or people who like outdoor sports.

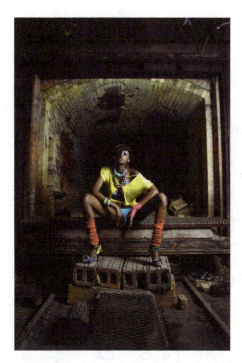

Figure 1.9
A stylist should always be scouting shoot locations in the back of his or her mind. An old trailer can provide a great background along with some simple accessories as props.

Freelance Stylists

Freelance fashion stylists work for clients that hire them. As freelancers, they are self-employed and in control of their own careers. They find jobs, they handle their own marketing and networking, and they are responsible for all the aspects of managing a business, including expenses, taxes, and paperwork. A freelance stylist may choose to be represented by a creative talent agency. These agencies help stylists find jobs in exchange for a portion of the stylist's pay. Agents also help with billing and scheduling, which frees the stylist up so that he or she can focus on fashion.

The pros of being a freelancer include scheduling flexibility, variety in the day-to-day routine; getting to work with a wide range of photographers, hair and makeup artists, and talent; opportunities to exert creative control; the chance to work with many different types and styles of clothing and accessories; and the constant potential of getting hired for a great job. Cons include not having a steady paycheck, potential lapses of time between jobs, worrying about finding work, and struggling to make a name in the industry. Freelance stylists don't get the benefits such as health insurance and paid vacations that full-time employees get. Although freelancers theoretically can decide which jobs to take and which to turn down, the reality is that they have to earn enough money to pay their bills. This can mean they have to take a less interesting job if that job pays more.

PERSONALITY TRAITS THAT A STYLIST NEEDS TO SUCCEED

Fashion styling is a profession that requires certain personality traits. How do you know if you have what it takes to succeed in the business? If you are serious about becoming a fashion stylist, here are some important questions you must ask yourself.

Do You Enjoy Teamwork?

Styling is a job that involves constant collaboration and the ability to compromise. Every job includes the input of many people, including art directors, photographers, and, above all, the client. The client who hires the stylist ultimately needs to be pleased with the outcome, and a stylist must be willing to take direction, accept suggestions, and deal with changes, even if it means adjusting his or her creative vision.

Do You Have an Eye for Detail?

If you're a fashion stylist, attention to detail is your calling card. It's your job to notice how many designers are sending what styles and colors down the runway. It's also your job to note what's on the verge of trending in the real world: how street-style bloggers are cuffing their jeans, what shoes skateboarders are wearing, how pop stars are parting their hair. On set, it's also your job to watch for any issue with the clothing and accessories you've pulled together for the client: Is there a stray thread hanging from a coat hem? A bathing suit strap that's twisted? Does the talent have socks to wear with his shoes? Is there a makeup smudge on a shirt collar? It's up to you to watch everything like a hawk before, during, and after a shoot.

Are You Self-Motivated and Self-Reliant?

Freelance stylists find their own work, do their own billing, maintain a studio and/or office, and build their own professional contacts. They also maintain their marketing efforts, including keeping websites and portfolios current and posting to social media as often as possible. These tasks are time-consuming and can be all-encompassing. They might also seem daunting at first, and it can be easy to procrastinate. Stylists need to have or cultivate the discipline to use free time productively.

Do You Have Good Verbal, Written, and Visual Skills?

As fashion stylists are out in the community meeting people, they need to put their best foot forward. Good communication skills and an extroverted personality are imperative. This doesn't just apply to face-to-face social situations like meeting new people. A stylist must be able to convey information in both words and pictures. For example, a stylist may have to show a client images to convey how he or she plans to approach a job. Or, a stylist may have to resolve a dispute over billing or a damaged garment, and the ability to write an effective email or letter can be critical to being able to resolve such matters in a way that doesn't damage an important relationship or the stylist's reputation.

Do You Have Personal Style?

Personal style is the first thing that people notice, and if you "look the part," you will feel more confident, and this confidence can help you get more jobs. This doesn't mean that you have to follow the latest runway trends or be covered head-to-toe in designer labels. Just because you work in fashion doesn't mean you have to be a slave to fashion. What it does mean is that you should strive to look neat, clean, and professional at all times. This means wearing flattering, current, and tasteful ensembles that show some thought and convey a point of view. (See Figure 1.10.)

Do You Have Strong People Skills?

Being approachable is important for anyone professionally, especially when freelance or self-employed. Approachable people smile, make eye contact, and ask questions to stimulate conversation. Being able to make others see your point of view without alienating them is important.

Are You Adaptable?

It is important to be open to new ideas and to other people's creative input. In the end, stylists must please the clients who hire them. However, it is also important to know when not to adapt to someone else's idea, especially if the final image or outcome is something the stylist doesn't want to be associated with.

TEN HOW-TO SKILLS A FASHION STYLIST NEEDS TO POSSESS

All fashion stylists have a fundamental love of fashion. Often the best stylists are the ones who see fashion as an art form that can be studied, understood, and interpreted. While some stylists seem to have been born with an innate fashion sense, talent alone isn't enough. Success depends on a skill set and a knowledge base that anyone can learn with dedication and hard work. Here are the skills stylists need to learn:

Figure 1.10
Brad Goreski is a great example of a stylist who has a memorable personal style without being gimmicky or overly trendy.

1. **How to Flatter Different Body Shapes with Clothing:** Fashion stylists dress a wide variety of people. Every body is different, and no one is perfect, not even top models. It's up to the stylist to understand measurements, proportion, and shape and be able to flatter everyone with the right clothing and accessories. This is covered more extensively in Chapter 4.
2. **How to Properly Use Color:** In addition to flattering body types, stylists need to understand various skin colorings and which color palettes flatter them. Color palettes are covered more thoroughly in Chapter 4.
3. **How to See Things Through a Camera Lens:** Things look different when seen through the lens of a camera. Different clothing and accessories call for their own camera angles

and distances when photographed. Stylists should understand what fabrics and materials look best on film. Chapter 9 covers some basic photography tips.

4. **How to Efficiently Source Clothing and Accessories:** Stylists need to have a wide variety of professional contacts to be able to borrow merchandise from showrooms, design houses, boutiques, and department stores. This is covered in more detail in Chapters 2 and 9.

5. **How to Use Technology:** With more fashion designers streaming their shows online and even some designers debuting their collections only on Instagram and social media, stylists must know how to access fashion information online. Also, an online presence via a website and such social media sites as Instagram and Snapchat are imperative not only for marketing but also for networking. Additionally, there are many cloud-based business tools that make office tasks like maintaining merchandise records, invoicing clients, and keeping track of expenses much easier.

6. **How to Spot Trends:** Clients hire stylists for their understanding of current trends. They trust the stylist's eye and sense of what is relevant in fashion. They are relying on the stylist's sense of the overall direction of fashion, something the stylist gleans from keeping up with designers, street style, celebrity style, movies, music, television, art, and influential subcultures like skateboarders, rappers, club-goers, drag performers, and more.

7. **How to Stay Informed:** Essential things for stylists in the know include the latest designer collections, fashion trends, entertainment industry news, popular art, new and old cinema, fashion history, and current world events.

8. **How to Stay Within a Budget:** Styling usually means sticking to a client's budget for a shoot. Knowing how to accomplish a lot with a small amount of money is an important skill, and a stylist must be able to account for such "hidden" expenses as mileage and parking when driving to retailers to borrow merchandise, postage expenses to send sample merchandise back and forth, and the cost of replacing any kit materials used on the shoot.

9. **How to Build a Professional Reputation:** Networking doesn't include only photographers and potential clients. It also includes other stylists. If a stylist gets offered a job he or she can't take, he or she might pass it on to another stylist out of professional courtesy. The self-promotional materials covered in Chapter 7 are essential for networking.

10. **How to Organize an Office:** Stylists need to stay on top of billing and paperwork. If an invoicing and billing system isn't organized, it can cost time and money. Also, it is essential to keep an organized calendar of past and upcoming jobs. A stylist saves all job-related receipts, which can either be billed to a client or taken as a business tax deduction with the IRS.

How to Spot Current and Emerging Trends

It is important for stylists to be able to identify trends and know what they are at any given time. Print and online media are teeming with articles on the subject, and it isn't hard to get up to speed rather quickly. Picking out trends involves looking at runway collections, retail advertising campaigns and seasonal shipments, and street fashion. Street fashion has become especially influential, and the sidewalks outside of Fashion Week venues get almost as much coverage as the collections themselves. Fast fashion retailers are able to reflect runway trends almost immediately because of efficient production. This is why looking at all three areas gives a complete picture of current trends.

Note-taking and sketching are great ways to pick out trends. Observations can be typed into a memo app or photographed on a smartphone or tablet. Some people might prefer to jot down notes or sketches in a notebook. Key things to look for in the note-taking process are new themes such as silhouettes, colors, fabrics, and patterns.

If a theme has been around for more than one season, it can still be relevant but not as fresh as it once was. Older themes from past seasons aren't found on the pages of fashion magazines. In the past they might have been seen in distilled forms at mass-market clothing retailers long after they vanished from the fashion forefront. Current fashion moves at a faster pace, and mass-market retailers can produce and evolve with trends at a much more efficient rate.

Knowing how to wear trends is equally as important as spotting them. If a bare midriff is in style one season, how it is worn can make or break the look. There is a big difference between showing the entire midriff and revealing only the upper part. If flannel shirts influenced by the 1990s are trendy, it is important to know how to wear them so that they look current. Today's versions might be tailored differently than the ones worn in the past. In the nineties it might have been fine to wear a baggy flannel with baggy ripped jeans and combat boots. Today's men and women might instead pair a flannel with skinny jeans and sleek ankle boots.

Recommended Reading:
Fashion Editorial Publications

The following magazines have been selected based on the strength of their fashion editorials and how influential they are within their target markets. It is important for a stylist to be acquainted with editorials not only for their styling techniques, but also for their overall storylines. In addition to being accessible in print and online, the following publications can be followed through websites and social media channels. Also, be sure to check out other countries' versions of these magazines. *American Vogue* is wonderful, but so are *French Vogue* and *Vogue Italia*.

- Esquire and esquire.com: This men's magazine covers fashion, style, and entertainment, with a dash of current event commentary.
- Harper's Bazaar and harpersbazaar.com: One of America's leading women's fashion magazines, this also has a retail component that showcases new and popular designers.
- *GQ* and gq.com: This men's magazine showcases men's style, from fashion and grooming to music, sports, and food.
- *Vogue* and vogue.com: Considered by many to be the world's leading fashion magazine, its iconic September issue is the must-buy magazine of the year.
- *W* and wmagazine.com: An offshoot of *WWD*, this magazine features dramatic and fashion-forward editorials influenced by art and film.
- *i-D* and i-d.vice.com: Specializing in chronicling cool since 1980, this magazine covers emerging pop culture trends and tastemakers across music, fashion, clubs, and more.

INDUSTRY INTERVIEW

Interview with Allison St. Germain

Allison is a NYC-based fashion stylist originally from New Orleans. She currently resides in Brooklyn with her husband, son, and two kitties.

Website: *www.AllisonStGermain.com*
Instagram: *TheBeastlyBeast*

What celebrities, companies, or high-profile clients have you worked with?
Saks, Lord & Taylor, Dooney & Bourke, Dr. Oz, Lykke Li, Santigold, Andrew Rannels, Christine Taylor, various luxury magazines.

How did you get into the fashion industry? Did you have formal training, or is it something that evolved or you fell into?
I kind of fell into this. I moved to NYC from New Orleans at twenty-one. One of my roommates who always borrowed my clothes told me I should be a fashion stylist. I didn't even know what that was at the time. I did a little research and found my calling.

Did you go straight into styling, or did you assist first?
I assisted many different stylists from celebrity to still life to find out more about each avenue of styling.

Now that you are styling, what qualities do you look for in an assistant?
A good personality, can-do attitude, hard worker, not a diva, problem solver, and of course a good fashion sense.

What kinds of job duties did you do when you first started working?
Steaming clothes, closet organizing, pickups, returns, and schlepping.

Do you have any funny or horror stories of when you first started?
I didn't know how to use a steamer, or even turn it on for that matter. The stylist was watching me and I was trying to act like everything was fine and was searching for the on button. I figured it out and she never said anything, but I was mortified.

What's something you wish someone had told you before you started? What advice would you give your younger self about styling?
I would have told myself not to work with some of the crazy nasty people that I assisted. I guess I learned how not to treat people because of them, but it's never ok to be nasty to your assistants.

What do you feel is a common mistake that many people make when they first start out in the industry? Or a common misconception about what you do?
People think it's a glamorous job when it isn't. Stylists are the first to arrive and the last to leave on set. I'm often crawling around the set to pin the wardrobe. We prep days and weeks before the job happens to get clothes. Pounding the pavement with a thousand shopping bags, and dealing with rotten attitudes from sales associates.

What's your philosophy of styling or dressing a client?
Get to know them and what they're looking for. Mood-boards are a great way to understand someone's aesthetic.

Where do you like to shop?
When I'm prepping jobs, I like to go to Saks, Bloomingdales, and Barneys. They have a great studio service program. I can shop, take photos for my clients, have the wardrobe I've chosen hung up on a

rack, and actually think about what I'm purchasing. In a store that doesn't offer this service you'll find me flying through the store like a wild woman buying everything in sight before the sales associate asks if I'm a stylist.

What are some of your favorite designers?
J Brand, Acne, Comme des Garcons, Rag & Bone, Helmut Lang, and Public School to name a few.

What are some hidden gems or offbeat places where you pick up stuff for jobs?
Tokio7 and beacon's closet are always fun for a special vintage piece.

How much of your own personal style can be influenced on a job?
If the concept of a shoot isn't particularly my style, I'll find a way to make it mine.

Who are your muses? How or where do you find inspiration?
I love old Hitchcock films for inspiration and putting together mood boards from Fashion Week. Patti Smith is my fashion icon.

What's something that you don't like about being a stylist? If you could change something about the industry, what would it be?
I don't like the returns. Dealing with angry sales associates when they see me coming with a giant bag of returns. Some rules need to change about ecom. It's a lot of work and pays the least but people are shopping more and more online so I feel like companies should be investing more money into ecommerce sites.

It can be difficult keeping track of so many items on a big job or when juggling a multitude of shoots. How do you keep organized? Do you have a special system, so to speak, that you like to use?
I use Excel and make copies of my receipts. When sorting through the returns we just check off the lists until everything is accounted for.

You work a lot in ecom; what are some of the differences between working on a fashion shoot and working on an ecommerce shoot?
Fashion shoots are about selling a mood or a feeling. You want the reader or customer to want this lifestyle. Ecom is strictly about selling the clothes.

A styling tip when working for ecommerce—
Drink water, pace yourself, and breathe.

How do you network? Why is it important to build relationships in this industry?
Almost every job I've ever gotten is because of a recommendation. I'm always pleasant on set and try to continue relationships with people outside of work.

How do you present your work (e.g., website, portfolio, comp cards)? How did you establish your aesthetic or brand?

I have a website, iPad portfolio, and comp cards. The cards, I'm sure, go right in the trash, but they're fun to hand out. I edit my iPad portfolio to each client that I'm meeting with. I'm not going to show my ecom work for an advertising job.

How have technology and social media changed the styling profession and fashion industry?

Social media has been a game changer for sure. Now everybody is a stylist because they're a social influencer. It doesn't necessarily mean that they are able to dress a forty something woman for a pharmaceutical advertisement, though, or correctly pin a size 6 sample to a size 2 model. I think clients are figuring that out now.

Do you have any tips for working as a freelance or independent contractor (anything from tax tips to professional practice, like contracts and insurance, getting paid, setting rates)?

Keep all receipts and make spreadsheets!! I'm being audited as we speak and having those receipts and my calendar still available from that year is really saving the day.

Once you are awarded a job, you must insist that the client give you an advance for the wardrobe budget. I've had a client file chapter 11 after I shopped the wardrobe, completed a shoot, and paid my assistant.

INDUSTRY INTERVIEW

Interview with Eryka Clayton

Eryka Clayton has been successfully working as a style director and creative producer since the mid-nineties. With her extensive skill set, creative vision, and timeless, elegant style, she has been instrumental in helping brands, artists, and actors define their image and bring it life. Her editorial and advertising work has appeared in numerous magazines internationally, and her celebrities have graced the major award show red carpets and landed on the best-dressed lists.

Eryka is currently based in New York, where she serves as the editor-in-chief and fashion director of *Collective Magazine*.

Website: *erykaclayton.com*
Instagram: *@erykaclayton*
Twitter: *@erykac*

What celebrities, companies, or high-profile clients have you worked with?

Design Within Reach, The Waldorf Astoria Hotel, OceanDrive Magazine, Sarah Hay, Jason Statham, Gerard Butler, Lynn Collins, Bryce Dallas Howard, Kat Graham, Nora Zehetner, Rachel Bilson, Mischa Barton, Christie Brinkley, Sarah Wayne Callies, The Conrad Hotel, The Roosevelt Hotel, AT&T, Omega, Saks Fifth Avenue, Time Inc., Lancome, Tyler Ellis, JJ Watt, Josie Natori, Steinway, John Tavaras, Gillette, The Olympics, Annalynne Mccord, Sarah Hyland, Kate Nauta, Rodrigo Santoro, Jessica Lowndes, Nastia Liukin.

How did you get into the fashion industry? Did you have formal training, or is it something that evolved or you fell into?

I was shopping in my home-town of Rockville Centre, New York, at the local boutique. The owner approached me about modeling in a BCBG fashion show they were producing in exchange for store credit. I was fourteen and the pants I wanted were expensive, so I obviously said yes. Backstage at a show, I was getting my makeup done and the fashion show director was buzzing around checking in on everything and giving multiple people direction. I was watching her and realized I wanted to be her one day. So I asked her if I could come be a fly on the wall sometime. She said no. She said I could apprentice. Sweep floors, get coffee, etc. and soak up all that I could. I did that for three years through high school. We worked on many fashion shows together. I walked as a model in some and worked all of them. Getting the perspective from filling many roles allowed me to learn about different facets of the industry. For college I went to New World School of the Arts in Miami, where *Ocean Drive Magazine* was at the epicenter of the social culture. I wanted to work there. I gave myself a five-year timeline to make that happen. Two years later I was their youngest hire. At the time I was twenty years old, and I knew nothing. Thanks to my bosses Michelle Addison and Rich Santelises, after about a year I knew something. One thing led to another, and between then and the age of twenty-six, I worked my way up to editor-in-chief of *Signature Los Angeles Magazine*. Along the way I consulted, working with brands and celebrities to help create their image, shaping their marketing, and had a blast the whole way through. Fast-forward to today, the scope of what I do may be slightly different, but the work is pretty much the same.

Did you go straight into styling, or did you assist first?

I started styling when I was editor-in-chief of *Signature Los Angeles Magazine*. I fashion-directed all of our cover and editorial shoots and in some cases also styled them. I had great relationships with various showrooms from working as an editor, so the transition was easy.

Now that you are styling, what qualities do you look for in an assistant?
I look for:

- Critical thinkers who are doers
- Honest, kind and quick with a positive attitude
- In great health and physical shape so they can carry multiple garment bags for over a mile if need be
- Organized
- Team player and a leader
- Someone who has a keen attention to detail
- Style savvy and an ability to sew well are prerequisites

I took stage management in college, and now I realize all the qualities of a stage manager are also the qualities of a great assistant. They are multitaskers and organized, but don't micromanage. Like us, they have a handle on everything that is going on in a production. We work with many personalities because we are dealing with various people such as models, producers, photographers, and studio managers, so the ability to thrive as an interpersonal communicator is key. This aptitude can be fine-tuned but not taught.

What kinds of job duties did you do when you first started working?
Folding and sweeping, stuffing gift bags, ordering lunches, that kind of thing.

Mailings, client reach outs, collecting checks from clients, scoping out potential clients, taking notes in meetings, organizing productions, etc.

Organizing the fabric rooms, keeping inventory of props and materials for shows, helping out with castings and such.

What's something you wish someone had told you before you started? What advice would you give your younger self about styling?
The work doesn't get done unless your soul is being fed. Sometimes you don't need to do every job. It is important to do things for you. I travel, watch sunsets, find peace and quiet (which is not always easy), etc.

Give yourself the opportunity to find your inspiration. It will keep the spark in your work.

What do you feel is a common mistake that many people make when they first start out in the industry? Or a common misconception about what you do?
Bending to the client. If a client hires you, do not try and meet them where they are, but stay true to your vision. They hired you for a reason. In other words, don't sell out. Your vision is valuable. You can be nice and say no. Just make sure you present a stellar proposal that you can deliver.

What's your philosophy of styling or dressing a client?
Bringing the essence of the client forward in an authentic, timeless way so you can look at a photograph in 40 years and still appreciate the look. Timeless style is still at the core of everything I do.

Where do you like to shop?
Everywhere. Little boutiques I will never remember the name of in cities and villages I travel through, vintage shops like 10 ft Single by Stella Dallas in Brooklyn, Intermix, etc. I prefer to shop when I see a special piece. I am typically drawn in by windows; it doesn't matter much the brand or store.

What are some of your favorite designers?
Christian Dior, Oscar De La Renta, Celine, Tom Ford, Carolina Herrera, Escada.

What are some hidden gems or offbeat places where you pick up stuff for jobs?
Street Vendors in SoHo for jewelry. There is a guy who makes handmade African beaded pieces off Spring Street that I love. 10 ft Single by Stella Dallas and other vintage stores are great when I need things for a job with a specific time period theme. Flea markets in Paris are always a great choice. H&M, Zara, Saks, and Bloomingdales work really well for ad clients.

How much of your own personal style can be influenced on a job?
Of course it has its place, because after all it is me. Essentially, I'm the lens on the object.

Who are your muses? How or where do you find inspiration?
Models that I have worked with over and over again through the years. They have become like sisters, best friends, and art partners. We work together, laugh, cry, etc. They truly help inspire me. I find inspiration being a speck in this universe, and the world around me. I have a childish curiosity for the world. I often can be found staring up at the clouds during a sunset. I travel a ton because the things I see and experience from being around other cultures offer inspiration over and over again. You never know how things connect or when something will trigger a memory. For example, I went to Tulum a while back and they had a huge amount of seaweed washed up on the shore because of an oil spill. Seeing the locals pulling the seaweed up into huge piles, I realized the damage we do and the delayed impact our actions can have. The memory of that has made me way more mindful of my contribution to consumer waste in my day to day. These kinds of experiences are invaluable and really shape me as an artist and as a human being.

What's something that you don't like about being a stylist? If you could change something about the industry, what would it be?
Literally always carrying a boutique's worth of wardrobe with me. If there could be a way to teleport my pulls, it would be the perfect job.

I would also love to see everyone compensated for their true value. This is something that is true at a very high level all the way down to the manufacturing. It is something we can do something about.

Additionally, I would like to see a change towards bettering the planet. I would like to see businesses lessen their footprint. Using fair trade, natural materials, and socially responsible business practices. Hopefully making fast fashion companies smaller. Do we all really need 50 basic $10 T-shirts? I would argue not. This change can happen by educating for the consumer and letting them decide what to buy. The beauty industry has a focus on educating the shopper, so maybe we can take cue from that.

It can be difficult keeping track of so many items on a big job or when juggling a multitude of shoots. How do you keep organized? Do you have a special system, so to speak, that you like to use?
Lists: more specifically an Excel document called Wardrobe Breakdown_"client name." I learned how to create one in college while working in the costume shop. An inventory system, by look and by talent that can be scaled up or down as necessary. I label everything. Garments on the inside of the back of the collar, ziploc bags with tags, extra buttons get labeled. These kind of organization practices have saved me so much time and immense resources over the years.

Name two styling tips.
Safety pins (black, white, gold, silver, every size, in every color, at all times in your kit).

Use a natural white cotton sock over your steamer so you don't burn yourself or get the garment wet.

You work in both the fashion and lifestyle sectors of styling. What do you think are the main differences between the two?
Lifestyle uses fashion. So fashion is the inception where innovation happens and creatives fly. Lifestyle is how you incorporate fashion into the day to day, making it your own. I have a strong interest in working with celebrities and brands to help them present their personal style using fashions we love!

Anything else you would like to add?
Have fun! We are not saving the world with what we do, but we are coloring it. Really be free and play.

On a more practical note, your money is never a guarantee in this business. You are working freelance. Paychecks vary. Ecommerce work is a great way to make bread and butter money. However, if you are like me and prefer to create brands, work on advertising campaigns, craft marketing, and work with celebrities; then paychecks will be bigger but maybe less often. Invest. Your financial health is worth it.

SUMMARY AND REVIEW

Fashion styling is much more than just putting outfits together. It is a dynamic and fast-paced career that can be extremely rewarding. The three main areas of fashion styling are print, the entertainment industry, and image management. There are many types of stylists beyond fashion, including runway stylists and those who work with props, sets, and other designed products.

There are two types of paid styling jobs: salaried and freelance. An example of salaried styling job is that of a magazine editor or a style director of a major retailer. These jobs are often steady and predictable, and benefits can include health insurance and paid vacations. The downside, however, is that stylists can have restrictions on creativity and how they use their time. Freelance stylists, on the other hand, are self-employed, so they can pick and choose the jobs they work. As with many self-employed people, freelancers might work around the clock and at odd hours. When they aren't shooting, they might be working on billing, maintaining their home offices, reading magazines to stay up on trends, or polishing their personal appearances.

All stylists need to possess certain personality traits. An ability to work as part of a team, communication skills, and an extroverted personality are essential to success. In addition, skills such as dressing to flatter figure and skin tone are important. Good fashion stylists love fashion and don't mind surrounding themselves with it. They eat, breathe, and sleep fashion and are constantly looking for the next great thing.

KEY TERMS

- client
- editorial styling
- effective image
- entertainment industry
- fashion styling/fashion stylist
- food styling
- image management
- lifestyle styling
- print styling

- prop styling
- runway styling
- set styling
- styling
- styling kit
- talent
- themes
- wardrobe styling

REVIEW QUESTIONS

1. List three possible clients for a freelance editorial fashion stylist.
2. What does the term *talent* mean?
3. How do fashion stylists influence the general public?
4. List the three main types of fashion styling.
5. Describe two challenges that wardrobe stylists face.
6. Name two areas of styling outside of fashion.
7. Where might a salaried fashion stylist work?

8. What are two drawbacks to being a freelance stylist?

9. What is a personality trait that you possess that would make you a good fashion stylist, and why?

10. Name three general places a fashion stylist should look to stay up-to-date on current trend and themes.

LEARNING ACTIVITIES

Learning Activity 1.1: Search magazines and online sources for current fashion photographs. Find one common theme among this season's looks and copy/paste or cut it out. Attach five examples of the theme to a piece of paper. The examples can be from either the runway or street fashion. Be sure to include the designers' names next to runway pictures. Include a short paragraph describing the theme.

Learning Activity 1.2: You can often find fashion stylists listed on modeling and talent agency websites. Conduct an online search for a fashion stylist portfolio. Try to find a stylist who has at least two different categories in his or her portfolio, such as a stylist who has prop styling and celebrity styling photos posted on his or her site. Write a short paragraph about what type(s) of portfolios the stylist is showing and describe them in one typed, double-spaced page.

Learning Activity 1.3: Go to a supermarket and look at what is for sale. Look at the packaging on different items. Jot down five unexpected examples of styling on packaging—anything from a person on the front of a cereal box to a picture of dishes on a bottle of dish soap. List the specific brand, briefly describe the package, and explain whether you think the packaging displays an effective image and why or why not.

RESOURCES

"Acrylic Ice." Trengrove Studios. http://www.tengrovestudios.com.

"Art Director: What Do Art Directors Do?" Mediamatch. https://www.media-match.com/usa/media/jobtypes/art-director-jobs-402675.php.

"Challenges of Shooting in Remote Locations." Nadia Pandolfo Photography. http://www.nadiapandolfo.com/blog/2015/1/6/challenges-of-shooting-in-remote-locations.

Cox, Susan Linnet. *Photo Styling: How to Build Your Career and Succeed.* New York: Allworth Press, 2006.

"Fashion Calendar." NYMag.com. http://www.nymag.com/fashion/fashioncalendar/fashionweek.

Fashion Trendsetter. http://www.fashiontrendsetter.com.

"Food Styling Tips, Tricks, and Techniques—Food Styling Tips for Food Photographers." Food Photography Blog. http://www.foodportfolio.com/blog/food_photography/tricks_of_the_trade.html.

"4 Reasons on Why Stylists Are the Most Important People in Fashion." SchoolofStyle.com. http://schoolofstyle.com/blog/4-reasons-on-why-stylists-are-the-most-important-people-in-fashion/.

"How to Make It: Tips for Becoming a Successful Fashion Stylist." ComPlex. http://www.complex.com/style/2013/04/how-to-make-it-tips-for-becoming-a-fashion-stylist/.

"An Interview with Neiman Marcus Fashion Director Ken Downing." Philly.com. http://www.philly.com/philly/blogs/style/An-interview-with-Ken-Downing-of-Neiman-Marcus-.html.

left brain / right brain, LLC. *Stylebook* [Computer software, Version 7.0]. Apple App Store, 2016. http://itunes
.apple.com/us/app/stylebook/id335709058.

Looklet. http://www.looklet.com.

"Making Magic: Stylists in the Fashion Photo Shoot." Smugmug.com. https://news.smugmug.com/making-magic
-stylists-in-the-fashion-photo-shoot-87dd58ecd1b.

Style.com. http://www.style.com.

"This Is Every Hollywood Stylist's Worst Nightmare Before a Major Red Carpet Event." InStyle.com. http://www
.instyle.com/news/hollywood-stylist-red-carpet-prep-nightmare.

"Types of Styling from a New York Stylist." Ms. In the Biz. http://msinthebiz.com/2013/06/04/types-of-styling
-from-a-new-york-stylist/.

WeConnectFashion. http://www.weconnectfashion.com.

WGSN. http://www.wgsn.com.

"What Is Style Sight?" Stylesight. http://www.stylesight.com.

"What We Offer: Overview." Trendstop. http://www.trendstop.com/en/fashion_trend_analysis/womenswear
/trend-forecasts-w-10.html.

Wright, Crystal. *The Hair, Makeup & Styling Career Guide.* Los Angeles: Motivational Media Productions, 2007.

2 Photo Styling

In this chapter you will learn:
- The two main areas of photo styling
- The differences between editorial and lifestyle styling
- Fashion magazine timetables
- How fashion stylists source clothing
- The fashion calendar and production schedules
- The fashion stylist's responsibilities before, during, and after a shoot

PHOTO STYLING 101

Photo styling is a diverse field with varied potential for work. **Photo shoot stylists** work on photo shoots for different publications, including fashion magazines, nonfashion magazines, brochures, clothing catalogues, websites, and print and online advertisements; they also shoot stock photography. Photo styling can be broken down into two basic types of jobs: editorial and lifestyle. These two types of jobs have different target markets and therefore portray vastly different types of clothing. Despite their differences, they have several elements in common. (See Figure 2.1a–b.) The similarities between editorial and lifestyle shoots lie in their organization and preparation. Many freelance stylists specialize in both areas. In fact, some freelance **print stylists** also branch out into other areas of styling like personal styling, prop styling, and designer collaborations to keep their incomes consistent; these areas will be explored more in Chapter 5.

Editorial Styling

Editorial styling tends to be more fashion-forward. Most editorial styling takes place for online or print fashion magazines. These are often stylists' dream jobs where they get to flex their creative muscles. The outfits aren't necessarily wearable on the street, but they are visually stunning in the finished image. When

Figure 2.1a–b
The work of (a) editorial print stylists may seem more glamorous and high-profile than the work of (b) lifestyle print stylists, but the two jobs are remarkably similar in the nuts and bolts of organization, preparation, and many of the basic tasks on the shoot.

styling for this type of shoot, a stylist is going beyond everyday looks. The look of an editorial shoot is about pushing the envelope and creating an image with impact. Often editorial styling reflects the hottest trends and the newest merchandise to hit stores. Sometimes it focuses on high-end designers, but it's not a necessity. Editorial styling is more about unexpected combinations and current looks.

Editorial look is a term that describes a look that is more fashion-forward than the everyday look. (See Figure 2.2.) A model can have an editorial look, and so can an outfit, hair, or makeup. For example, a model with an editorial look might have an intriguing facial feature or haircut. A model with a lifestyle look is more classic and can appeal to many audiences.

Lifestyle Styling
Lifestyle photography can include shoots for online or print brochures, catalogues, and advertisements. Lifestyle styling encompasses everyday looks, such as khaki pants with a polo shirt. Lifestyle hair and makeup look more natural, while editorial hair and makeup may be designed for more impact. (See Figure 2.3.) Freelance stylists frequently work in both editorial and lifestyle styling. Lifestyle styling is generally considered to be less creative, but the tradeoff is that it pays well. While the resulting images may not bring much sizzle to a stylist's portfolio, lifestyle jobs are great for keeping money coming in. In fact, it's not uncommon to see well-known magazine editors dabbling

Figure 2.2
Model Cara Delevingne has what may be considered an editorial look. Her fashion-forward hairstyle and delicate facial features make for a beautiful, unusual, and memorable combination.

Figure 2.3
Model and actress Marissa Miller has a look that is well suited to lifestyle work, such as catalogues and advertisements. She has the quintessential "California girl" beauty.

in lucrative lifestyle work, like *Vogue Magazine* former creative director Grace Coddington, who signed for an advertising styling job with Tiffany & Co. after leaving *Vogue*.

Lifestyle jobs not only pay better on average, but they can last longer, too. A clothing-catalogue shoot can last for a week or more. In addition, the stylist doesn't need to source clothing for the catalogue because it is already provided. This is a huge benefit, since the process of sourcing clothes is always time-consuming and often stressful.

Influential Editorial and Lifestyle Stylists
It is important for professional stylists to know the most influential names in the industry. Here is a short list of the most well-known editorial and lifestyle stylists working today:

- **Grace Coddington:** Former creative director of the American edition of *Vogue* magazine, her mane of red hair is legendary in the industry, as is her whimsical, painterly style.
- **Edward Enninful:** Currently the editor of the British edition of *Vogue*, Enninful became fashion director of *i-D* magazine at the age of eighteen and also served as fashion and style director at *W*. He is widely considered to be one of the most talented stylists in the business.
- **Joe Zee:** Editor-in-chief of *Yahoo Style* and former creative director of *Elle* magazine, this approachable, engaging stylist has become a media personality thanks to stints hosting a podcast and a television show. He also wrote the book *That's What Fashion Is*.
- **Carine Roitfeld:** This legendary French stylist has become a fashion icon for her edgy, sultry

personal style. She's been at the top of the masthead at the French editions of *Elle* and *Vogue* and now serves as editor-in-chief of her own magazine, *CR Fashion Book.*

- **Kate Young:** A freelance stylist who got her start at *Vogue* and later *Teen Vogue*, she has styled for editorial shoots and ad campaigns and has a roster of celebrity clients. Considered one of the most powerful stylists in Hollywood, she launched a capsule fashion collection for Target in 2013.
- **Lori Goldstein:** This versatile New York City–based stylist has worked with the greats of fashion photography and has styled ad campaigns for fashion houses ranging from Prada and Dolce & Gabbana to Vera Wang and Yves Saint Laurent. She's also worked with Madonna, Michael Jackson, Rhianna, and Beyoncé. She's currently fashion-editor-at-large at *Elle* magazine, the author of *Lori Goldstein: Style Is Instinct,* and the designer of a fashion line for QVC.
- **Patricia Field:** This flame-haired stylist earned her reputation as a fashion maverick through the eclectic indie boutique she owned for more than fifty years in downtown Manhattan, but Field earned international fame through her styling work in the entertainment industry. She was the fashion visionary behind the *Sex and the City* costuming and won an Emmy for her work on that show (plus another for *Ugly Betty*). She also was nominated for an Oscar for her wardrobe styling on the movie *The Devil Wears Prada*. She continues to work and also runs an ecommerce site featuring the work of indie designers.
- **Katie Grand:** Named by Britain's *The Daily Telegraph* newspaper as one of the most powerful stylists in the world, Grand is the creative director of Marc Jacobs and has styled runway shows for major international brands like Ungaro, Loewe, and Louis Vuitton. She's the founder and editor of the biannual fashion magazine *Love.*

"What's not publicized about a lot of people in fashion is how they got to where they are. Really read up on the people who inspired you, and learn from their journey. Find out about them, and find out how they got from point A to point B. It can be really inspiring."
—*Meghan Blalok, managing editor,* Who What Wear, *http://stylecaster.com/how-to -break-into-fashion/*

How Much Do Photo Stylists Make?

Freelance photo stylists bill the client according to a **day rate**. This is the amount of money they earn for a day of work, and a standard working day of shooting lasts between ten and twelve hours. Freelance stylists can also charge for the time before and after the shoot while they are preparing for and wrapping up the job. Typically, time spent on pulls and returns is billed to the client at a half-day rate; however, this can always be negotiated.

Editorial freelance stylists' day rates range between $500 and $1,000 a day. A select few top-level stylists can earn up to $5,000 per job. Lifestyle styling jobs for catalogues and commercials often pay significantly more, and rates typically start at $1,000 per day. Also, a stylist working on a lifestyle job like an advertising campaign can sometimes receive extra payments, like a travel allowance, travel stipend, or a per diem rate, to cover the expenses of travel and meals during longer shoots.

Budgets are generally set by the job, and those who earn more do so because of the strength of their résumé and their past work. This is where having an agent can literally pay off. A talent agency does not charge the stylist; rather, it tacks its fee—usually a percentage of the total amount billed—onto the bill that the client pays. But a good agency can handle all of the negotiating for you, making sure that you earn what you're worth and what the market is paying and that you're on course to earn more in the future.

Even though the day rates for photo stylists can be generous, the national average or median income for a photo stylist is about $47,000 per year according to payscale.com. This is because print stylists experience periods of unemployment between paying jobs, and also stylists working outside of major cities will not make as much money. For seasoned freelance fashion photo stylists working in Los Angeles and New York City, editorial work can easily earn them a six-figure income; lifestyle work can boost that salary to seven figures.

For big jobs and long shoots, a lead stylist might request an assistant. Assistants typically make $150 per day on an editorial shoot and between $250 and $350 a day on a lifestyle shoot. But it's also not uncommon for an assistant to work for the experience, meaning no pay. Unlike the stylist's salary, the assistant's day rate is generally set and is non-negotiable.

If a stylist is on staff at a company or at a magazine, of course there is no day rate, just the stylist's annual salary that is set by the company. This varies widely depending on the size of the publication and the location, but in New York City in 2014, a fashion editor for a print publication typically earned nearly $70,000 a year; working for the magazine's website boosted that salary slightly. The editor at the top of the masthead, the magazine's creative director, could expect an average annual paycheck of more than $160,000.

FASHION MAGAZINE TIMETABLES

Sitting is another word used in the magazine industry to refer to an editorial shoot. Generally editorial shoots, or sittings, take place three months before a magazine's publication. This means that the September issue of a magazine that hits newsstands in August was shot in May. The September issues of magazines show upcoming fall/winter styles, but the editorials were shot at the end of the preceding spring.

Publication is synchronized with retail deliveries. After all, the fashion magazine is there to generate publicity for the clothes. **Editorial credits** are the descriptions and prices of clothing listed on each editorial page. Documenting and submitting editorial credits is the stylist's responsibility and is done immediately after the shoot. When the reader wants to buy a garment, he or she needs to be able to see the price and where it can be purchased. If a magazine publication isn't synchronized with retail clothing availability, the clothing won't sell as well. Magazines are powerful publicity machines, and much of their power lies in their timing.

Runway to Retail: The Fashion Manufacturing Time Line

Approximately eighteen to twenty-four months prior to the show:

- The season's color, fabric, and silhouette trends are identified by trend-forecasting companies and presented to fashion designers. These companies are made up of market-research professionals who analyze statistical data such as consumer expenditures to gauge future trends. They are not choosing trends; rather, they are connecting and synthesizing trends that are arising from high culture (theater, fine art), pop culture (movies, popular music), and street culture (fashion blogs, social media).

- Once trend-forecasting agencies identify colors and popular types of fabrics for the coming season, mills begin designing and producing fabrics that they will sell at upcoming trade shows.

Approximately twelve months prior to the show:

- The newly produced fabric is shown at trade shows such as Première Vision in Paris and New York or Pitti Filati in Florence, where fashion designers and design houses purchase sample yardage for upcoming collections. Fabric often comes before the design.

Approximately three to six months prior to the show:

- Designers sketch more designs than will be produced. Sketches are done either on paper or digitally using drawing or drafting software such as Adobe Illustrator or CAD, and then many of the sketches are discarded before they get the chance to be made into samples.
- Samples from approved sketches are made from inexpensive muslin fabric.
- Drape and fit are adjusted on these muslin samples. At this point, either the idea is scrapped or the design is made with the more expensive sample yardage that has been purchased.

Approximately one month to as little as one hour prior to the show:

- Final samples are made for the upcoming show by in-house patternmakers and sewers.
- Production managers begin to coordinate production costs and manufacture dates with factories beforehand, but production will not begin until after the show. Production is not begun until after it is known how the customer will react!

At and after the show:

- Magazine editors and retail buyers attend.
- In the weeks after Fashion Week, buyers place orders and editors scope out designers and clothing for future issues.
- Clothing goes into production. Design changes may be made to clothing to make it more marketable to consumers. Revised samples are made before clothing goes into full-scale production. Production problems such as quality control are addressed during this period.
- Magazines photograph samples about three months before the clothing arrives in stores. By the time the magazine hits newsstands, the clothing is ready to be purchased in stores or online.

DISRUPTING THE TIME LINE: SEE-NOW, BUY-NOW

The logic of showing clothes months before anyone can buy them, as well as filling stores with merchandise that's not always in sync with the seasons, has long been criticized inside and outside the fashion industry. Also, social media have contributed to the public's growing desire for instant access to everything. People were growing tired of waiting for clothing to arrive in stores when they'd been seeing images of it for months online.

Figure 2.4
When a shoot follows a specific theme like evening gowns, it is often helpful if the stylist has time to put together a specialized styling kit.

In 2016, it seemed that these problems could be solved thanks to a new fashion production time line called **See-Now, Buy-Now**. Under this system, clothing sent down the runway during Fashion Week could be bought by both retailers and real people shortly after the show. At the Ralph Lauren Collection runway show in September 2016, guests only had to wait a few minutes before being able to buy the looks they'd just seen. The show took place right in front of Lauren's flagship Upper East Side boutique, and after his customary walk down the runway to greet friends and family, the smiling designer personally opened the doors to invite the lucky attendees inside to shop the collection in person or even from their phones, as it also had become immediately available online.

Among the fashion brands that joined Lauren on the See-Now, Buy-Now bandwagon were Tom Ford, Burberry, and Tommy Hilfiger. Moschino, Lela Rose, and Alberta Ferretti also signed on, albeit with capsule collections. How does this change affect the manufacturing and editorial photo shoot time line? Simple: Showroom samples are made available before the fashion show rather than after.

With such important global brands on board, it seemed like the much-criticized fashion calendar was finally on its way to being a fashion footnote. By 2017, however, the shift to the new model had slowed, and many in the industry said it was still too early to declare the new model a success. It remains to be seen whether the See-Now, Buy-Now approach will catch on across the industry, what its impact on designers' creative processes will be, and just how fast it might happen and how far it will go.

Preparation: A Key Responsibility

Proper preparation is crucial to being organized and ready for the day of the shoot. **Prep work** for print photo shoots is the many responsibilities of the stylist before every shoot; it will be explored more in Chapters 9 and 10, but here is an overview.

Sometimes the stylist has the luxury of having days or weeks of lead time before a shoot. In that case, the preparation process can include preliminary meetings to discuss the shoot, the construction of mood boards, and model fittings and alterations. A stylist might even have the chance to put together a specialized styling kit for the job and to save money by having merchandise sent via two-day mail instead of overnight or by courier or Uber. (See Figure 2.4.)

Other times a stylist might have only half a day's lead time before a shoot. That means that the stylist is frantically running around town pulling and buying as much merchandise as possible, hoping that the **talent** actually matches the measurements that the client provided.

There are certain tasks that a stylist can do during downtime to make preparing for a shoot easier. One task is making contacts with local retail owners and managers. Having contacts established often allows stylists to **pull** merchandise at a moment's notice. *Pulling* is another term for **sourcing** an item from a retailer, designer, showroom, or PR agency. Other prep tasks include maintaining the **styling kit**, which is an on-the-job toolbox (see Table 9.1), conducting fashion research between jobs to understand the most current looks, catching up on billing and recordkeeping, and perhaps even creating and scheduling social media posts so they can be uploaded quickly and easily even when things get busy.

The following are a few important steps in the preparation process.

Preliminary Meetings

The date, time, and location of the shoot must always be clearly established before shooting begins. Similarly, the stylist must confirm who is producing the shoot. Key players include all decision makers, such as the **photographer** and the **art director**, as well as hair and makeup stylists. For print jobs, the client should know the date that the photos will be published or go live. The stylist can sometimes request multiple copies of the publication for his or her portfolio.

Before shooting the stylist should also get to know some basic information about the talent. This includes their coloring, measurements, and clothing and shoe sizes. Last but not least, the stylist's budget for the shoot must be established before shopping begins. As already noted, even if a stylist can borrow merchandise, it may not be free. Preliminary meetings do not always happen before a shoot because there may not be enough lead time. If the stylist is hired right before the shoot, all preliminary information must be exchanged quickly over the phone, or via email or text. The stylist must be prepared to ask all the right questions at a moment's notice. This is also where an agent can come in handy, because the agent is in a good position to ask many of these questions long before a booking is confirmed.

This is also a good time to ask about the client's social media policy. Photo shoot sets make great social media posts, as do selfies with models and snaps that show off designer labels. Find out what information about the shoot can be revealed and to what extent. If the client says it's okay to post photos, it's nice to ask for the client's hashtags so that everyone can share in the social media love.

Seasoned stylists have mental checklists of important questions and necessary kit supplies embedded in their brains from experience. For those starting out, especially for a test shoot, it would be wise to prepare a written list, including spaces to quickly jot down notes.

Establishing a Story

Another responsibility of the stylist is to meet with the photographer and/or art director to discuss the theme or **story** of the shoot. A story is the central theme on which the shoot is based. Some stories can be as broad as mod styles from the 1960s or as specific as a particular movie, such as *Breakfast at Tiffany's* or *Titanic*.

Sticking to a story can unify multiple pictures from one shoot because each image is centered on the same idea. Stories are especially applicable in editorial shoots. After a story is discussed, the stylist will create **storyboards** using tear sheets (published magazine editorials). Storyboards are tear sheets and inspiration pictures from magazines or the internet collaged together onto a board. The pictures can be used to show hair, makeup, poses, lighting, and fashion ideas. (See Figures 2.5 and 2.6.)

Although the story may seem to be set in stone, experienced stylists know that nothing is ever final until the final camera snap. It's critical that a stylist hit the agreed-upon creative mark, but it never hurts to have multiple additional options handy, just in case anything changes on the set.

[
"It's wonderful when a stylist has a vision, sets up mood boards, etc. But don't micro-manage your hair and makeup team. It's important everyone is on board with a cohesive story, but the greatest shoots always happen when everyone is left to what they do best."
—Rachel Toledo, makeup artist, www.rachelmakeup73.com
]

Pulling for an Editorial Shoot

Retailers usually want to lend their merchandise when they know they will receive editorial credits in a magazine. But they won't just hand merchandise over without a paper trail and a guarantee that someone will take responsibility for its care and safe return. This is the function of a **pull letter**. This is an actual letter (or a PDF of one) written on the client's letterhead that confirms the stylist has been hired for the specific job and that the client and/or the stylist will assume responsibility for the items borrowed. In editorial styling, the more common term is a **letter of responsibility** or LOR, and these tend to be more open-ended rather than job-specific, but the function is the same. Even though there may be a client or an insurance policy promising to pick up the tab for any damage, pulling merchandise is still a big responsibility. A stylist must understand that his or her reputation is on the line with every pull.

Pulls often begin with an email. Send an email to the brand PR contact or showroom manager introducing yourself with your website or some sort of online portfolio; setting forth a description of the job, including the theme, the magazine assigning the job, and the anticipated date of publication; and then listing the team members, especially if there is anyone who is well known in the industry, including a popular photographer or a professional model. Then, set forth exactly what you're looking for. This could be a theme such as "evening gowns" or "red dresses" or specific look numbers from the most recent runway show, but if you're being specific, be ready to set forth a number of options in case some of the samples are not available. Be sure to discuss plans for getting the clothes: if you'd like to pick them up in person, or you'd like the items to be shipped. Provide a FedEx number, in case the agencies will not ship them to you at their expense, and an anticipated return date, which should be as soon as possible.

Figure 2.5
This storyboard was used in an editorial photo shoot. It was the starting point for the fashion, hair, and makeup styling seen on the model.

Figure 2.6
Storyboard for print

Finally, attach a PDF of the pull letter to the email. Do not hesitate to follow up if there has been no response in a few days, but be as polite as possible and always be working on alternative pulls in case any one source falls through.

> "Clients like to see editorial work, and editorial photography gives your portfolio diversity."
> —Dana Goldenberg, stylist. Marlena Trafas, "Ask a Fashion Stylist, an Interview with Dana Goldenberg," Lone Wolf Magazine, August 1, 2015, https://lonewolfmag.com /ask-stylist-dana-goldenberg/.

Pulling for a Lifestyle Shoot

Lifestyle photo shoots are typically used to promote or advertise a nonfashion brand. This could include anything from a print advertising campaign for an insurance company to a person appearing on a cereal box. The goal is often to show real people, so shoot stylists usually pull real clothes. There are two reasons why lifestyle shoots don't often use designer samples. First, there is no incentive for the designers to loan out their samples because there are no fashion credits; no one seeing these photos would know who designed the outfit pictured. Second, all designer samples are made in **sample sizes**, meaning they're designed to fit models who are either a size 0 or a size 2. Because lifestyle shoots are commonly designed to reflect real life, the models look more like real people, meaning they're not always thin enough to fit into the sample sizes.

If the client has a big budget, the stylist can just buy what he or she needs. Most of the time, however, a stylist buys the necessary merchandise and then brings it back for a refund after the shoot. It seems easy, but there are risks to this practice. As with borrowed merchandise, the stylist is responsible for making sure nothing happens to the merchandise during the shoot and that all items are in return-ready condition after the shoot. That means that garment tags are reattached, dress shirts are refolded and pinned, and shoes and handbags are perfectly repacked and stuffed. The goal is to never give a retailer a reason to refuse a return.

> "People I met were impressed when they learned I worked at Vogue. . . . [But] I would lie awake at night, wondering how I would walk into the office (again), face the beautiful skinny women (again), and find new ways to make fun of myself (again)? When I left fashion editorial and started working in commercials and advertising with real women, actors and models, women with imperfect bodies and limited resources, I began to feel a different connection to my work."
> —Stacy London, television personality. Stacy London, The Truth About Style (New York: Viking, 2012), 52.

FASHION PR AND WHY IT MATTERS TO STYLISTS

Public relations firms are often hired by designers to represent their clothing lines. These firms do everything from setting up **Fashion Week** shows, trade shows, and special promotional events, to acquiring and providing stylists with sample garments for shoots as requested. Here are five reasons why fashion PR firms are important to stylists:

1. Fashion PR representatives are the hook up for editorial **samples**. When designers create a collection for the runway, they only make a few garments in each look for models to wear when showing to buyers and editors; these prototype garments are called samples. The designer won't send a look into production until a retailer orders it, so until that happens, only one or two samples of a runway look may exist, and PR reps often control which stylists get to pull them and in what order. This can be important, because the sooner a stylist can access a sample, the better condition the sample will be in.
2. Contacts within these firms can get stylists into important fashion shows and events. This is especially true during Fashion Week. Stylists can typically register with an organizer of a particular city's Fashion Week to get a badge to attend the event in general, but the actual shows are almost always individually ticketed, and the tickets (or invitations) are doled out by the publicists and the designer. While Fashion Week organizers do provide a list of designer contacts to email invitation requests to, it's always better to have a contact rather than to send a request to a general mailbox.
3. Fashion PR firms are great places for aspiring stylists to do internships. They can witness the process of lending out sample garments for editorial shoots. Fashion PR firms also connect aspiring stylists with magazine editors and other useful contacts in the industry.
4. The people who work at fashion PR firms love fashion, too, and chances are they're also working on building their careers in the industry, meaning they'll likely move to other agencies, get promoted, and maybe even launch their own agency or fashion brand someday. Building and maintaining relationships with ambitious agents will always pay off.

> "I knew Prabal Gurung when he was an assistant at Bill Blass. It's cool to grow up with people, but also it's important to remember that today's intern is tomorrow's PR director, designer or big stylist. That's important because people get caught up in, 'Oh they're just this,' or whatever. That's b————."
> —*Sally Lyndley, stylist. Eliza Brooke, "5 Key Career Tips from Successful Stylists," Fashionista, https://fashionista.com/2014/11/stylist-career-advice.*

Fashion Public Relations Agencies

The following fashion PR agencies have offices in New York and Los Angeles. They are great places for fashion students to look for internships. They vary in size, and some of them offer other services in addition to PR.

- Alison Brod Public Relations (alisonbrodpr.com)
- AMP3PR (amp3pr.com)
- BPCM (bpcm.com)
- Haan Projects (haanprojects.net)
- HL Group (hlgrp.com)
- Karla Otto International (karlaotto.com)
- KCD (kcdworldwide.com)
- Krupp Group (kruppgroup.com)
- Michele Marie PR (michelemariepr.com)
- Paul Wilmot Communications (paulwilmot.com)
- Pierce Mattie Communications (piercemattie.com)
- PRC PR Consulting (prconsulting.net)
- Seventh House Public Relations (seventhhousepr.com)

The Fashion Calendar

The traditional manufacturing time line means that each Fashion Week is followed by three to four months of production and delivery time. During this time, buyers place orders, clothing is put into production, and finally, finished garments are delivered to retailers.

There are multiple Fashion Weeks throughout the year, and each corresponds with a different season and/or market. **Ready-to-wear** refers to clothing that is manufactured according to standard sizes that is sold in a store. The main ready-to-wear seasons or markets are Spring, Fall, and **Resort/Cruise**. **Couture** is clothing that a client must order, and it is custom-made to that client's specific measurements. Men's clothing has traditionally been shown at separate Fashion Weeks, but designers are increasingly showing both men's and women's ready-to-wear on the same runway.

There are four main cities where Fashion Weeks take place. These cities show in the same order each season, every year. The order is New York, London, Milan, and finally Paris.

Once Fashion Week wraps, it's time for **Market Week**. This is the time when retail buyers inspect the collections more closely and place their orders for the upcoming season. This is also when buyers can make changes in the runway styles, either to offer exclusives to their customers or to make a garment more marketable. Hemlines might be shortened, or fabric colors might be changed. Depending on what buyers order, some pieces of the collection may not even go into production.

Couture differs from ready-to-wear because each couture garment is individually ordered and custom-made for a particular customer. Couture is not mass-produced in factories or sold off the rack, so it doesn't have a Market Week.

- **Spring ready-to-wear shows:** September/October
- **Spring/summer Paris couture shows:** Late January

- **Spring/summer merchandise deliveries to retailers:** Begins in February
- **Fall ready-to-wear shows:** February/March
- **Resort/cruise shows:** May/June
- **Paris haute couture shows:** Early July
- **Fall/winter merchandise deliveries to retailers:** Begins in July

How the System Works

Designer Showrooms

Designer showrooms are places where buyers come to place orders. Some designer showrooms are located in the design offices and staffed by in-house brand representatives. Other showrooms are spaces leased by designers; they represent a variety of designers under one roof and are staffed by their own sales representatives. Small brands that cannot afford to staff their own showroom can arrange to be represented by a multibrand showroom that manages sales orders for multiple noncompeting brands for a commission. (See Figure 2.7.)

Stylists work to cultivate relationships with the people who run these showrooms. Two good ways to gain access are assisting more experienced stylists and interning for PR firms. Lead stylists are experienced and have a lot of contacts in showrooms. They might borrow clothing from the showrooms for shoots. Sometimes a designer will have an in-house PR team and showroom but will outsource some PR work.

Figure 2.7
Designer showroom

The Day Before the Shoot

A **call time** is the time that shooting is set to begin. Call times can run rather early in the morning, so being prepared the day before will help to ensure a timely arrival. The day before shooting begins can be busy as last-minute items are prepared. As previously noted, sometimes a stylist won't even have a day to prepare and is hired for the job only hours ahead of time.

If the job has lead time, getting the car packed the evening before helps to speed things along in the morning. Everything but clothing can be put in the car early. Clothing shouldn't be put in the car until the last minute to prevent wrinkling, which will save time fixing it during the shoot. The evening before is also a good time to double-check directions, traffic, and road conditions, to make sure the car has plenty of gas to get to the shoot location, and to ensure that all electronic devices are charged.

In more urban locations, the stylist who is working under a small budget might have to plan on using public transportation to get to and from a job. In a larger city where people don't always drive, a client with a larger budget might reimburse for other transportation, such as a rented or hired car. A stylist should have multiple ride-share apps like Uber, Lyft, and Via at the ready and be able to know how early to order a car to avoid delays and surge pricing.

Cheat Sheets

Cheat sheets are typed summaries of outfits and accessories for each scene or shot. As stylists prepare for a shoot and plan how clothing will coordinate, they should be taking notes. (See Figure 2.8.) The notes should read like editorial credits and include clothing descriptions, designer names, prices, and retailer information. It is best to type the notes and print them out the night before shooting. If and when there is a change in the sequence or arrangement of clothing, the changes can be handwritten on the notes. (See Figure 2.9.) This is a neater and more organized approach than typing everything out after the shoot is over. Not only does this help to keep things organized before and during the shoot, but it also prevents mistakes when having to recall clothing by memory.

The Importance of Knowing Fashion Terminology

Fashion terminology is the wording used to describe the details and construction of clothing. Knowing terminology is important for verbal and written communication, especially when writing accurate editorial credits. When designers lend their merchandise for a shoot, they are trusting that they will receive good publicity. If the clothing, designer, or retailers are described incorrectly in the credits, the editorial doesn't look polished. It can also cast doubt on the stylist's skill level.

The stylist is responsible for writing editorial credits. This means that the cheat sheets will have to be properly documented. It also means that the verbiage must be thoroughly proofread after the shoot is over. Improper terminology will be noticed by editors and will reflect the stylist's level of expertise. The stylist must note the price of each item. If a price is not available because the garment is a sample or a boutique does not want to publicize its price, the stylist may write "price available on request." If a stylist uses a sample that does not end up being put into production, the stylist may still credit the designer but include terminology such as "similar styles available at" before listing the retailer.

Melody Acree

PO BOX XXX • New York • New York • 10008 • 555.340.1955 • info@melodyacreefashionstylist.com

PUBLICATION: FLAIR
SHOOT DATE: January 8, 2017
PUBLICATION DATE: March 4
STORY: SPRING FASHION
LOCATION: Bright House Networks Field

PHOTOGRAPHER: Susan Jeffers
FASHION STYLIST: Melody Acree
FASHION ASSISTANT: Blake Glover
MAKEUP/HAIR STYLIST: Lindsey Matacchiero
MODEL: Kelly Maida, Level Model & Talent Management

SHOT #1
SET: Bleachers
Chiffon polka-dot blouse w/ruffled sleeves and tie waist, by Anna Paul from LaFrance, $124.00. White tie-front linen shorts, by Theory, from Saks Fifth Avenue, $175.00. "Scotty" dog pin, $58.00, Circles necklace/bracelet set (bracelet not shown), $88.00, all from LaFrance. Hat: $56.00, LaFrance. Ballet Flats, Thierry rabotin (lowercase intentional), Deborah Kent's, $286.00.

SHOT #2
SET: Baseball Nets
Shorts as above worn with white eyelet kimono sleeved tunic wrap, by BCBGMAXAZRIA, $198.00, available at Saks Fifth Avenue. Worn with silver ballet flats by Juicy Couture, $365.00, available at Saks Fifth Avenue. Green disc earrings, LaFrance, $34.00.

SHOT #3
SET: Wooden Bench
Floral print peasant-style top has ribbon trim and novelty buttons, by Theory, $260.00, available at Neiman Marcus. Worn with Seven for All Mankind Jeans, $280.00, available at Neiman Marcus. Chocolate platform sandal, Tory Burch, $450.00, available at Saks Fifth Avenue. All jewelry, stylist's own.

Figure 2.8
Cheat sheets are typed summaries of outfits and accessories for each scene or shot.

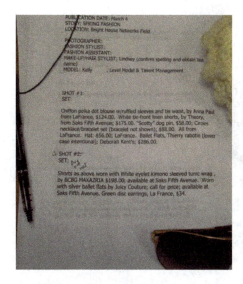

SHOT #1:
SET:

Chiffon polka dot blouse w/ruffled sleeves and tie waist, by Anna Paul from LaFrance, $124.00. White tie-front linen shorts, by Theory, from Saks Fifth Avenue; $175.00. "Scotty" dog pin, $58.00; Circles necklace/bracelet set (bracelet not shown); $88.00. All from LaFrance. Hat: $56.00; LaFrance. Ballet Flats, Thierry rabotin (lower case intentional); Deborah Kent's; $286.00.

SHOT #2:
SET:

Shorts as above worn with White eyelet kimono sleeved tunic wrap , by BCBG MAXAZRIA $198.00; available at Saks Fifth Avenue. Worn with silver ballet flats by Juicy Couture; call for price; available at Saks Fifth Avenue. Green disc earrings, La France, $34.

Figure 2.9
If and when there is a change in the sequence or arrangement of clothing, the changes can be handwritten right onto the cheat sheet.

If you are working for a specific editorial client, try to find out the house citation style so that your credits can be written in a way that makes editing easy on the staff. For example, does the publication include the "www" preface on websites or is only "website.com" written? Are the addresses of retail shops listed with the designer and price or later in a "where to shop" list? Of course, it goes without saying that a stylist must spell everything correctly, from the type of fabric to the designer name. Be sure to double-check everything.

Styling Kit Check

The day or night before shooting, it is good practice to check styling kits one more time to make sure they are fully stocked and that nothing is missing. It might be easier to place the kit box or boxes into the car the night before to save that step in the morning.

Protecting Shoes

Like clothing and accessories, shoes are often borrowed or purchased for shoots, which means they must be returned in perfect condition so that they can be sold to customers. (See Figure 2.10.) Stylists are financially liable for damaged footwear unless they have a pull letter from the client. The key to keeping shoes pristine is masking tape and timing.

All shoes brought on set must be **masked**, which is the process of covering the soles with masking tape to prevent scuffing or other damage caused by contact with the ground. This is easy to do the day before a shoot.

Different stylists have different approaches to masking. Some like acid-free tape from art supply stores, and some use regular standard beige tape. Another option is blue painter's tape. While any tape that's migrated off a heel or sole will be immediately apparent in a photo, the blue can also help a photographer during the postproduction process because the color makes the stray piece of tape easier to notice than if it were a neutral shade. The best approach is to have both types of tape in the kit and to ask the photographer which he or she prefers.

It's also important to gauge the appropriate thickness of the tape layer. If the model is sitting or standing in one place, a single layer may be fine. If the model is moving or if the shoot is outside, it may be necessary to tape a layer or two of cardstock to the bottom of the shoe. Some stylists swear by maxipads to protect shoe soles; the thong-sized pads seem to be shaped perfectly for stiletto soles.

Timing also helps to keep shoes in perfect condition. The stylist usually doesn't put shoes on the model until the last possible minute. Typically, the model will bring a pair of flip-flops, sandals, or thick socks and wear them while walking from the dressing area to the shoot spot. The stylist will carry the shoes and put them on the model while the photographer tests lighting and remove them the minute the photographer has finished shooting the look.

Figure 2.10
Stylists are responsible for providing options for the shoot. Here, options come in the form of a wide variety of shoes to choose from.

Ironing and Steaming Clothing

Clothing will more than likely have to be ironed and/or steamed repeatedly before or during the shoot, but it's good to do a preliminary once-over in the days before as well. (See Figure 2.11.) It can save valuable time on the day of shooting and keep the stylists from feeling too frantic. If the shoot is taking place at a location without electricity, then clothing needs to be prepped and packed as carefully as possible beforehand.

The Day(s) of the Shoot

On the day of the shoot it is best to arrive earlier than call time. When call time arrives, it looks best if the stylist is already on set and available rather than still making trips to and from the car. The kit should have been double-checked the night before. Studio or indoor shoot locations should be able to provide the stylist with a cart and rolling racks for transporting merchandise and a table and chair for the work area. However, this shouldn't be expected. Having an organized kit and your own rolling racks, cart, or dolly and even a folding card table makes the process a lot easier and will ensure that you stay organized and efficient.

Dress for Function

Because stylists don't often get to sit down for long periods of time, they tend to dress practically for work. They might wear flats or sneakers along with clothing that isn't constrictive; it's critical to be able to bend, kneel, and move. This is not to say that stylists shouldn't dress fashionably. Looking good is particularly important because clients are now shooting behind-the-scenes video for social media and as additional online assets. Sometimes the client even hires additional people just to photograph, video, and livestream what's happening on set, and chances are strong that the stylist will get swept up in this coverage.

Figure 2.11
Ironing and/or steaming the clothing will more than likely have to be repeated during the shoot, but it's good to do a preliminary once-over beforehand, too.

"People have this idea of me running around in heels and going to fashion shows, and really, I'm running around in sneakers on photo shoots, unpacking 10 trunks of clothes and repacking them."
—Annie Ladino, celebrity stylist. Interview with celebrity stylist Annie Ladino by Molly Borter for The Muse, https://www.themuse.com/advice/how-i-broke-into-styling-a-qa-with -celebrity-stylist-annie-ladino.

Call Times and When Shooting Takes Place

Photographers often prefer either early morning or late afternoon light for outdoor shooting. The strong overhead light of the middle of the day is sometimes hard to work with. This means that call time might be hours before sunrise, and the stylist will have the model ready to shoot before the sun comes up. Studio shoots may have more flexible hours, but stylists still can't afford to be late for call times.

Shoot Etiquette

It is expected that the stylists will stay close to the model but on the sidelines and out of the camera's view while the photographer shoots. It is the stylist's job to keep an eye out for any adjustments that need to be made. (See Figure 2.12.) If imperfections with the model's clothing or accessories are not fixed on set,

Figure 2.12
Set work includes adjusting and checking the fit of clothing during the photo shoot.

the photographer or the client must spend extra time and money to fix them in postproduction.

When a stylist needs to step into the shot to make adjustments, he or she must tell the photographer. Creative input from the stylist is always welcome. However, the stylist doesn't have the ultimate say, and teamwork is more important. Etiquette for the print shoot will be explored more in Chapters 9 and 10, which cover planning for and executing the shoot.

Keeping Track of the Clothing

All merchandise must be accounted for when arriving on set and before leaving. It's also the stylist's responsibility to keep track of all tags, stuffing, packaging, and boxes in order to be able to correctly re-package and re-tag merchandise. It is best to account for everything while everyone is still on set. If people have left and things turn up missing, there is less hope of retrieving them. (See Figure 2.13.)

Key Players on Set

It is important for the stylist to be aware of who is calling the shots on set. There may be more than one decision maker there, but ultimately the stylist must satisfy the client's needs. Here are the key players listed in their order of importance.

Client

The client employs everyone on the shoot. It is the client who pays the bills and who must ultimately be pleased with the outcome of the shoot. The amount of client involvement varies in the hiring process for a shoot. With a smaller company, the client is more likely to be hands-on in hiring the crew. Clients can include catalogue companies or business owners who want to advertise.

Art Director, Producer, or Production Manager

An art director, **producer**, or **production manager** is sometimes a freelancer hired by the client. Other times this person is a part of the client's in-house staff. Depending on the size of the shoot and its budget, one person or more fill these roles. It is this person's responsibility to oversee the shoot and communicate the client's wishes. (See Figure 2.14.) He or she will hire the photographer, who in turn might hire the stylist. Other times, this person might have a particular stylist he or she likes to work with.

Figure 2.13
Fashion stylists always arrive at a shoot with more clothing than necessary. There need to be alternative options in case something doesn't photograph well or there is time to take extra shots. Fashion stylists use foldable rolling racks to hold clothing.

Photographer

Photographers are often responsible for hiring the stylists and talent for a shoot. They will sometimes also have their own assistant. The photographer's opinion holds a lot of sway, since he or she is the one looking through the camera lens.

Figure 2.14
The art director oversees the shoot and makes sure the client's wishes are represented.

Stylist

The stylist falls right below the photographer in the pecking order of the shoot. That means that the client, art director, producer, and photographer all have more say in big decisions such as model casting and shoot location. Collaboration should be enjoyable, but the stylist also needs to know that his or her input might not affect the final shot.

Talent

Talent is usually the model but can include anyone in front of the lens. The talent is there to enhance the product and adjust poses according to direction from the photographer.

The Day after the Shoot

Shoot days can often be long and exhausting, and it is tempting to procrastinate on completing the **wrap work** that needs to be done.

Wrap work includes returning clothing (as soon as possible to maintain a good working relationship with the retailer, designer, showroom, or PR firm), billing the client, restocking the kit, removing tear sheets from the storyboard and filing them for later use, and writing and submitting editorial credits. It is best to schedule an open day on the day after a shoot so that final tasks can be completed, and this time can often be billed to the client. Postshoot responsibilities will be explored more in Chapters 9 and 10.

INDUSTRY INTERVIEW

Interview with Adam Drawas and Jennifer Walker
Website: *http://www.walkerdrawas.com/*

Walker Drawas PR does work for some amazing brands—Revole, Lucky Brand, Gant, True Religion, Jinny Kim, and Charlotte Ronson, to name a few. How do you decide if a label is the right fit for you and your clients?

Adam: Jennifer and I come from brands that consumers want in real life. We work with a lot of street brands and high-end day wear. More life-focused than red carpet. For us a lot of these brands need to activate in the marketplace. In more unique ways we are experts at, like, celebrity dressing and working with media and editors that fit that mold.

Jennifer: I think it's important when we sit down with all of our clients or potential clients we sort of vet them on their understanding, willingness, or hunger to think outside the box. And be respective to our expertise in terms of moving the needle. We know that traditional types of fashion PR and marketing mechanisms very much exist; however, it's more the adventurous brands that really want to be innovative and different that pave the way that we are really excited to be working with.

Can you give a basic explanation of what your role is in relation to working with fashion bloggers and stylists who pull clothing from your press showroom?
Adam: Our role is to place product on fashion stylists, bloggers, tastemakers, and celebrities and work with media publications and editorial outlets to place product in the consumer market place. So the consumer can understand what's out there and available from a fashion style perspective.

How'd did you get into the fashion industry? Did you have formal training, or is it something that evolved or you fell into?
Adam: I went straight into working with brands in various capacities. I started out in London, working in everything from fashion PR to show production. I kind of forewent a lot of formal education and learned on the job. I knew the industry much more as a trade and I apprenticed as many people as possible. It gave me an understanding of how the industry worked and which facet of the industry I connected with most. And that kind of led to another and so on. . . .

Jennifer: I moved to NY out of college. I started my career in-house at Ben Sherman. Starting this way was a great way for me to learn a grassroots type of fashion marketing, as those brands were pretty scrappy in the best way possible. I found the experience extremely valuable to be able to do things I would do later in my career. I also knew that after working there for four and a half years I needed more technical training. I went to go with a very established fashion PR firm in NY working with brands like H&M and Matthew Williamson. This experience helped me to think long-term. Here I also learned a plethora of skills with producing events and NY fashion week shows. I also learned to work with contemporary designers with what their day-to-day process was, as well as working with the LA agency and the celebrity side of fashion. From there I went back to an in-house job with All Saints. Then in 2009 social media started to amp up. Instagram started to get going and this whole influencer and celebrity influence became a lot more substantial beyond the red carpet. I saw a lot more power being generated by the influence of these outlets. I then moved to the West Coast and joined forces with Adam. We realized with both our talents we were stronger together.

How important do you think it is for stylists to get their clothes on celebrities?

Adam: I think it's everything nowadays. With social media the viewership is how the consumer absorbs what's going on with the marketplace. Those are the vehicles. It used to be the primary avenue of fashion was through magazines. Then in the early 2000s people started taking more notice with celebrities. A lot of it started on the red carpet. As paparazzi grew and people seeing what celebrities wore day to day grew, people were more interested to know what that "it girl" was wearing rather than what the model was wearing. It's not to say that magazines and media aren't working; both are extremely vital but equally parallel. It shows what is hot at the moment. Celebrity fashion endorsement, whether it be the formal campaign or what they wear down the street, is critically important to what the consumer wants. Consumers want to see a different perspective and a little more approach to style. There's a little more democracy in what people want to wear. Nowadays, it's about multiple people's perspective in what is shown. For the consumer, [it's about] being able to see style in your size, in your shape, in your ethnicity, and style choices. . . . you don't need to conform to what one editor in a magazine says what you need to wear; more people can say, "This is what is hot, this is what's cool." When working with a celebrity, it's never one note; it's about finding the right fit.

How have technology and social media changed the styling and fashion industry?

Adam: What has happened over the last two years has been an insane surge of content. The consumer has a very short attention span because there are constant visuals happening. If you think about it, when you are watching TV and it goes to the commercial, the most likely thing that's happening is that you are grabbing your phone and scrolling through social media. The consumer is consuming much quicker. There is a lot more access and a lot more out there.

Jennifer: Yes, to add to Adam's point: where we used to shop a lot of retails, we now shop a lot in terms of authority. So people used to flip the pages of *Elle* or *Vogue* as a source of information of what's cool or hot. Now the fandom has changed; now we have influencers and Instagramers who are becoming more influential than celebrities in that way because the people/audience are looking to them to teach them what to wear and to tell them how to shop. People are ultimately trying to become and live this lifestyle. Bloggers' influences are being driven out through all their social channels.

Adam: One thing to add: There is another bridge being built. Social media are talking about what's hot but now you can buy it immediately. You literally can go from perusing what's out there to getting your hands on it in a matter of seconds. The access and the lead-time of wanting something and purchasing it, are minutes. So the consumption rate has grown so fast and because of that the competition is greater and greater and the price points are more cost effective. This is also why the industry has shifted so much to the importance of social media when it comes to fashion. Ten years ago you would see a runway show and have to wait six months to get it in store. Now, people talk about the aesthetic and you can get it in 24 hours; it's the doors to access. It has changed drastically.

What advice do you wish someone had told you before you got into the fashion industry, and what advice would you give to your younger self?

Adam: Something no one ever told me before I got into the industry is that it is an industry of smoke and mirrors. The fashion industry promotes and puts a spotlight on glamour and style to showcase what fabulous lifestyles are out there, but those who work in it are just the purveyors of that; we are not the ones living it. Buckle up because it's not that glamorous. Someone once said many years ago, "You are either a workhorse or a show pony," but in the fashion world, you have to be both. You need to put on the show and throw around the dazzle, but at the end of the day you need to wake up first before anybody.

Jennifer: I always have people comment on how fun and awesome my life looks. I get to travel and go to the Super Bowl and Coachella and hang out with celebrities and throw fun parties, but really it is a lot more work than everybody thinks it is. Although it looks like a lot of fun but it is a hustle and a grind. It is very rewarding as well, but it is in no way a cakewalk!

I'm sure you have some pet peeves of people who come to your showroom and borrow things. Do you have any advice for new stylists on how to approach a fashion PR properly? What are some no-no's?

Adam: Respect and transparency. At the end of the day, say what really the job is. Say what is happening with honesty and clarity and say it with respect. More importantly, you are only as strong as your relationships. I think our relationships are a testament to who we are as people. If a stylist needs a favor, if we have a good relationship, we will make that favor in a blink of an eye. Maintain that respect so people always know what they are getting from you. Also you need to make people feel comfortable. I believe that being able to enjoy the process with people will make the situations so much easier.

Jennifer: My one thing is never burn a bridge. You never know who you are going to work with later down the road or the opportunities that are going to open up to you. Keep your integrity and your ethics intact.

What happens if a stylist loses a garment? Do you have any funny or horror stories? What happens if a garment gets ruined? How does a stylist deal with that? What's the proper etiquette?

Adam: A way that you move on from them is that you deal with them and never bring it up again. Be real and handle your business and do everything in your power to fix the situation even if there isn't a perfect result.

Do you have any other words of wisdom or advice for those dreaming of entering the world of styling for fashion?

Adam: This industry is competitive and at times cutthroat. You have to love fashion. You have to love pop culture in all of its forms as it's a long-haul type of industry.

Jennifer: Get some rest!

Interview with Brandy Joy Smith

Brandy Joy Smith is from northern California and began working as a stylist in 2009. Brandy resides in Brooklyn, New York, with her chorkie Bambi and fiancé Tyler. She draws inspiration from her many travels. Some of her favorite places to visit are Paris, Tulum, and Copenhagen. In her spare time Brandy finds passion in other hobbies such as baking pastries and candies, hiking, and reading. She prides herself in her ability to execute visual storytelling through wardrobe and finds her job as a stylist to be extremely rewarding.

Website: *www.brandyjoysmith.com*
Instagram: *@brandyjoysmith*
Twitter: *@brandyjoy*

What celebrities, companies, or high-profile clients have you worked with?
Andy Cohen; J. Cole; Sasheer Zamata and Aidy Bryant of SNL; Jessica Williams; Fred Armisen; Chloe and Halle; Maye Musk; Linda Wells; The Gap; Elle; Harper's Bazaar; Marie Claire; L'Officiel

How did you get into the fashion industry? Did you have formal training, or is it something that evolved or you fell into?
I started at a CDFA award-winning jewelry company in marketing and PR. During that time, I began doing some styling for our marketing materials and it ended up morphing into my realization that I had an artistic passion towards the idea of becoming a stylist.

Did you go straight into styling, or did you assist first?
I did assist first. I started interning for a stylist named Kerri Curtis, and it soon turned into assisting before venturing out on my own and creating my business.

Now that you are styling, what qualities do you look for in an assistant?
The most important qualities I look for in an assistant are a positive attitude and drive. The hours can be long and exhausting, so it's very important to me that my assistant continually has a positive attitude amidst the hectic schedules. We like to keep a motto of #nobadvibes in our work environment. The second key factor being the abstract concept of "drive" because everything else about the job is teachable.

What kinds of job duties did you do when you first started working?
I steamed clothes, picked up clothes, inventoried samples, set up, broke down, grabbed coffees, took out the trash. You learn quickly if you want to stand out as an assistant that you have to be willing to do it all, and do it with a smile on your face.

Do you have any funny or horror stories of when you first started?
In my first year working as a lead stylist, I was styling a wedding spread in Texas for fall. The male model was wearing a dark navy velvet tuxedo jacket (did I mention this was in the middle of a summer heat wave?). The aforementioned jacket was extremely expensive and had been loaned from a retailer. Both models were standing on a small hill, and as the photographer began to shoot, the male model fainted from the heat and fell down the hill. After checking to see if he was okay, my next worry was the blazer. Luckily, the company paid to have it dry-cleaned and it was able to be returned to the retailer, but I admittedly was a nervous wreck until then.

What's something you wish someone had told you before you started? What advice would you give your younger self about styling?
In the beginning, you are really stressed about all the logistics of the job and that can overwhelm you. Though I'm extremely organized and detailed, I have to remind myself I'm not saving lives; no one is going to die on my watch. I'm playing with clothes, and if I'm not having fun then I've missed the entire point of having this creative job.

What do you feel is a common mistake that many people make when they first start out in the industry? Or a common misconception about what you do?
I get a ton of interns that think we are going to just be on set everyday, doing something glamorous. The reality of the job, however, is far from that. We are on our feet shopping or going to showrooms daily, packing and unpacking samples. It's a physically demanding job and you need to be ready for it. On that note, so glad sneakers are in style now.

What's your philosophy of styling or dressing a client?
My philosophy is dress for your body type. Once you do this, you'll be surprised at what you can pull off. I do like to nudge clients out of their comfort zone sometimes when I think it's something they haven't tried before, and it's rewarding to see what an eye-opening experience it can be for them and their confidence.

Where do you like to shop?
Personally, I like to shop at Sandro Paris, & Other Stories, Bloomingdales, and Saks. Typically I only shop for myself if I see something when shopping for a client. I'm always in the Soho area jumping in and out of stores. I also love some Brooklyn locals like Catbird, In God We Trust, and Bird.

What are some of your favorite designers?
Some of my favorite designers and brands are Alexander Wang, 3.1 Phillip Lim, Sandro Paris, Whistles, Stella McCartney, & Other Stories, and Reformation. I like to shop high and low; I'm all over the boards. Mostly for dressing myself, I like things that are not overly feminine.

What are some hidden gems or offbeat places where you pick up stuff for jobs?
I call these places my "connects" (rental houses). Mostly they are industry places for shoes. My go-to stop is Montana Rader; she has locations in NY and LA. It's basically like walking into shoe heaven. For clothing I like to visit Eric from Cloak [Luxury Wardrobe Rentals]. His service and inventory are first class.

How much of your own personal style can be influenced on a job?
I really separate my personal style from my clients. I have a marketing and PR background and that history really allows me to see things from the client's side. I typically wear mostly muted colors, but I find my work has a ton of color in it.

Who are your muses? How or where do you find inspiration?
In early life I would say my grandmother was one of my muses. She was a cocktail waitress, and I would look at all of her pictures of her getting glammed up to go to work. She always had that perfect balance of sleek and trendy. Today, I find my inspiration in old movies and people in the streets. New York is filled with such creative style, I always find myself being inspired by perfect strangers whenever I decide to take a casual walk.

What's something that you don't like about being a stylist? If you could change something about the industry, what would it be?
As we have entered the digital age, it seems the amount of work one has to produce has rapidly increased. Although this is great for your pocketbook, it can be frustrating for your creative curative process. The projects can seem very rushed; that's why I feel it's important to create projects for yourself just to stimulate your creative juices and express without limitation or expectation.

It can be difficult keeping track of so many items on a big job or when juggling a multitude of shoots. How do you keep organized? Do you have a special system, so to speak, that you like to use?
My best secret for organization would have to be my ability to prioritize what's important. More often than not, I'll have a detailed list of what I need to do that day, and in one second it can all change and my team and myself all have to switch gears. Once you can prioritize the most important tasks at hand, the flow of things becomes a lot more evident.

Do you have one or two signature styling tips?

I think it's important for a stylist to be able to separate her own wants and style from the client at hand. Once the ability to do this is second nature, you'll find you can be creative in a different way than what you're used to. For dressing, it's definitely about dressing for your body type and style. Understanding what you can and cannot pull off is huge. I think people should understand the difference between what they think is cute on a hanger and what they know will look good on them and do something for them. Once you have your style down, you will finally achieve the ever elusive concept of looking "effortless."

How do you network? Why is it important to build relationships in this industry?

I usually try to create relationships on the jobs I work on by being present and just engaging in conversation with the client and production team. I've been able to create some very rewarding friendships that go beyond work. At this point in my career, positive word of mouth goes a long way in connecting with new clients.

How do you present your work (e.g., website, portfolio, comp cards)? How did you establish your aesthetic or brand?

I put work on my website, and I have an online portfolio. Since everything is digital these days, it's a better way to present my past jobs to the masses. Also, I try my best to reduce the amount of paper we use in the office.

How have technology and social media changed the styling profession and fashion industry?

It's definitely picked up the pace for jobs. We'll have back-to-back work now without a break for months. Since social media and technology influence people's ideas, you constantly need to keep up with what is happening to know the trends that are created in seemingly the blink of an eye. What's cool in March, for example, won't necessarily be cool in a couple of months.

Do you have any tips for working as a freelance or independent contractor (anything from tax tips to professional practice, like contracts and insurance, getting paid, setting rates)?

Personally, I have an agent to do the negotiating side of things because I don't want that to get in the way of my personal client relationships. Other tips for being a freelancer are keeping organized, having your paper trails, and have a constant system and a trustworthy squad.

Anything else you would like to add—quotes or words of wisdom?

I try to enforce to my team that I don't have all the answers. But, if they find that they learn from my experience, then I will be an open book to them. I think it's important to keep sight of what holds value for your own life, and to not only place goals, but work as hard as you can until you meet those goals. People would be surprised at how much they can achieve once they put it in their head that it is possible.

Summary and Review

Photo styling is a field with many varied options. Photo stylists work with both high fashion and everyday looks, depending on whether they're doing editorial or lifestyle work. In the best-case scenarios, stylists have time to plan for the shoot ahead of time. Sometimes, however, they are hired for jobs at the last minute and have only hours to prepare. Pay rates vary depending on the type of shoot and the photo stylist's level of experience.

Prep work includes tasks such as ironing or steaming clothing, writing cheat sheets, and making sure the styling kit is fully stocked. On the day of the shoot the stylist should arrive a little earlier than call time to prepare a work space. It is advisable to dress for comfort, since stylists stay on their feet for long periods of time. Also, the stylist should be prepared to stand on the sidelines during shooting and jump in to make adjustments when necessary. Wrap work includes billing, returning borrowed clothing, and restocking the styling kit.

The business of fashion follows lengthy production timetables pegged to seasons and international fashion show calendars. These production timetables also dictate when magazines can photograph and publish new collections. Recently, a production trend has emerged called "See-Now, Buy-Now" that makes fashions available immediately after they are presented on the runway. It remains to be seen whether this new trend will be embraced across the industry.

Key Terms

- art director
- call time
- cheat sheets
- client
- couture
- day rate
- designer showrooms
- editorial credits
- editorial look
- fashion terminology
- Fashion Week
- letter of responsibility
- Market Week
- masking
- photo shoot stylist
- photographer
- prep work

- print stylists
- producer
- production manager
- pull
- pull letter
- ready-to-wear
- Resort/Cruise
- sample
- sample size
- See-Now, Buy-Now
- sitting
- sourcing
- story
- storyboard
- styling kit
- talent
- wrap work

Review Questions

1. What are the two main areas of print styling, and how are they different?
2. How far in advance do editorial shoots take place before magazine publication?
3. Why is it important to stick to a story when shooting?
4. Name two reasons that PR firms are important to aspiring and professional stylists.
5. Why are many in the fashion industry frustrated by the traditional fashion calendar? Do you think See-Now, Buy-Now is a good idea? Why or why not?
6. List three tasks that can be completed before the day of a shoot.
7. Why do stylists need to fix as many imperfections on the talent as possible during the shoot?
8. List three ways a stylist could earn more money on a shoot.
9. Discuss two ways professional relationships can help a stylist prepare for a shoot.

Learning Activities

Learning Activity 2.1: Use pictures from magazine editorials to create a storyboard for a photo shoot. The photo shoot can be an imaginary shoot or a real test shoot that is being planned for a future date. There should be enough pictures to fill either two 8.5 × 11 inch pages or one 11 × 17 inch page. The pictures should all center on a specific theme or story that can be executed in a photo shoot.

Learning Activity 2.2: Select a current fashion magazine and flip to the back of the magazine where the editorials are located. The editorials will have pictures of models in a multipage story. Find the names of the fashion editors or stylists of the editorials. Research each editor or stylist and write a two- to three-sentence summary of his or her background. This might include past publications or famous personalities that this person has styled.

Learning Activity 2.3: Find a fashion editorial in one of the major fashion magazines. Write at least a half-page paragraph summarizing the story. Describe the inspiration, types of clothing shown, color palettes, model poses, and setting of the shoot.

Resources

"About Patricia Field." Patricia Field ArtFashion. https://patriciafield.com/pages/bio.

"All About Becoming a Fashion/Wardrobe Stylist." The Fashion Spot. December 16, 2003. http://forums.thefashionspot .com/f90/all-about-becoming-fashion-wardrobe-stylist-2-a-118317.html.

Collings, Kat. "The REAL Salaries of Fashion Editors May Shock You," WhoWhatWhere.com. August 26, 2014. http://www.whowhatwear.com/fashion-salary/slide8.

Cox, Susan Linnet. *Photo Styling: How to Build Your Career and Succeed*. New York: Allworth Press, 2006.

Dingemans, Jo. *Mastering Fashion Styling*. Philadelphia: Trans-Atlantic Publications, 1999.

"Fashion Stylist Salary." PayScale. http://www.payscale.com/research/US/Job=Fashion_Stylist/Salary.

"Fashion Stylist Salary." PayScale. http://www.payscale.com/research/US/Job=Fashion_Stylist/Hourly_Rate.

Friedman, Vanessa. "How Smartphones Are Killing off the Fashion Show." *The New York Times*. February 11, 2016. https://www.nytimes.com/2016/02/11/fashion/new-york-fashion-week-smartphones-killing-off-runway-show.html.

"The Federation." Fédération de la Haute Couture et de la Mode. https://fhcm.paris/en/the-federation/

Holgate, Mark. "Ralph Lauren Goes to See-Now-Buy-Now Format—Check Out His Clothes Here First." *Vogue.com*. September 12, 2016. http://www.vogue.com/article/ralph-lauren-new-york-fashion-week-show-buy-now-fall-2016.

"How Much Should You Make as a Stylist?" School of Style.com. February 1, 2014. https://www.youtube.com/watch?v=J89hXZTNfWs.

Jones, Sue Jenkyn. *Fashion Design*. London: Laurence King Publishers, 2011.

Lyndley, Sally. "How Much Money Does a Stylist Make?" YouTube. October 1, 2014. https://www.youtube.com/watch?v=_-2ukuOtFwQ.

Matthews, Erica. "Mastering Pulling/Calling in Clothes & Sending Emails." YouTube. February 10, 2016. https://www.youtube.com/watch?v=bAOSmFsj4Qw.

Maxwell, Kim. *Career Diary of a Fashion Stylist*. Chicago: Garth Gardner Company, 2007.

"9 Editorial Stylists to Admire." School of Style.com. http://schoolofstyle.com/blog/9-editorial-stylists-to-admire/.

"NYC Fashion Market Weeks." NYC Fashion. http://www.apparelsearch.com/terms/m/market_week_term.html.

Paton, Elizabeth. "Fashion Shows Adopted a See-Now, Buy-Now Model. Has It Worked?" *The New York Times*. February 7, 2017. https://www.nytimes.com/2017/02/07/fashion/see-now-buy-now-business-fashion-week.html.

Roche, Eddie. "Love Connection: Marc Jacobs & Katie Grand." *The Daily Front Row*. September 10, 2015. https://fashionweekdaily.com/love-connection-marc-jacobs-katie-grand/.

"10 Best Fashion Stylists." Netrobe.com. February 20, 2012. http://blog.netrobe.com/2012/02/10-best-fashion-stylists/.

Thomas, Pauline Weston. "Chambre Syndicale Fashion History." Fashion-era.com. http://www.fashion-era.com/chambre_syndicale.htm.

White, Jan. *Editing by Design: For Designers, Art Directors, and Editors—The Classic Guide to Winning Readers*. New York: Allworth Press, 2003.

Wintour, Anna. Introduction to *Stylist: The Interpreters of Fashion*, ed. Style.com, vii. New York: Rizzoli, 2007.

Wright, Crystal. *The Hair, Makeup & Styling Career Guide*. Los Angeles: Motivational Media Productions, 2007.

3 Styling for the Entertainment Industry

CHAPTER TOPICS CALL SHEET

In this chapter you will learn:
- The differences between wardrobe styling and costume design
- How film and television productions are produced
- How to create continuity throughout the film or television episode
- The differences between major movie studios and independent studios
- How a theater wardrobe department runs
- How to style a musician for a video or performance

WARDROBE STYLING FOR FILM AND TELEVISION

Many fashion stylists work in films, television series, television commercials, or theater productions. Fashion stylists in these industries can work under a variety of job titles. This book will refer to them as *wardrobe stylists*. (See Figure 3.1.) Wardrobe stylists work in costume or wardrobe departments under the job titles of **wardrobe supervisor** and **wardrobe assistant**. The wardrobe supervisor, once known as a wardrobe mistress or wardrobe master, oversees the entire cast's costumes, works closely with the director to execute the correct vision for the production, and ensures that the wardrobe stays within budget. Wardrobe assistants work under wardrobe supervisors, helping to source and organize costumes.

Wardrobe styling can present a different set of challenges from print styling. Working with moving images and an entire cast of characters can place heavy demands on a wardrobe department. Multiple people are usually hired to help make things run smoothly. This chapter outlines the job duties of wardrobe stylists and how they function within a production.

Wardrobe Stylists Are Not Costume Designers

Wardrobe stylists are not to be confused with **costume designers**. Costume designers in the purest sense

Figure 3.1
The wardrobe department of a film or television production, where all costumes are stored and inventoried.

are responsible for conceptualizing, illustrating, designing, cutting, and sewing clothing. Different productions require different levels of sewing from their wardrobe and costume departments.

Wardrobe Styling

At the very least, most productions require sourcing and purchasing a wardrobe, as well as making a few alterations if necessary. This is not like print styling, where a model's clothing can be clipped or pinned for a better fit. In print the clips can be hidden from the camera lens because it is a still picture. In film and television, the talent is moving in front of the lens, so there is no room for clips or pins. Clothing must fit properly from the outset, which means that talent must be fitted to their wardrobe by the wardrobe stylist.

Costume Designing

When a production uses costumes designed from scratch, it is the costume designer, not a wardrobe stylist, who plans and designs the wardrobe for the entire cast. An example of a production that would hire a costume designer is a historical film based in the 1600s. It is difficult to find preserved garments from that century, and usually they can only be found in museums. Also, it is almost certain that the cast members' body measurements would not fit an authentic historical garment. Therefore, it is necessary to either design costumes from scratch or find existing period costumes and make alterations if necessary.

Areas in Television Where Wardrobe Stylists Work

Television can provide a wide range of opportunities for stylists because there are so many types of productions and the production cycle is faster than on a movie. Wardrobe stylists work on television series, miniseries, made-for-TV movies, shopping channels, news channels, game shows, and commercials, to name just a few of the major areas. (See Figure 3.2a–b.)

Major Cities Where Wardrobe Stylists Find Employment

The major cities for wardrobe stylists to find employment are Los Angeles and New York. Many productions also take place in Chicago and Las Vegas, and Orlando, Austin, and Miami are well-known production spots. Unlike with print styling, it is hard to support oneself as a wardrobe stylist without living in one of these cities, and Los Angeles is preferable. Print stylists can diversify their skills and work in a variety of areas within editorial and lifestyle. Wardrobe stylists can only work where there is filming taking place.

Major Studios vs. Independent Studios

Major studios dominate production in Los Angeles and New York. They have the biggest budgets and the most star power. (See Figure 3.3.) However, it is difficult for an aspiring wardrobe stylist to get hired by a major studio from the outset. Small independent production companies are more likely to hire someone with little to no professional background. Working on an independent production can be a wonderful experience. Most likely, an aspiring stylist would be hired for the first time as a wardrobe assistant. However, in very small productions it is not unheard of for a first-time stylist to oversee the entire wardrobe department. This means that there is potential for a higher degree of creative input in smaller productions. (See Figure 3.4.) It can be a great place to start building a résumé, but expect to get little or even no pay in the beginning.

Figure 3.2a–b
Wardrobe stylists work in television on series, miniseries, made-for-TV movies, shopping channels, news channels, game shows, and commercials. A: Still from *Coco Chanel*. B: Still from *Cloverfield*.

Figure 3.3
Still from *Guardians of the Galaxy II*

Figure 3.4
Still from *Girls*

Internships are also a great way to build experience. Small independent production companies make good internship sites. Interns are participating for résumé experience and should not expect to be paid.

"I wanted to create a fashion editor portrayed by Meryl [Streep], so it was very important that I understood her body, her ideas, and so on. . . . I went into the archives of Donna Karan, because when she started in the '80s and the '90s, her silhouettes were classic, they held up in time, they fit women, they flattered women, they weren't difficult. You can't start putting difficult clothes on a person. They're actors: they have to move, they have to feel real. And Donna said 'Yeah, go to my archives.' I went to New Jersey where she has a warehouse and I went through racks and racks, and I brought a lot of pieces out from there, and we used a lot of those pieces."

—Patricia Field, costume designer for The Devil Wears Prada. *Julie Kosin, "Patricia Field on Creating the Look of 'The Devil Wears Prada,'" Harper's Bazaar, June 30, 2016, http://www .harpersbazaar.com/culture/film-tv/a16439/patricia-field-devil-wears-prada -10-year-anniversary-interview/.*

The Average Income for a Wardrobe Stylist

The national average income for wardrobe stylists is roughly the same as for print stylists (approximately $50,000 per year). There are advantages to working in this part of the industry. For one, there is more continuity when it comes to work time. Since film and television productions last longer than a print shoot, the stylist works more consistently. However, this means that a wardrobe stylist makes less per day than a print stylist. Another advantage is that there are professional guilds or unions available to support wardrobe and costume personnel.

A disadvantage of working in film or television is that stylists might not get as much creative control over the clothing. They are executing the vision of the director according to the script, and they are often working with everyday looks. This is much more specific than editorial styling, where stylists interpret general ideas and work with cutting-edge fashion.

Unions and Membership Societies

Unlike print styling, wardrobe styling has resources for those who are willing to be members of certain organizations. Here is a list of professional societies and unions for wardrobe and costume personnel:

- **The Costume Society of America:** An informative resource for costume history (www .costumesocietyamerica.com).
- **United States Institute for Theatre Technology's Costume Commission:** A good resource for networking. Other members can help with finding hard-to-locate items that need to be purchased for productions (www.usitt.org).
- **IATSE Union: Motion Picture Costumers Union Local 705 in Hollywood:** This union is divided up into trade specialty areas. Unions help to negotiate wages for costume professionals (www .motionpicturecostumers.org).
- **IBPAT: United Scenic Artists Union Local 829:** This union has offices in Chicago, New York, and Los Angeles. Like the IATSE union, it provides support to members and strives to improve wages and working conditions (www.usa829.org).

The Chain of Command

Understanding the chain of command on a film or television set helps the stylist know how to behave and where to address questions or concerns. This list sets out a typical chain of command, starting from the top:

- **Executive Producer:** Finds screenplay and secures funding
- **Producer:** Hires lead crew and staff
- **Director:** Responsible for the creative vision of the shoot; oversees everything on set
- **Assistant Director:** Assists director in everything, including hiring and overseeing crew
- **Production Designer:** The head of the art department who helps to create the overall look of the film

- **Costume Designer:** Oversees wardrobe for entire production
- **Costume Supervisor:** Involved in producing costumes for the production
- **Wardrobe Supervisor:** Makes sure that there are enough costumes, helps check for continuity, oversees wardrobe department
- **Key Costumer:** Assists costume designer, helps ensure wardrobe stays within budget, oversees fittings
- **Costumer or Costume Attendant:** Maintains costumes and dressing area, dresses talent

THE PHASES OF PRODUCTION

As in print work, the wardrobe stylist is active in planning (prep), set, and wrap work. In motion pictures and television these three phases are called **preproduction**, **production**, and **postproduction**. All of these phases are carefully planned and scheduled. Just like print stylists, wardrobe stylists must be prepared for any number of crises by the time shooting begins. Among other things, this means having backup costumes and a fully stocked styling kit.

There are some basics that wardrobe stylists need to know to effectively work on a film or television series. (See Figure 3.5.) For example, it is helpful to know the different phases of production as well as who the bosses are on set. If a novice stylist is entering the field, knowing these will help work run more smoothly.

Getting the Green Light

Before preproduction can begin, a project must get the **green light**. When a project gets the green light, it means that the producer and screenwriter have pitched their idea to a studio and the studio has agreed to provide funding.

Figure 3.5
As in print styling, the wardrobe stylist often needs to be observant of shooting. Adjustments often need to be made to the fit of the wardrobe, and the stylist must be ready to step in at any given moment. Wardrobe malfunctions can slow the production and can be frustrating for the cast and crew.

Preproduction

Preproduction begins after a project gets the green light. It is extremely busy and entails a great deal of organization and planning. A multitude of things need to happen in this time frame. The shooting schedule is created, cast and crew are hired, sets are created, shoot locations are scouted, budgets and accounting protocols are established, and production offices are set up. This is the time that the wardrobe supervisor and assistants are hired and costumes are planned, sourced, and purchased.

Storyboards

Storyboards are explained in the previous chapter, but storyboards for film, TV, or other types of video shoots follow a different format. When used for video shoots, storyboards are visual layouts of the script that are created in the preproduction phase. They are drawn by hand and are similar to comic books in their formatting. Directors use storyboards to plan scenes in advance during the preproduction phase. (See Figure 3.6.) They also help map out wardrobe changes. While a storyboard for an editorial shoot might simply have inspirational photos from magazines or websites, a storyboard for a film or commercial often has scenes sketched out individually.

Figure 3.6
Directors use storyboards to plan scenes in advance during the preproduction phase. Storyboards also help map out wardrobe changes.

Production

The production phase is also called **principal photography**. This is when all of the scenes are filmed with basic dialogue only. There are no sound effects added yet, and the scenes aren't necessarily shot in chronological order. In fact, a shooting schedule might dictate that a scene where a costume is destroyed gets shot before a preceding scene where the costume is intact. This means that the wardrobe stylist must have multiple versions of the same costume on hand—as many as three or four. Costumes can get stained or lost, or an additional garment may be needed for reshoots. The end of the principal photography phase is called a **wrap**.

Postproduction

Postproduction is when footage is edited into its final form. This is also when music and sound effects are added. At this point, much of the wardrobe is put away because shooting has wrapped. However, the wardrobe stylist must always be prepared in the event of **reshoots**. Reshoots occur when certain scenes are shot again with some changes. They are common in the film industry and take place after **editing** has begun. Editing involves arranging raw footage and changing the length of scenes. Sometimes, during the editing process, the director decides that certain scenes need to be reshot to enhance the final product. This means that the wardrobe stylist must be prepared with the exact costumes needed for each scene. The costumes must be organized, prepped, and easily accessible. Also, photographic documentation from the principal photography phase must be referred to so that characters retain a consistent look.

Wardrobe stylists use digital cameras, mobile phones, or other handheld devices to document looks for continuity. The photographs serve as quick references and visual reminders of how the costumes look on the talent. They also show things that might be done to costumes such as tearing, distressing, or applying fake blood splatter. The photographs are saved after principal photography ends in case they are needed for reference during reshoots.

Television Commercial Production

Television commercials follow a similar production process to television and film, but they are produced in a shorter amount of time and with a smaller budget. The crews of commercials, including wardrobe stylists, refer to a **creative brief** during preproduction. (See Figures 3.7 and 3.8.) A creative brief summarizes pertinent information about the client, the *product* being advertised, the *target market*, the *purpose* and *main message* of the ad, and the *production schedule*. The creative team refers to the brief to make sure they stay on target while generating ideas. The wardrobe stylist refers to the brief when making sourcing and styling decisions.

[
"In film, you have two to six or more months to prep. In TV you take exactly the same meetings, script breakdown, shopping, building, fittings and collaborations with producers, production designers, actors . . . but cram it all into seven or eight days. . . . Essentially you're making a movie every seven days."
  —Cynthia Summers, wardrobe stylist for the Lifetime Network show Unreal. Aleesha Harris, "On-Set Style: Wardrobe Stylist Cynthia Summers Talks 'Unreal,'" Vancouver Sun, July 5, 2016, http://vancouversun.com/life/fashion-beauty/on-set-style-wardrobe-stylist-cynthia-summers-talks-unreal.
]

ANATOMY OF A WARDROBE DEPARTMENT

The wardrobe department of a film or television production is where all of the costumes are stored and inventoried. The department is often housed in a trailer, whereas television productions have dedicated rooms for wardrobe storage. There are usually multiple people in the wardrobe department, from

Figure 3.7
A creative brief summarizes pertinent information about the client, the product being advertised, the target market, the purpose and main message of the ad, and the production schedule. The wardrobe stylist refers to the brief when making sourcing and styling decisions.

supervisors to assistants, each with a different set of responsibilities. Once the wardrobe for a production is decided upon and sourced, it must be carefully organized and catalogued so that it is easy to access for quick changes. There are some important aspects to the wardrobe department that define the wardrobe stylist's job.

Duplicate Costumes

Duplicate costumes are a must in film and television. The wardrobe department has to be prepared for items to go missing and get damaged. Each duplicate version is fitted to the talent's specific measurements. If the director calls for a reshoot, the wardrobe stylist needs to be ready with the right costumes. In addition, if a costume goes missing or gets damaged, the stylist must be ready with another.

Understanding Fabric Care and Knowing How to Sew

Because the costumes are fitted to the talent, it is important for the wardrobe stylist to have a basic understanding of alterations and also to work with a good tailor who can rework garments when needed but also make alterations that easily can be undone if a garment has to be returned to a store or a designer showroom. If a garment gets stained by mistake, it's a wardrobe stylist's responsibility to get the stain out. Although a larger wardrobe department may have laundry facilities, not every garment can be laundered, so it helps if a stylist has a basic understanding of fabric care and stain removal.

The Green Room

In smaller productions, the **green room** might double as the wardrobe-changing area. The green room gets its name because it traditionally had green painted walls. It is not necessarily green, but it is a place for talent to unwind before or after shooting. In larger studio productions, such as talk shows, the green room is separate from the wardrobe. It is a place for the talent to wait before shooting.

Buying vs. Renting Wardrobe

Some productions might rent part of the wardrobe, but at least a portion of it is purchased. Sometimes wardrobe is rented from a **studio services** department of a local retailer. Many retailers in Los Angeles and New York City offer this service. Bloomingdale's, Saks Fifth Avenue, Barney's, and Neiman Marcus are a few of the retailers that do. Arrangements vary: the production could rent or borrow a portion of the wardrobe and buy the rest or be charged a percentage of the total amount of the borrowed merchandise. It is important to keep in mind that borrowed clothing might not be able to be altered, which can be a limitation for the wardrobe stylist.

When it comes to uniforms or period clothing, wardrobe stylists often rent them from companies like the Cop Prop Shop in Los Angeles or the Warner Bros. Costume Department in Burbank. For example, if a production calls for police officers and firefighters, it's much easier (and far less expensive) to rent ready-made uniforms than buy everything from actual tactical supply companies. There are countless costume rental companies and prop shops that offer every type of outfit imaginable, from astronaut to Zelda Fitzgerald, and they often offer on-site tailors and laundry facilities, too.

Rack Dividers

The contents of the styling kit, detailed in Chapter 9, include rack dividers, sewing supplies, and other tricks of the trade. Rack dividers are some of the most important tools for wardrobe stylists. These are important in a wardrobe department that has many duplicate costumes for a large cast. Each divider lists the talent's name, so that the characters' costumes can be separated and organized. Clothing in each talent's section can be arranged by scene or sequence of shooting for easy access.

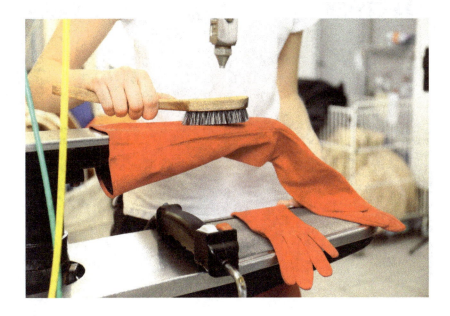

Figure 3.9
Special stain removal chemical solutions.

Costume Bible

The **costume bible**, or **continuity bible**, is a binder that holds all of the information pertaining to a production's wardrobe. Among other things, it has costume sources, talent's measurements, and budget information, and it lists the needs of the wardrobe department. Everyone in the department uses the costume bible, and the wardrobe stylist must update it continually to keep it current. (See Figure 3.10.)

Wrap

When the production goes into the editing phase, it does not mean that shooting is over. As mentioned earlier, reshoots are not an unusual occurrence. Clothing must be properly labeled and stored so it can be pulled easily.

Continuity

Continuity for the wardrobe stylist means that costumes look consistent if they are worn throughout multiple scenes. They must stay the same unless the script calls for changes. It is up to the stylist to catch inconsistencies in the characters' wardrobes and fix them before shooting.

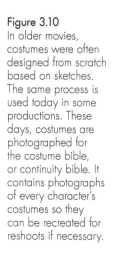

Figure 3.10
In older movies, costumes were often designed from scratch based on sketches. The same process is used today in some productions. These days, costumes are photographed for the costume bible, or continuity bible. It contains photographs of every character's costumes so they can be recreated for reshoots if necessary.

The Importance of the Script

One of the major differences between a print stylist and a wardrobe stylist is that wardrobe stylists must prepare for a production by reading a script. After they read it, they must do a **script breakdown**, which means that each aspect of the production gets color-coded or highlighted, including the cast members, extras, costumes, and hair/makeup in every scene. The color-coding system remains the same throughout the script. Each scene then gets compartmentalized into sections on **breakdown sheets**. (See Figure 3.11.) In many productions, the cast and crew will receive a script that has been broken down for them. However, some small independent productions might not furnish a broken-down script. In this case the wardrobe stylist would need to highlight costume changes and make notes before sourcing the wardrobe.

> "For me, it's about the script and understanding what the characters are saying to each other, what the setting is, what the mood or tone or feel of each script is and how I can help to tell the story of the characters through the costume design. The point of inspiration starts with these scripts."
> —Janie Bryant, Mad Men *Costume Designer.* "How 'Mad Men' Costume Designer Jamie Bryant Was a Storyteller Through Fashion," Huffington Post, May 14, 2015, http://www.huffingtonpost.com/2015/05/14/mad-men-costumes-janie-bryant_n_7277666.html.

The Importance of Staying Informed

Keep in mind that there will be changes made during production. The wardrobe stylist should expect this, and thus it is crucial to be adaptable. By staying alert and in the loop, the stylist can anticipate changes on set and be ready to avert a crisis, or simply meet the production needs when they arise.

STYLING FOR THEATER

Wardrobe styling for the theater and for Broadway is different than for television and film because clothing can't simply be purchased and used as is. Every costume, whether sewn from scratch or purchased from a store, must be adapted to make it easier to be worn again and again, in every production, for the show's entire theatrical run. Often garments are made or reinforced with several layers of fabric and lining to prevent wear and tear, including tears during quick changes. Antibacterial cotton dress shields also are frequently sewn into the underarms of garments to protect against sweat stains and odors.

The primary responsibility for development of all costumes falls to the costume designer. Like costume designers for television and film, costume designers working in theater must know how to illustrate, design, and sew. Once the director has approved the final costumes, the costume designer's job is done and wardrobe responsibilities shift to the wardrobe supervisor. It's the wardrobe supervisor's job to ensure that the costumes look as fabulous for the final performance as they did on opening night.

Figure 3.11
Script breakdown means that each aspect of the production gets color-coded or highlighted. Each scene then gets compartmentalized into sections on breakdown sheets.

"DESPERATE HOUSEWIVES"
by
Marc Cherry

WRITER'S FINAL DRAFT
AUGUST 12, 2003

TEASER

FADE IN:

EXT. SUBURBAN STREET - DAY

We're DRIVING down a tree-lined suburban street. We finally stop at a well-kept UPPER MIDDLE-CLASS house complete with white picket fence.

MARY ALICE (V.O.)
My name is Mary Alice Scott. When you read this morning's paper you may come across an article about the unusual day I had last week.

CLOSE-UP - MARY ALICE SCOTT

The camera pulls back to reveal an ATTRACTIVE WOMAN IN HER EARLY 30's wearing gardening gloves, emerging from the house. She crosses to the flower bed and begins pruning.

MARY ALICE (V.O.)
Normally there's never anything newsworthy about my life. But that all changed last Thursday.

INT. SCOTT HOUSE - KITCHEN - DAY

Mary Alice's HUSBAND AND SON are seated at a table. She is busy serving them BREAKFAST.

MARY ALICE (V.O.)
Of course everything seemed quite normal at first.

INT. SCOTT HOUSE - LAUNDRY ROOM - DAY

Mary Alice puts some clothes into the WASHING MACHINE.

MARY ALICE (V.O.)
I performed my chores.

EXT. DRY CLEANERS - DAY

Mary Alice emerges from a dry cleaners with some CLOTHING encased in PLASTIC.

MARY ALICE (V.O.)
I ran my errands.

EXT. SCOTT HOUSE - BACKYARD - DAY

EXT. HUBER HOUSE - BACKYARD - DAY

Mary Alice paints some LAWN FURNITURE.

MARY ALICE (V.O.)
I completed my projects.

INT. SCOTT HOUSE - KITCHEN - DAY

Mary Alice DUSTS bric-a-brac around the room.

MARY ALICE (V.O.)
In truth, I spent the day as I spent every other day. Quietly polishing the routine of my life until it gleamed with perfection.

INT. SCOTT HOUSE - LIVING ROOM - DAY

Mary Alice stands completely still in the middle of the IMMACULATE room.

MARY ALICE (V.O.)
Which is why it was so astounding when late last Thursday afternoon...

INT. SCOTT HOUSE - HALLWAY - DAY

Mary Alice stands on a chair and reaches up to the top shelf of the hall closet. She brings down a REVOLVER.

MARY ALICE (V.O.)
...I decided to take a loaded gun from the hallway closet and empty its contents into my head.

CLOSE on A GUN FIRING.

MARY ALICE falls to the floor.

We see what appears to be BLOOD spreading out over some tile. As a woman's HAND begins to wipe it away...

INT. HUBER HOUSE - KITCHEN - CONTINUOUS

...we PULL BACK to reveal it's the hand of EDITH HUBER, a plump woman in her late 40's, who has just spilled some TOMATO SAUCE onto her kitchen counter. She wipes it up when she suddenly HEARS something from outside.

MARY ALICE (V.O.)
My body was discovered by my next-door neighbor, Mrs. Edith Huber, who had been startled by what she would later describe to the police as a strange popping sound.

Wardrobe supervisors have a big job. They are responsible for how the costumes look on stage and what happens to them when the theater is dark. They keep track of all costume parts, from dresses and shoes to eyeglasses and pantyhose—where they are, how they're packed up between performances, and how often they need to be professionally cleaned. Wardrobe supervisors also must ensure that every costume is ready to go before every performance and that any necessary repairs to clothing, accessories, and shoes are made as soon as possible. If damage is minor, the wardrobe supervisor often handles the repair; if it's something more serious, the wardrobe supervisor usually sends the item out to be repaired and then handles any substitution that must be made until the repair is completed and the item is returned. If something must be replaced—pantyhose, shoes— the wardrobe supervisor must be able to source the same or a significantly similar item. During the production, the wardrobe supervisor also manages a staff of people called dressers who are hired to actually help the actors and actresses get in and out of their costumes, including during quick changes between scenes.

At the close of a production, the wardrobe supervisor oversees what's called a costume strike, which means that all costumes are cleaned, packed, and appropriately stored and that any rented costumes are cleaned, brought back to their original condition (meaning that alterations are ripped out), and returned.

> "Alice Gilbert is the most amazing wardrobe supervisor. I've worked with her before. I had to have her on *Wicked* because I thought, she's the only person who could under-stand the complexities of a monkey costume and a mask all the way to the most delicate piece of beaded chiffon."
>
> —Susan Hilferty, *Wicked* costume designer. "WICKED Costumes: Wardrobe Maintenance," YouTube, February 29, 2012, https://www.youtube.com/watch ?v=-u5lcCkYznY.

Styling for a Musical Performance

Many people think that styling a musician means picking spectacular clothes for performers like Beyoncé to wear on stage. Sometimes it does, but those jobs usually are handled by fashion design-ers who create one-of-a-kind pieces for each performance. But there are other types of musicians who hire stylists to help them put together looks to wear on stage, like concert violinists or jazz pianists. Here is a quick list of questions to keep in mind when fitting a musician for a stage performance:

1. If the musician is employed by an orchestra or band, what is the required dress code?
2. Does the musician have the required range of motion when wearing the clothes?

3. How sensitive is the fabric to perspiration, both immediately and over time?
4. How does the garment look when the wearer is in his or her performance position? For example, for a cellist, does the skirt elegantly fold around the instrument when the musician is seated? For a singer, are the jeans too tight for the musician to dance around?
5. Does the musician look and feel good in the clothes?

When styling a musician for a music video, the job is similar in scope to working on a television show or a movie. The wardrobe stylist collaborates with the director and sources the outfit that best fits with his or her artistic vision. That collaboration also may include input from the musician, especially if the musician is interested in clothing or has a very specific direction for the video.

INDUSTRY INTERVIEW

Interview with Victoria Barban

Victoria Barban is an international fashion stylist who lives in London. After spending her first few years buying and designing for some of the UK's most exclusive designers, Victoria made a natural transition to freelance fashion stylist. She has been featured in numerous publications, including *Hunger Magazine, You, Fault, Phoenix, Blanc,* and *Fiasco,* where Victoria was contributing fashion editor. Victoria is now in demand for style fashion shoots and for clients at home and overseas.

Website: *www.victoriabarban.com*
Instagram: *@victoriabarban*
Twitter: *@victoriabarban*

What celebrities, companies, or high-profile clients have you worked with?
Some of my biggest clients are Sony Music, Modest Management, and MTV, so I have had the pleasure of working with numerous artists from the music industry. I also really enjoy working with TV personalities and actresses; as an avid Game of Thrones fan, I was delighted to be asked to style Natalie Emmanuel.

How did you get into the fashion industry? Did you have formal training, or is it something that evolved or you fell into?
I studied for a B.A. in Fashion with Business studies, and although at the time I excelled in the creative side of my course—winning Designer of the Year—the business element has been really useful throughout my career. I finished my training at Central St. Martins in London, where I focused primarily on fashion styling.

Did you go straight into styling, or did you assist first?

After graduating I worked as a fashion buyer and then designer before finally focusing on my real passion, which was styling. Although I didn't assist other stylists, I did put in the yards by working throughout the industry, including working for a photographic studio, where I absorbed everything to do with my trade.

Now that you are styling, what qualities do you look for in an assistant?

Although a sense of style is important when selecting an assistant, it is far more important to have a "can do" attitude. I hate tardiness; I hate excuses. I ask that all my assistants turn up on time and ready to work. I once had a new assistant turn up wearing 6" heels; although they were beautiful shoes, they were totally inappropriate as she had been given her brief for the day, which involved traveling around London collecting PR samples.

What kinds of job duties did you do when you first started working?

When I started out, I did every element of the job by myself, so I understand fully what an assistant role entails. I dealt directly with the PRs, sourcing all the samples myself, and then collected and returned them all to the various press offices. This was long before I could drive, so I relied on public transport and a strong suitcase! Days were long, but I loved every minute. I cared for the garments on shoots, from steaming them to fitting them on models.

Do you have any funny or horror stories of when you first started?

Too many to mention! One horror story involved £4,000 worth of hats, which I left at a kiosk in a train station. Luckily I noticed before I boarded the train and quickly turned around. Someone was just about to pick them up when I swooped in and grabbed them. Another horror story involved an extremely delicate vintage dress and a rather well-known actress. I can still hear the sound of the 90-year-old lace tearing!

What's something you wish someone had told you before you started? What advice would you give your younger self about styling?

I think it's important to realize how challenging the industry can be but also to never give up. I have so many friends who have been about to give up when they suddenly get their big breaks—corny but true.

I think it's vitally important to realize how much hard work is involved and how competitive things are; some people are still under the impression that fashion is all glamor. You really do have to roll your sleeves up, muck in, and be part of the team; gratitude and satisfaction can sometimes feel a long time coming, but they are definitely worth waiting for.

What do you feel is a common mistake that many people make when they first start out in the industry? Or a common misconception about what you do?

When I started out, people didn't quite get what a stylist did. Some people thought I was a dresser, others thought I was a photographer's assistant, and my grandmother could never comprehend the role and thought a stylist was just another name for a hairdresser! With the exception of the hairdresser, I am often both of the former roles, though neither truly encapsulates what a stylist does. My role is about creating a picture for the artist to paint or in this case the photographer to photograph. This also applies to personal styling when the wrong stylist can really have an impact on a celebrity or client's career. It is worth pointing out at this point that no, you do not get to wear, keep, or borrow the samples for your own personal use, although sometimes you can be lucky enough to receive beautiful gifts.

What's your philosophy of styling or dressing a client?

When I am styling for an editorial, it is often more about adapting the model to fit into the story; this can often be why more neutral models can be in high demand as opposed to those with distinctive features. When I am styling personal clients or celebrities, this rule is completely reversed, as I think it is important to show who the individuals are and what their priorities are in life. My role is to help interpret their personality and ensure this comes across in a natural manner; the worst look is when someone looks totally uncomfortable in his or her own skin.

One of my clients is a manager for an extremely popular boy band; her wardrobe needs to fit in with her exceptionally busy lifestyle and the various climates that she has to cope with.

Where do you like to shop?

Although I love fashion and still get genuinely excited at the thought of viewing the latest designer collections, I am a stylist at heart. I like to create style; I like to take bits and pieces and mix it up. I love to take one great designer piece and pair it with high street or market finds. I still think vintage is a great way to get inspired, and I can spend hours trawling vintage stores across numerous continents.

What are some of your favorite designers?

I generally detest this question; it's like asking me to choose my favorite child; however, at the moment I am having a real love affair with Vilshenko, Bora Aksu, and Huishan Zhang. Ryan Lo and Ashish always make me smile with their use of color and sparkle.

Fendi has always been a favorite for continuity in great craftsmanship, sublime style, and keeping fashion fun. I recently met Anna for the first time; she continues to inspire and surprise.

What are some hidden gems or offbeat places where you pick up stuff for jobs?

To find great pieces you really need to be creative and open-minded in your search. I have found some great finds from hunting through prop houses, a retired costume designer's boudoir, flea markets, army surplus stores, and beyond . . . odd is interesting; you'd be surprised where you can find it.

How much of your own personal style can be influenced on a job?

On the rare occasion I get to style someone who has similar taste to myself, it is very tempting to make it overly personal; however, I believe everyone should have his or her own individual style.

Who are your muses? How or where do you find inspiration?
I am lucky enough to live in London and also get the chance to travel to some great countries. I find real people so inspiring, and now with even more access to street style through social media I think there is a real move away from having a celebrity crush.

What's something that you don't like about being a stylist? If you could change something about the industry, what would it be?
I have always had a real concern about the level of support given to new talent. Although I feel the industry has gotten better over recent years, there is still room for improvement in terms of creative acknowledgment and financial rewards. There is a danger that we don't give credit where credit is due; creativity has a price, and this should always be recognized.

It can be difficult keeping track of so many items on a big job or when juggling a multitude of shoots. How do you keep organized? Do you have a special system, so to speak, that you like to use?
I have a room I like to call my dressing-up room with multiple rails where I try to keep each job separate. From very early on in my career I have been taught that if something is "old bread"—in other words, if you have used it on a shoot—then get it back to the PR or designer ASAP. Not only does this help keep your space organized, but it also helps nurture vital relationships with integral people in your network. The longer things stay around, the greater chance of damage.

Name two styling tips.
Recognize your body type. I am rather petite, but when I was younger I was such a tomboy. I cringe when I look back on all those old photos where I am totally lost inside some huge baggy overalls.

Spend time on accessorizing. I think this is something that has gotten lost over the years. I am not talking about making everything matchy-matchy; I mean really complement your outfit. More often than not I see the wrong shoes with a great outfit.

Tell us a little about what you did for Fiasco Magazine.
As contributing fashion editor at *Fiasco Magazine*, I would work as part of the fashion department. I would come up with ideas for within the designated theme for each issue. I would select the appropriate team, consisting of photographer, hair, makeup, models, etc., that I thought would execute the particular concept. Selling my ideas to the editor-in-chief to overseeing the final layout was all part of my role. An integral part of my role was also keeping a finger on the pulse. What's new? Who is the new kid on the fashion block? What are the next trends or brands to watch?

How do you network? Why is it important to build relationships in this industry?

When I started out on my own, I jumped straight in. I never assisted; therefore, it was vital to network. Social media is great for this, but you also have to get out there, attend events, press days, presentations. Someone once told me you are only as good as your last job, and this is so true. You are judged not only on your work but also on the person you are; you have got to be able to work with different teams on a daily basis. There are no two days that are the same.

How do you present your work (e.g., website, portfolio, comp cards)? How did you establish your aesthetic or brand?

When I first started styling, portfolios consisted of a large A3 book of printed images. I have watched this evolve, and today everyone now carries their portfolio on their i-pad or tablet. In a presentation I enjoy working from i-pad, but my website is the true heart of my business; it is the main focus for my energy and ideas, and it is vital that it is nurtured and properly maintained. I do think it's important to keep your identity in your brand and work; this is something that will become clearer to you the more you work and grow in the industry.

How have technology and social media changed the styling profession and fashion industry?

Social media has had a greater impact on fashion than on any other industry. Social media and fashion work so well together; they are both fast-paced and instant. With designers producing more collections than ever before and people becoming accustomed to having everything immediately, social media is the perfect platform for this.

Do you have any tips for working as a freelance or independent contractor (anything from tax tips to professional practice, like contracts and insurance, getting paid, setting rates)?

I would advise anyone wanting to enter this industry to do your research, especially for things such as insurance. People trust you with their possessions; more often than not these items are invaluable. Make sure your insurance covers this; always err on the side of caution. I have traveled a lot with clothing samples, jewelry, and hard drives containing images. Things can get lost; you need to make sure you can replace those things where possible. Also from experience, I would say never start working on a job without having a copy of your T & Cs [Terms and Conditions] signed by your client; no one wants to work for nothing.

Final note: always be available. I'm still kicking myself for having to turn down a meeting with the girl band Little Mix due to an unfortunate diary fail!

Summary and Review

Styling actors, actresses, and musicians for film and video shoots and performances involves concerns that are unique to the field. Stylists who work in these industries are called wardrobe stylists. It is important for wardrobe stylists to understand the type of production that they're working on and their roles within that system.

On movies and television shows, preproduction is the time before shooting begins. In this time the crew is hired, the shooting schedule is arranged, and the wardrobe for the production is planned. During the production or principal photography phase, the wardrobe stylist is mainly concerned with dressing talent and keeping the wardrobe department organized. As in print styling, the wardrobe stylist is expected to remain on the sidelines during shooting and keep an eye out for costume imperfections. During postproduction, the stylist is wrapping up and cataloguing all wardrobe items. The wardrobe stylist should be ready for reshoots, which are common.

On stage, wardrobe stylists handle everything involving costumes apart from the actual design and sourcing. Because costumes are worn over and over, maintenance is a large part of this job.

Wardrobe stylists who work with musicians performing in music videos also work directly with the director and the creative team overseeing production. When a musician is performing live, there are many special concerns, such as whether a musician can move in a garment.

Key Terms

- breakdown sheets
- continuity
- continuity bible
- costume attendant
- costume bible
- costume designer
- costume supervisor
- costumer
- creative brief
- duplicate costume
- editing
- green light
- green room
- key costumer
- postproduction
- preproduction
- principal photography
- production
- reshoots
- script breakdown
- storyboards
- studio services
- wardrobe assistant
- wardrobe styling
- wardrobe supervisor
- wrap

Review Questions

1. List two differences between wardrobe stylists and costume designers.
2. Why are small independent movie studios and student films good places for novice stylists to look for job and internship opportunities?

3. What does it mean when a production gets the green light?

4. Why are reshoots common, and how do wardrobe stylists prepare for them?

5. Explain continuity and the contents of the continuity bible.

6. Find and list the websites for three costume sources for police uniforms, including one company not located in Los Angeles.

7. Find an example of a costume from a recent Broadway musical and list the different parts of the costume.

8. List two reasons why a female cellist might favor wearing a long black velvet dress.

9. Why do wardrobe stylists need to have duplicate costumes?

10. What are two differences between wardrobe styling for film and for television?

LEARNING ACTIVITIES

Learning Activity 3.1: Using the Internet, find a union that serves people in the movie industry and answer the following questions:

1. What is the name of the union, and where is it located?
2. Who is eligible for membership in this union?
3. Why or how does this union benefit its members?
4. List two ways to gain membership in the union.

Learning Activity 3.2: Search online for a script from a popular television show. There are websites that publish scripts from multiple shows in one place. Try to choose a script that is less than forty pages. Read through the script and jot down costume changes. Look for times when new characters are introduced or when a character is in a new setting that requires a costume change. Create a numbered list of costume changes in order, with the character's name and a few words to summarize the reason for the change. The objective is to get an idea of how many costume changes can occur in one television episode.

Learning Activity 3.3: Make a collage for one outfit for a character from a favorite television show or film. Use online stores to source the clothing. Copy and paste the outfit into one document, along with a picture of the character on the same page. Then write a short summary of the television show and the character's personality. Describe how your outfit reflects the character's personality and lifestyle.

RESOURCES

American Theater Wing. "The Wardrobe Supervisor (Career Guides)." YouTube. October 18, 2013. https://www.youtube.com/watch?v=i7JT7Nt7K3w.

Association of Independent Commercial Producers. http://www.aicp.com.

The Bias Cut. http://www.thebiascut.blogspot.com.

Bureau of Labor Statistics. "From Script to Screen: Careers in Film Production." Summer 2013. https://www.bls.gov /careeroutlook/2013/summer/art02.pdf.

Bureau of Labor Statistics. "Occupational Employment and Wages, May 2016: 39-3092 Costume Attendants." http://www.bls.gov/oes/current/oes393092.htm.

"Concert Dress." The Violin. http://www.the-violin.com/concert-dress.

"Costume Attendants: Salaries." MyPlan. http://www.myplan.com/careers/costume-attendants/salary-39-30 92.00.html.

"Costume Designer." Get In Media Entertainment Careers. http://getinmedia.com/careers/costume-designer-live.

"Custom Report for: 39-3092.00—Costume Attendants." O*NET. https://www.onetonline.org/link/custom /39-3092.00.

4Filmmaking. http://www.4filmmaking.com.

"Example Creative Brief 2017." AdCracker. http://www.adcracker.com/brief/Sample _Creative_Brief.htm.

"How to Break Down a Script." Pixel Valley Studio. https://en.wikipedia.org/wiki/Breaking_down_the_script.

Lyndley, Sally. "Studio Services: Barney's New York." YouTube. July 22, 2014. https://www.youtube.com/watch ?v=n7QSrn2_SIA.

"Nightmare on Elm Street Reshoots." Filmstalker. http://www.filmstalker.co.uk/archives/2009/12/nightmare_on _elm_street_reshoo.html.

"'Red' Screens for Critics, Willis, Malkovich Return for 'Red' (Re)Shoot(s)." Moviefone. https://www.moviefone .com/2010/08/22/willis-malkovich-red-re-shoot/.

Schlemowitz, Joel. "Glossary of Film Terms." http://www.joelschlemowitz.com/glossary-of-film-terms.

"Wardrobe Assistant—Film, TV or Theatre." PlanIT Plus. http://www.planitplus.net/careerzone/areas/default .aspx?PID=nf&TOPL=20&SECL=20dt&ID=641.

"Wardrobe Supervisor." Get In Media Entertainment Careers. http://getinmedia.com/careers/wardrobe-supervisor.

"Wardrobe Supervisor." Wikipedia. https://en.wikipedia.org/wiki/Wardrobe_supervisor.

"What Do Costumes/Wardrobes Do?" Media Match. http://www.media-match.com/usa/jobtypes/costumes -wardrobe-jobs-402697.php.

Theatrical Wardrobe Union Local 764, IATSE. http://www.ia764.org.

Zee, Joe (Host). *Unbuttoned #2: Meet the* House of Cards *Costume Designer* [Audio podcast]. March 6, 2015. https://www.yahoo.com/style/unbuttoned-2-meet-the-house-of-cards-costume-112879044613.html.

4 Image Consulting

CHAPTER TOPICS CALL SHEET

In this chapter you will learn:
- The basics of personal styling
- How personal styling is different from personal shoppers and celebrity stylists
- About the importance of fabrics and fit
- Education and certification for image consultants
- Basic elements and principles of design, such as line and shape
- Different body types and what flatters them
- How to analyze different personal style categories
- How to decipher an individual's personal color palette
- How personal stylists develop their clients' style
- Why a stylist's personal appearance matters

IMAGE CONSULTING 101

Image consultants, also known as personal stylists, are professionals who work with clients to cultivate and refine their personal images. Image consultants often help clients to improve more than their wardrobes. They do everything from helping clients dress for special occasions to revamping entire wardrobes and, in the case of wealthy clients, managing multiple wardrobes across more than one home. **Image consulting** is a uniquely challenging area of the styling industry because every client comes with his or her individual needs, personalities, preferences, and unique body shape. (See Table 4.1.)

In this book image consultants and **personal stylists** are referred to in the same fashion context. **Personal shoppers** also fall under the image consulting umbrella. Other names for professionals in this field are **wardrobe consultants** or **style consultants**. Unlike print or film stylists, image consultants work with normal, everyday people. Because image consultants' clients are real people and the clothing is worn in day-to-day life, image consultants have different considerations than print or entertainment stylists when selecting clothing. Clients' personal tastes and body types play a much more prominent role in image consulting jobs than they do for print stylists, for example, who work with models. Clients' budgets and lifestyles also influence image consultants. After all, a client might not have the budget for the high-end clothing seen in an editorial shoot and might predominantly need a conservative career-oriented wardrobe rather than an edgy fashion-forward one.

Most image consultants are freelancers working for private clients who pay by the hour. Personal shoppers, however, are most often employed by a retailer, and they are paid by that retailer to give one-on-one assistance to the retailer's clients.

Both image consultants and personal shoppers have similar goals: to make sure the client looks and feels fantastic, and for the client to come back for the stylist's assistance again and again.

Finding Work and Building a Client Roster

It takes a long time for personal stylists to build a steady client base. Jobs come via word of mouth and self-promotion. Word of mouth is gained through talent, reliability, past successes, and people skills. The best ways to get recognized for these attributes is to work in a fashion setting. Retail sales and management, especially high-end retail, are great ways to meet people who might hire a personal stylist. Other ways include doing visual merchandising, facilitating fashion show production, and assisting an established stylist.

Self-promotion and marketing are critical for earning new clients. This means always having business cards ready to hand out and maintaining on-brand social media accounts that can be linked or shared at all times. It is good practice for personal stylists to be able to list the specific skills they have to offer. After all, they are being hired based on their expertise. If they can't describe what they have to offer, then why would someone pay for their services? Examples of personal styling skills include building a professional wardrobe and putting together formal looks for special events.

Being able to verbally summarize the benefits of personal styling services is a good asset. For example, a women's professional networking event (see Figure 4.1) or a men's fashion charity event is a great setting for a short presentation. A presentation like that can give the stylist a great marketing opportunity and the ability to reach a large audience.

It is equally critical for a stylist to turn these initial client engagements into repeat business, building a stable stylist-client relationship. The goal is for the client to continually rely on the stylist, and the stylist in turn can get to know the client on a deeper, more thorough level to be able to anticipate wants, needs, and style preferences.

"Working in fashion is not always as glamorous as it seems. Just like any other highly competitive industry, you put in long hours and a lot of hard work to get where you want to be. It's easy to confuse loving fashion with wanting to work in fashion, but they are two totally different things."
—Lauren Conrad, media personality, https://laurenconrad.com/blog/2015/08/ask -lauren-tips-for-getting-into-the-fashion-industry.

Where Personal Stylists Also Work

High-end boutiques and department stores are great workplaces for aspiring stylists. The customers are often willing and able to spend a good deal of money to make an impression. These customers might potentially hire stylists. The next reason is that what the client is wearing will get noticed by his or her friends and hopefully send more customers to the store. The third reason is that successful independent boutiques often participate in local fashion shows. A fashion show might end up as a chance for a salesperson to select some or all of the outfits seen on the runway. This is a great opportunity to show off styling skills in front of a large audience.

Figure 4.1
Unlike print or film stylists, image consultants work with "real people."

Personal Shoppers

Often personal shoppers and personal stylists are one and the same person, and the client dictates the services they offer. Luxury and higher-end department stores like Barneys New York, Saks Fifth Avenue, and Nordstrom often hire personal shoppers to assist their customers. A personal shopper for a department store works one-on-one with a client to assist the client in buying merchandise from that store. A personal shopper may help a client find a single pair of shoes or be intimately involved in building, organizing, and maintaining a wardrobe. Clients appreciate that a personal shopper can speed up and streamline the shopping process (something that can be especially important for men) and that personal shoppers are able to act on the client's behalf, either to reserve a popular size before the collection hits the sales floor or to snap up a great deal when a sale begins. Because personal shoppers have a deep knowledge of the brands that their stores carry, including the fit and cut of different designers, they are able to guide their clients to merchandise that makes them look their best. The personal shopper's goal is to build a relationship with a client that results in repeat visits and also additional business from referrals.

The personal shopping relationship begins with an appointment. At that time, the personal shopper will find out the reason for the visit—what does the client need to buy?—and some basic information about brand and wardrobe preferences, sizes, and budget. Most personal shoppers work from an office that is dedicated to personal shopping services. This area usually has its own private dressing rooms. It is not uncommon, however, for personal shoppers to meet clients at their homes, offices, or hotels.

A personal shopper preps for a client appointment like a stylist preps for a photo shoot: he or she pulls merchandise from the sales floor and arranges it in the dressing room to present to the client. If the client is pressed for time, it can be helpful to have everything ready to try on, meaning that dress shirts and suits are unbuttoned and shoes are unpacked from their boxes and ready to wear. A personal shopper also works closely with the store's alterations department and can summon a tailor at any time during an appointment. At the close of the appointment, the personal shopper will ring up all purchases and help the client with the shopping bags, which can range from simply carrying them to the parking lot and putting them in the client's trunk to arranging for a messenger to take the bags to the client's home or hotel.

Because personal shopping is a service that department stores offer to their customers, personal shoppers do not charge a fee, nor do their clients ever pay a fee. Rather, personal shoppers earn a salary as employees of the store. In addition to their salary, however, many personal shoppers earn a commission or other incentive based on their sales.

"To help women move their style forward while still retaining their identity and comfort, I took a triangulated approach—the classic threefer, if you will. I generally pulled three groups of items: those that were too easy, those that were too hard, and something in the middle. This line of attack worked especially well with people who when they came to me were as unsure of themselves as fawns on new legs."
—Betty Halbreich, personal shopper, Bergdorf Goodman. Betty Halbreich, I'll Drink to That: A Life in Style, with a Twist (New York: Penguin Press, 2014), 143.

"When I take my clients shopping, I always have a wish-list for them which consists of:
- Need to have—essentials
- Nice to have—pieces that reflect the season's trends
- Bonus pieces—things that will look absolutely stunning but aren't necessary"
—Lucy Plevin, personal shopper. Lucy Plevin, "10 Top Tips from a Personal Shopper," My Style Companion, http://www.mystylecompanion.com/blog/10-top-tips-from-a-personal-shopper/.

Celebrity Stylists

A **celebrity stylist** is a personal stylist who works with well-known individuals to clothe them for appearances at events. The type of event can vary—maybe it's a red carpet premiere, a charity luncheon or a press conference—but usually it is a situation where the celebrity will be photographed or his or her appearance will be publicly documented in some way. A celebrity stylist must ensure that the celebrity looks flawless, both in person and in photographs. The celebrity stylist is responsible for every single element of an outfit, from socks to Spanx, and often collaborates as part of a creative team with studios, designers, jewelers, and a "glam squad" of hair and makeup artists, nail technicians, and others. As celebrities have received more attention for their clothing, so have their stylists. Petra Flannery, Jessica Paster, Monica Rose, Rachel Zoe, Phillip Bloch, and Kate Young are just a few prominent stylists seen in the media. (See Figure 4.2.) While it seems glamorous, celebrity styling is actually incredibly demanding because it brings together all three types of styling: editorial styling, entertainment industry styling, and personal styling.

Like editorial stylists, celebrity stylists work with showrooms, designers, fashion PR people, and studio services departments to either pull merchandise for their clients or have it made. The celebrities generally do not keep the clothes unless they want to buy them, so the stylist is personally responsible for the safekeeping and prompt return of every item. The celebrity stylist also has a duty, albeit unofficial, to make sure the celebrity is photographed in any borrowed or specialty items so that the designer or retailer can use the photograph for promotion. This is seen as the trade-off for the loan, and the celebrity stylist's reputation can hang on this "quid pro quo."

In today's media world, celebrities aren't just photographed; they're filmed, too. There's also paparazzi waiting eagerly to click away if the celebrity trips, experiences a wardrobe malfunction, or even exits the car in a way that may reveal too much. It's a celebrity stylist's job to make sure that the celebrity can move, walk, pose, and sit with ease, that the outfit looks perfect from all angles, and that plunging necklines and straps stay put.

Figure 4.2
Celebrity stylist Rachel Zoe is known for her signature bohemian style.

Finally, the celebrity stylist is like a personal stylist in that he or she must dress a real person, not a model. When models are hired for a shoot, it's their job to be there on time and to wear whatever the stylist asks them to put on without complaining. Successful models do not let their personal problems or personal preferences interfere with their job. Not so with real people. Celebrities can require even more patience and preparation, especially if they don't have a lot of time for fittings or they have a "diva" reputation.

Celebrity stylists, like personal stylists, must be able to dress all body types. While many actors and actresses are indeed thin, they're not always uniformly proportionate in the shoulders and hips like models, and they can be taller or shorter than a model. This means a celebrity stylist must understand garment construction, tailoring, and alterations. For example, for an actor who is very muscular, a celebrity stylist might sew snaps between the buttons on a shirt to make sure it stays closed. For a very tall actor, the arms of a shirt might need to be lengthened by adding extra fabric at the elbows.

Celebrity stylists who work with actors and actresses usually are hired by the movie or television studio, or by the celebrity's publicist. A celebrity stylist can be hired by the day, by the job, or by the look. For example, the celebrity stylist might charge a day rate to find a dress for a celebrity for a personal appearance, or he or she might charge for the look if he or she is putting a wardrobe together for a multiday media tour called a *press junket*. It is not uncommon for the stylist to attend an event with the celebrity, remaining on call in case of a wardrobe emergency. Rates for styling celebrities vary. Stylists can earn from $1,000 to $1,500 a day to as much as $10,000 a day. It all depends on the celebrity's reputation, the stylist's reputation, and the nature of the event.

Celebrity styling is a hard career to cultivate because it requires having connections within the entertainment industry, connections within the fashion industry to access the most amazing merchandise, and an established office with the ability to process a lot of incoming and outgoing merchandise and to safeguard expensive designer items that can include fine jewelry. The best way to get into celebrity styling is to work for a celebrity stylist as an assistant. Internships at a magazine, at a fashion house, or with a PR firm are also good ways to get the connections and the experience that lead to an assistant stylist position with a celebrity stylist. The fashion industry runs on connections, so the goal is to be in a position to be recommended or to network toward a recommendation for an opening with a celebrity stylist.

Concierge Service and the Stylist

Concierge service involves providing highly personalized, on-demand service for a limited number of clients. Many basic characteristics of this service can be found in both personal shopping and celebrity styling: availability, retail/showroom/designer connections, versatility, organization and anticipation, and knowing a good seamstress or tailor.

AVAILABILITY

Availability entails assisting clients at short notice and at odd hours. For example, a client might be attending an event and at the last minute decide that he or she wants help shopping. Stylists need to be able to work these types of demands into their schedules. Sometimes stylists hire assistants to help carry some of the workload.

RETAIL, SHOWROOM, AND DESIGNER CONNECTIONS

Having strong fashion-industry connections allows stylists to find clothing and accessories at short notice. Personal stylists usually know what is in the stores and what is available online during any given season or any given month. This allows them to be prepared when a client calls. They need to know where to shop right away without having to scour an entire city for the right clothing.

VERSATILITY

A versatile personal stylist can provide a variety of options, is adaptable to change, and possesses diverse skill sets. For example, a customer might ask a personal clothing stylist for some hair and makeup ideas. Or a customer might have a change of heart about what to wear or his or her physical size or situation may have changed since the last fitting due to a weight gain, a pregnancy, or even an injury that requires a cast or crutches. It is the stylist's responsibility to make sure that the client always has alternatives.

ORGANIZATION AND ANTICIPATION

A freelance stylist must be organized to keep track of client preferences and past wardrobe purchases. Sometimes a client might even ask a stylist to shop for family members, and a stylist must be able to do this. This means that a stylist should be a good listener and be able to anticipate clients' needs. Anticipating needs is easier when a good client relationship is formed.

KNOWING A GOOD SEAMSTRESS OR TAILOR

A personal stylist should know a good seamstress or tailor who can get things done at short notice. Often being available to clients at the last minute also means last-minute alterations.

UNDERSTANDING SIZING

It's a stylist's job to find clothes that fit the client, but this is easier said than done. There is no uniformly accepted international size standard for clothing, shoes, or undergarments. For example, a dress in the United States will not be the same size in Japan, France, or England. It is critical that a stylist memorize domestic and international sizing, especially if he or she works with higher-end designer clothes and shoes, many of which come from international labels.

To make matters more complicated, there are often fit differences within a single size. This is due to a practice called **vanity sizing**, when a designer or manufacturer skews sizes downward to make the customer feel better. Psychological studies actually have shown that women feel better about themselves and about the clothing brand when they are able to wear a smaller size. There was once a system that attempted to standardize women's sizes; however, it was discontinued in 1983 because of serious flaws in the methodology of the measurements. This left clothing manufacturers free to set their own definitions of size, and many started practicing vanity sizing. For example, if a garment label showed a skirt was a size 12 in 1958, a skirt with the same measurements could today be found bearing a size 6 tag. While sizes still provide a general guide, there can be as much as a five-inch difference between the same-sized clothing made by different designers. A stylist therefore must develop a feel for the fit of popular labels to know whether, for example, a client who fits into a 6 in Michael Kors would wear a bigger or smaller size in Dolce & Gabbana or Ralph Lauren.

A Feel for Fabric

It is also important for a personal stylist to be able to understand and be able to accurately describe fabric and clothing construction. Cheap fabrics have a different look and feel than expensive ones. There is a big difference between polyester satin and silk satin, and acrylic tweed feels different from wool tweed. Important fabric characteristics are hand, luster, drape, and wrinkle resistance. Key terms and concepts related to fabric include the following:

- **Hand:** The hand of a fabric is how it feels. Fabric can be described as having a soft hand, rough hand, or smooth hand, to name a few expressions. It is important for a stylist to be able to determine the quality of a fabric by simply looking at it and feeling its hand.
- **Luster:** Luster describes the amount of shine in a fabric. Matte fabrics have little to no luster.
- **Drape:** Drape describes how a fabric lies when held vertically. It describes how many pleats there are and how they fall.
- **Wrinkle resistance:** Wrinkle resistance describes whether a fabric wrinkles easily. A good test is to grip the fabric with a closed fist for a few seconds. When released a fabric with poor wrinkle resistance will have creases. Sometimes this isn't a bad thing. For example, linen in the summer is fine when a little wrinkled because it's expected and reflective of the casual mood of the season.

Textiles have many more properties than the ones listed here. Flame resistance, oil affinity, and water affinity are a few. *J. J. Pizzuto's Fabric Science* and FabricLink.com are great resources for further information on fabrics, including care and stain-removal tips.

Image Consulting Education and Certification

Of all the areas of specialty within fashion styling, image consulting has the most educational resources for those aspiring to enter the profession. Some schools provide additional training to image consultants. Many image consultants choose to get certified by the **Association of Image Consultants International (AICI)** (www.aici.org). The certification requires knowledge of current industry practices and ideas, and some stylists feel it adds to their credentials. Certification is obtained through paying a fee to take an examination. The exam is based on numerous style books, including *The Triumph of Individual Style* by Carla Mason Mathis and Helen Villa Connor and *Wardrobe Strategies for Women* by Judith Rasband. The examination questions are centered on the physical and mental aspects of personal style. For example, a physical aspect of personal style is knowing what would be appropriate dress for a white-tie-and-tails event. An example of a mental aspect of personal style is how clothing communicates on a nonverbal level. There are also many schools across the world that offer training in image consulting. The training is often found as part of a fashion design or fashion marketing curriculum.

WHAT EVERY IMAGE CONSULTANT MUST BRING TO THE CLIENT

To be a successful fashion stylist in an area of the profession, a basic understanding of the principles and elements of style is essential. These include elements and concepts such as line directions in clothing, body types, personal style, and color.

The Stylist–Client Relationship

Once a client contacts a stylist, it is important for the stylist to have a clearly defined idea of services and pricing. It might be tempting for a personal stylist to offer discounts to get a job, but this can ultimately cause problems. If two acquaintances or friends pay different prices for the same service and find out about it, the stylist's reputation can be damaged. If a potential client asks for a discount, it is best to politely explain that the rates are standard for the industry and describe the valuable services that are available for the price. It simplifies billing if a client pays directly after a service. This helps eliminate any misunderstandings about how much time was spent at the consultation, since it will still be fresh in everyone's memories.

When a personal stylist meets with a client for the first time, it can be helpful to bring a questionnaire. The stylist can make a basic questionnaire for all clients and edit it over time when necessary. The client might fill it out, or the stylist might ask the questions and fill it out for the client. It is essential to find out the client's full name and contact information. Beyond that, the client's birthday is helpful so that a card can be sent. Proper stationery or greeting cards are great investments for a personal stylist. Even if the client only hires the stylist once, sending a birthday card is a nice way to remind the client that the stylist is still available for hire. The same also applies to holiday cards, as long as they are kept nonreligious. Also, it is nice to send a thank-you card to thank the client for business after a first consultation or after a consultation that happened after a long lapse.

Other information that can be gathered from the questionnaire pertains to body type and style preferences. Personal stylist consultations often take place in the client's home or in the client's closet. This is good because it allows the stylist to see how the client's home is decorated. A person's interior decorating tastes often translate to his or her wardrobe. For example, a client with a traditional-style house filled with antiques and oriental rugs might have a classic or preppy wardrobe. It is the stylist's job to get to know the client's tastes thoroughly. Also, because stylists are often privy to clients' personal lives, it is important that the stylist not gossip and be very careful about posting photos on social media. The stylist needs to be trustworthy, discreet, and above all, professional.

TABLE 4.1 Three Career Paths for the Image Management Stylist

	Image Consultant	Personal Stylist/ Shopper	Celebrity Stylist
Employer	Self-employed freelance	Self-employed freelance, but also can be part of a high-end retailer's personal shopping services	Self-employed freelance; almost exclusively lives and works in Los Angeles or New York City
Job Overview	Shops for the client's wardrobe needs and also helps refine other aspects of image	Styles and organizes client's wardrobe and helps edit or throw away unsuitable items. May shop for the client and present findings for client's selection. Helps client prepare for special formal events or helps busy clients compile work wardrobes	Usually works with high-profile clients to find clothing for special events. Can style client for occasions as needed. Can sometimes be a major influence in a celebrity's public persona
Clothing Sources	Local retailers/ecommerce	Local retailers/ecommerce or the retailer that employs the shopper	Local and global retailers, ecommerce, designer showrooms, PR firms, designer ateliers
Type of Clothing Styled	All types depending on clients' needs; can be mid-priced or high-end	All types depending on clients' needs; can be mid-priced or high-end	Usually high-end, designer, couture, or exclusive designer vintage
How to Break into the Industry	High-end retail sales or assisting in the personal shopping service department at a high-end retailer; may also be helpful to gain certification	High-end retail sales or assisting in the personal shopping service department at a high-end retailer	Intern at fashion PR firm or fashion magazine, assist fashion editor at magazine, assist editorial stylists and simultaneously build portfolio
How to Build Client Roster	Stay at same retail sales job for a long time, promote services through social media, cultivate relationships with local salons	Stay at same retail sales job for a long time, promote services through social media, cultivate relationships with local salons	Network and assist established stylists to build relationships with designers, showrooms, and celebrities

Recommended Personal Style Books

Personal style books are written to help people understand wardrobe essentials and proper garment fits and to help readers cultivate their own unique styles. They often also discuss different body types and what silhouettes best flatter them. It is a good idea for image consultants to have a library of books about personal style, fashion designers, or anything else that provides inspiration.

- *How to Get Dressed* by Alison Freer
- *The Cool Factor* by Andrea Linett
- *Living in Style* by Rachel Zoe
- *Design Your Life* by Rachel Roy
- *The Art of Dressing Curves* by Susan Moses
- *The Pocket Stylist* and *Style Evolution*, both by Kendall Farr
- *The Little Black Book of Style* by Nina Garcia
- *The Truth About Style* by Stacy London
- *The Wow Factor* by Jacqui Stafford
- *Dressing the Man* by Alan Flusser
- *Nordstrom Guide to Men's Style* by Tom Julian

Basic Elements and Principles of Design

Every fashion stylist must develop a sharp eye and work with the following:

BASIC ELEMENTS OF DESIGN

- Line
- Form, shape, and space
- Texture
- Pattern
- Color

BASIC PRINCIPLES OF DESIGN

- Balance
- Emphasis
- Rhythm
- Proportion
- Unity

Adapted from *Fashion by Design* by Janice Greenberg Ellinwood, Fairchild Books, 2011.

Line Direction in Clothing

Line is one of the most basic elements of design; thus, it serves as a great example of the kind of detail that every fashion stylist must work with. Color, pattern, and texture can influence line. The four main **line directions** found in clothing are **horizontal**, **vertical**, **diagonal**, and **curved lines**. Line direction in clothing is created by surface fabric patterns, blocks of color, seams, hems, or other design details. For example, a contrasting top and bottom creates a horizontal effect where the two hues meet. If a contrasting top stops at the hip area, then a horizontal line will fall there. Other design details that influence line include buttons, princess seams, pockets, and necklines. Each of the four line directions affects the way the wearer's body is perceived. It is important to remember that these four types of lines are neither positive nor negative. They are simply different, and they can be used to different advantages.

Horizontal Lines

Horizontal lines tend to widen the areas where they are worn. (See Figure 4.3a.) They can be a disadvantage if, for example, an apple-shaped woman wears them across the widest point of her midriff. The horizontal line in this case will accentuate this area, drawing attention that might be unwanted. On the other hand, horizontal lines can be an advantage to a pear-shaped woman who wears them across her shoulders or bustline. In this case, the horizontal line can widen and therefore balance a narrow shoulder against a heavier hip and thigh area. Examples of horizontal lines are horizontal stripes, hemlines of tops and bottoms, belts, shoulder pads, bateau or boatneck tops, puffed sleeves, and cap sleeves.

Vertical Lines

Vertical lines tend to elongate the areas where they are worn. (See Figure 4.3b.) Like horizontal lines, they can be used to advantage or disadvantage. A solid-colored, hip-length sleeveless shirt can be elongating on someone with a fuller torso. The column of color from shoulder to hip that contrasts with the wearer's skin tone creates a vertical line.

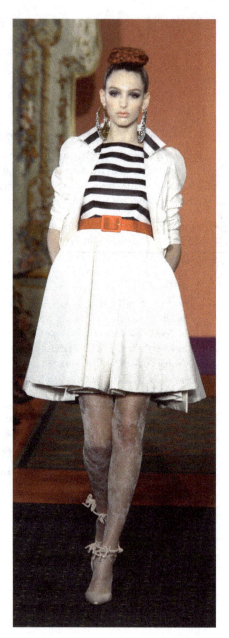

Figure 4.3a
Horizontal lines tend to widen the areas where they are worn.

Adding horizontal elements such as cap sleeves or a belt diminishes the vertical effect. Examples of vertical lines are vertical stripes, button-down shirts, vertical pleats, and princess seams.

Diagonal Lines

Diagonal lines tend to direct the eye to a point. (See Figure 4.3c.) They can also camouflage flaws by moving the viewer's eye to another point. An example of this would be an A-line skirt worn by a woman with full hips. An A-line skirt flows away from the hips and disguises their fullness. The eye might either move up to the waist or down to the shoes, depending on the rest of the outfit and what the wearer has chosen to accentuate. Other examples of diagonal lines are asymmetrical hemlines and diagonal lines printed on fabric.

Curved Lines

Curved lines tend to soften a look and can sometimes add bulk. (See Figure 4.3d.) They are great for very thin people who want to appear curvier. Examples of curved lines are ruffles and bubble skirts.

Understanding Body Types

As with any area of styling, it is important to understand different women's body types and what flatters them. Personal shoppers tend to work with clients who have typical bodies, whereas in editorial and celebrity styling, the client is often a woman who is tall and thin or devotes a lot of time to fitness. This is not necessarily the case with everyday women. The three main body types are **apple**, **pear**, and **hourglass**. Many style books break body types down into further, more detailed categories, but for our purposes we will keep the classifications simple. (See Figure 4.4.) The goal when styling is always to balance proportion, to enhance what's most attractive, and minimize problem areas.

Apple

An apple-shaped body carries weight in the torso, or midsection. The torso includes the stomach, chest, back, and

Figure 4.3b
Vertical lines tend to elongate the areas where they are worn.

Figure 4.3c
Diagonal lines tend to direct the eye to a point.

Figure 4.3d
Curved lines tend to soften a look and can sometimes add bulk.

sides. This person's shoulders are often wider than his or her hips. Often apple-shaped people complain that they can never find good blouses when shopping. Conversely, bottoms are easy to find, and they might be able to wear a wide variety of jeans, leggings, shorts, and skirts.

An apple-shaped body typically benefits from elongation in the top or torso. Fabrics like bulky knits and stiff wovens only add more bulk to this area. Slinky, loose-fitting knits and fluid wovens are good bets for tops. Tunics, sleeveless tops, and drop-waist tops are great silhouettes for this shape. Any hemline, design detail, or accessory placed near the thickest part (often the waist) only accentuates what one typically prefers to diminish. As for pants, this body type can fit into a variety of styles. Tunics or drop-waist tops with leggings are great looks. Often wide-leg pants can make the legs appear fuller and balance the torso.

Pear

Those with pear-shaped bodies hold weight in the thighs, hips, bottom, and legs. This body shape's shoulder is narrower than the hip. These bodies have the benefit of fitting into a wide variety of tops but have a tougher time with bottoms.

A pear-shaped body needs to balance a smaller torso with a fuller lower half. This body can wear bulky knit sweaters or crisp woven-fabric tops more easily. Nipped waists, cap sleeves, and ruffled necklines are great silhouettes for this shape. Tight pants, including leggings and skinny jeans, draw attention to the lower half of the body and create a visual imbalance. Wide-leg and boot-cut pants balance the hip and thigh area and can be more forgiving. Design details to avoid in bottoms are big pockets and pocket flaps.

Figure 4.4
Style books use a
variety of descriptions
to categorize different
body shapes.

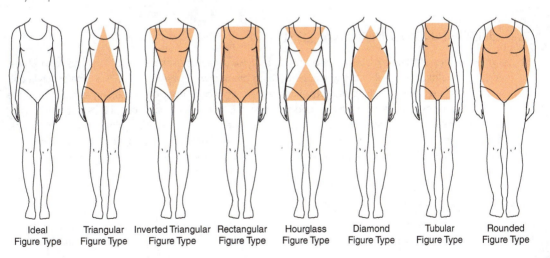

| Ideal Figure Type | Triangular Figure Type | Inverted Triangular Figure Type | Rectangular Figure Type | Hourglass Figure Type | Diamond Figure Type | Tubular Figure Type | Rounded Figure Type |

Hourglass

Hourglass bodies have a defined waist with a full chest and full legs. This body shape holds weight uniformly everywhere. Usually the shoulder and hip are approximately the same width. This shape can be a great asset because weight gain isn't as obvious since it's distributed across the entire body.

This body type has the benefit of looking outstanding in tight-fitting, bias-cut, and draped knit tops and dresses. However, if voluptuous, this body type can be easily overwhelmed by too many design details in clothing like ruffles or bows. As for balancing tops and bottoms, the hourglass body has a little more room to play.

Body Type Challenges

A stylist must not only consider one of the three basic women's body styles just listed but must also account for women who are not a standard height and weight. There are a range of tricks and techniques that a personal stylist must know to make these women look their best.

Petite

A stylist's goal when dressing women five feet, four inches tall or shorter is to make them look taller and to ensure that clothing fits and does not overwhelm their smaller frame. Stylists must pay close attention to proportion, avoid fabrics with large prints, and be ready to employ a good tailor to adjust jacket sleeve lengths and hemlines.

Plus Size

Also called full-figured, this woman typically wears a size above a 12 or 14. The goal is to look long, lean, and proportionate. Stylists must pay close attention to fit, because loose, baggy, and billowy garments can make the client look larger than more form-fitting garments.

UNDERSTANDING PERSONAL STYLE

One of the key elements of being a good personal stylist is the understanding of different personal styles. Many books and websites about wardrobe-building break down personal styles into different **style categories**: different types of styles that define someone's wardrobe. People can belong to more than one style category, and outfits can be mixed and matched from a variety of influences. It is important for stylists to have a defined and memorable personal style. This means having a good grasp of style categories. This book breaks style into eight categories: **Modern Classic, Romantic Vintage, Rock 'n' Roll, Bohemian, Creative Edgy, Glamazon, Minimalist Modern,** and **Urban Sporty**. (See Figure 4.5a–g.) Some of these style categories apply more to one gender than the other, as noted at the beginning of each category.

Modern Classic (Men and Women)

Modern Classic is a timeless style category, and it encompasses understated yet versatile looks that can be worn for work, play, or a night out. Celebrities with Modern Classic style include Victoria Beckham,

Gwyneth Paltrow, Reese Witherspoon, George Clooney, and Ryan Reynolds. This style includes items such as solid-color button-down shirts with dress pants for men, and simple sheath dresses for women. Designers specializing in this look are Hermès, Céline and Ralph Lauren; retailers include J. Crew, Brooks Brothers, Banana Republic, and Madewell.

Romantic Vintage (Women Only)

Romantic Vintage is a very feminine style defined by delicate fabrics, embroidery, lace, and vintage inspirations. This style is difficult to pull off head to toe without looking like a costume, so it is important to incorporate modern silhouettes and, if actual vintage pieces are used, to mix them with current pieces. Celebrities who have worn notable Romantic Vintage looks are Anne Hathaway, Sienna Miller, and Alexa Chung. Anna Sui and Vera Wang are two designers known for Romantic Vintage clothing, and this style can be found at the retailer Anthropologie.

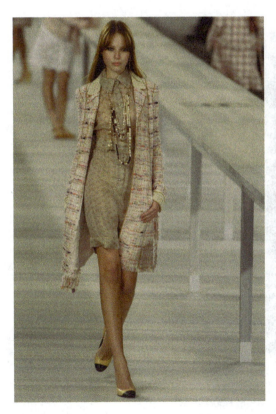

Figure 4.5a
Modern Classic is the most timeless style category.

Figure 4.5b
The model Karen Elson is known for her Romantic Vintage looks.

Rock 'n' Roll (Men and Women)

Rock 'n' Roll style is known for the color black, for a mix of hard and soft fabrics like leather and lace, and for a liberal use of studs, silver, and skull and biker motifs. Staples of this style for men and women include the black leather motorcycle jacket, combat boots, black jeans, and vintage concert T-shirts. This style is heavily influenced by bands like the Rolling Stones, Metallica, and Joan Jett and the Blackhearts, and celebrities known for this look include Kate Moss, Gwen Stefani, and Justin Theroux. Design houses that continually incorporate this style are Alexander McQueen, Balmain, and Philipp Plein, and this style can be found at the retailer AllSaints.

Bohemian (Men and Women)

Bohemian style is similar to Romantic Vintage in that it encompasses fluid fabrics and feminine silhouettes for women. However, it differs in that it is more sixties- and seventies-inspired and frequently references what people wore to the original music festival Woodstock. Examples of Bohemian style are ikat or

Figure 4.5c
The model Kate Moss is a famous Rock 'n' Roll style icon.

Figure 4.5d
Bohemian style is similar to Romantic Vintage in that it encompasses fluid fabrics and feminine silhouettes.

paisley blouses paired with cutoff jeans for women, or vintage button-down shirts for men. Nicole Richie is famous for her bohemian style, as are Kate Hudson and Owen Wilson. Chloe is a design house that channels an easy, breezy look every season, and Lucky Brand and Free People are two mainstream brands (and retailers) known for their Bohemian looks.

Creative Edgy (Men and Women)

Creative Edgy style is about interesting silhouettes, imaginative prints, nontraditional color combinations, and innovative construction techniques. This style is often synonymous with fashion risk-taking, and stars known for this style include Sarah Jessica Parker, Katy Perry, and Pharrell Williams. Larger brands known for Creative Edgy approaches are Prada, Marni, and Moschino, but it's important to know smaller, niche brands, too, like Hood by Air and Novis.

Figure 4.5e
Creative Edgy style is about interesting silhouettes or clothing construction techniques. Asymmetrical hemlines or unexpected sewing details define this look.

Glamazon (Women Only)

Glamazon style is about sex appeal and not being afraid to be noticed. Figure-hugging dresses and feminine silhouettes define this look. Some notable Glamazons on the red carpet are Salma Hayek, Kim Kardashian, Jennifer Lopez, and Christina Hendricks. Some women adopt the Glamazon look for special events but keep their day looks more simplified. Other women prefer the look every day, although they might tone it down for daily life. They might wear figure-hugging, curve-revealing dresses for events and fitted pants, blouses, stilettos, and noticeable jewelry in their everyday looks. Labels to look for include Herve Leger and Azzedine Alaia.

Minimalist Modern (Men and Women)

Minimalist Modern style is about a very simple, neutral color palette of black, white, navy, cream, and grey. What makes this simplicity work is the quality of the garment, the quality of the fabric, and the fit on the body. Calvin Klein and Giorgio Armani are designers known for a crisp, minimalist aesthetic. The actress Jennifer Aniston and actor Daniel Craig often wear classic, minimalist looks. Vince and Theory are two well-known brands that specialize in this look for men and women.

Figure 4.5f
Glamazon style is about sex appeal and not being afraid to be noticed.

Figure 4.5g
Minimalist Modern style is about a very simple neutral color palette. What makes this simplicity work is the quality of the garment, the quality of the fabric, and the fit on the body.

Urban Sporty (Men and Women)

The sporty look is about traditional roomy cuts. For example, sporty shirts are larger rather than fitted, and jeans are relaxed fit instead of straight leg. Sporty men might wear athletic apparel as casual wear and might not shy away from jewelry that is meant to be noticed. Michael Jordan and Derek Jeter are good examples of men who have a sporty style. Sporty women often mix different pieces with athletic apparel. For example, model Gigi Hadid has been known to wear Adidas pants with a leather motorcycle jacket.

Personal Style Self-Assessment Quiz for Women

1. If I had $10,000 to spend on clothing, I'd like to go shopping for (don't be afraid to look up brands you haven't heard of):
    a. Brands like Diesel, Vetements, and Balenciaga
    b. Brands like Betsey Johnson, Beyond Vintage, and Johnny Was
    c. Brands like J.Crew, Madewell, and Theory

     d. Brands like Elizabeth and James and DKNY

     e. Brands like Chrome Hearts and Trash & Vaudeville

     f. Brands like Lucky Brand, Joie, and Free People

     g. Brands like Roberto Cavalli and Herve Leger

2. If I had to choose one of these to wear to a dressy event, I'd choose:

     a. A menswear tuxedo-inspired jacket with a funky dress and ankle boots

     b. A delicate drop-waist lace slip dress with embroidered details and strap heels

     c. A neutral shift dress with simple jewelry and heels

     d. A solid-colored dress with an asymmetrical hemline paired with stacked heel ankle boots

     e. A leopard print dress with a leather jacket, extra-high heels, and big earrings

     f. A flowy late-1960s-inspired dress with lots of voluminous fabric, stacks of gold bangles, and dressy flat sandals

     g. A fitted bandage dress with a built-in bustier and stilettos

3. Of all of the people listed below, my favorite style inspirations are:

     a. Gwen Stefani, Rihanna

     b. Dita Von Teese, Karen Elson

     c. Reese Witherspoon, Jennifer Aniston

     d. Angelina Jolie, Rooney Mara

     e. Kat Von D

     f. Nicole Richie, Rachel Zoe

     g. Kim Kardashian, Jennifer Lopez

4. If you look at the clothes in my ideal imaginary closet, you'll see:

     a. Some experimental and unusual clothing silhouettes

     b. Feminine dresses, slacks, and blouses inspired by the 1920s, 1930s, 1940s, and 1950s

     c. A few edgy shoes and accessories and a lot of basic pieces that can take me to many different occasions

     d. Simple clothing that is unique yet understated, such as jackets with large, exaggerated lapels or T-shirts with asymmetrical hemlines

     e. Leather pants, fur or leather vests, old band T-shirts, scarves, and motorcycle boots

     f. Distressed jeans, moccasins, breezy sundresses, flowy dresses, and tops that are loose and comfortable

     g. A lot of black, red, and leopard print, satin fabrics, fitted/tight pants, a bustier or two, and a lot of form-fitting tops

5. If my living room reflected my ideal closet, it would have:

     a. Sleek, modern pieces mixed with bold pieces: for example, a contemporary white sofa, chrome-and-glass coffee table, with a chartreuse armchair, a patterned shag rug, and an Andy Warhol print

     b. Thrift store and flea market finds mixed with antique reproductions and home accessories from past decades

     c. Simple, functional, but stylish furniture that is somewhat modern with a hint of tradition

     d. Very sparse contemporary furniture mixed with unexpected elements, such as Lucite armchairs and interesting sculptures

e. Antiques mixed with contemporary furniture, with lots of comfortable throw rugs and blankets and some old concert posters on the wall

f. Comfortable thrift store or flea market–inspired furniture, globally inspired accent pieces, and patterned textiles, such as pillows, curtains, and blankets

g. Posh, well-made pieces with metallic accents and luxurious upholstery

6. My ideal imaginary shoe collection is mostly made up of:

a. Any and everything, including ankle booties, shoes with stud embellishments, spike-heel boots, and brightly colored heels

b. Some different vintage-inspired heels and flats that are feminine and often embellished or patterned

c. Basic black and nude heels, flats, basic sandals, and a couple pairs of knee-high and ankle boots thrown in for good measure

d. Sandals and boots with interesting details and silhouettes

e. Motorcycle boots and stud-embellished heels

f. Flat strappy sandals, moccasins, and suede boots

g. All shoes with some type of heel, and usually a pointy toe

7. If I could choose any one of these handbag options, I'd choose:

a. An unusually shaped messenger bag

b. A beaded clutch with satin lining

c. A nude clutch or shoulder bag that can match a lot of different things

d. A satchel with no visible logos or brand identity

e. A bag with fringe

f. A bag with surface embellishments

g. A python-skin bag with shiny gold or silver hardware

8. If I could wear my hair in any style, I would:

a. Bleach it, wear it short, or wear it in an asymmetrical style; I'd love to change my hairstyle often

b. Style it in soft waves in a chin-length or shoulder-length bob

c. Keep it simple and long with highlights

d. Have it cut in a short pixie cut

e. Wear it long and wild with an unexpected color such as deep auburn

f. Keep it natural with some length and beachy waves

g. Keep it medium to long but with some volume at the top and possibly on the sides

9. My ideal jewelry collection would consist of:

a. Everything from plastic earrings to bold necklaces; some would be expensive, and some would be cheap

b. Delicate jewelry with flowers and different gemstones

c. Diamond studs, a couple of good watches, such as Cartier or Rolex, a nice versatile diamond necklace

d. Unique jewelry from lesser-known designers

e. Chain-link earrings and leather-cuff bracelets

f. Stacks of gold bangles and armbands

g. Big diamonds, lots of rings, and lots of sparkly jewelry (no fakes)

10. If I had to work one of the following accessories into my look every day for the next month, I'd choose:
    a. White plastic hoop earrings
    b. An enameled locket with a flower motif
    c. Pearl stud earrings
    d. A funky gold cuff bracelet from an art fair
    e. A leather cuff with studs
    f. A bracelet worn above the elbow as an armband
    g. A huge gold and diamond cocktail ring

If you answered mostly:

A you are mainly Creative Edgy.
B you are mainly Romantic Vintage.
C you are mainly Modern Classic.
D you are mainly Minimalist Modern.
E you are mainly Rock 'n' Roll.
F you are mainly Bohemian.
G you are mainly Glamazon.

Personal Style Self-Assessment Quiz for Men

1. If I had $10,000 to spend on clothing, I'd like to go shopping for (don't be afraid to look up brands you haven't heard of):
    a. Brands like Diesel, rag & bone, and Ben Sherman
    b. Brands like J.Crew, Banana Republic, and Theory
    c. Brands like Calvin Klein and Armani
    d. Brands like True Religion and Lip Service
    e. Brands like Lucky Brand and American Eagle
    f. Brands like Nike and Adidas
2. If I had to choose one of these to wear to a dressy event, I'd choose:
    a. A fitted tuxedo-inspired jacket with contrasting slim-fit pants
    b. A basic two-button gray suit with a colorful wide-stripe tie
    c. A sleek two-button suit jacket with slim-cut pants and dress shirt with no tie and top button unbuttoned
    d. Suit jacket, worn jeans, untucked shirt, bandana, and boots
    e. Vintage leather jacket, patterned button-down shirt, and slacks
    f. A classic striped suit with a twist such as a bold tie and dress shirt, a necklace, or some cuff links
3. Of all of the people listed below, my favorite style inspirations are:
    a. Kanye West, Harry Styles
    b. George Clooney, Tom Cruise
    c. Brad Pitt, Tom Ford

d. Dave Grohl, Anthony Kiedis
e. Lenny Kravitz
f. Deion Sanders, Derek Jeter

4. If you look at the clothes in my ideal imaginary closet, you'll see:
    a. A mix of leather pants, jeans, bold sneakers, a lot of black, and a lot of pieces by lesser-known labels
    b. Basic sweaters that I can layer over a collared shirt, black and gray two-button suits, khaki pants, polo shirts, loafers, basic sneakers, relaxed-fit jeans
    c. Sleek slim-cut suits, pants, jeans, and fitted tees, all in neutral colors
    d. Ripped jeans, old band T-shirts, Converse
    e. Leather pants, vests, old band T-shirts, scarves, and motorcycle boots
    f. Relaxed-fit jeans, basic hoodies (perhaps with team names on the front), baseball caps, tennis shoes that are unique but not too outrageous

5. If my living room reflected my ideal closet, it would have:
    a. Sleek, modern pieces mixed with bold pieces: for example, a contemporary sofa, chrome-and-glass coffee table, big, bold paintings on the wall, and unique one-of-a-kind home accessories
    b. Simple, functional, but stylish furniture that is somewhat modern with a hint of tradition, such as Restoration Hardware or Pottery Barn
    c. Very sparse contemporary furniture and a lot of natural materials such as stone and wood
    d. Antiques mixed with contemporary furniture with lots of comfortable throw rugs and blankets and some old concert posters on the wall
    e. Comfortable thrift store or flea market–inspired furniture, globally inspired accent pieces, patterned textiles, such as pillows, curtains, and blankets
    f. Well-made, heavy, traditional furniture pieces with luxurious upholstery

6. My ideal imaginary shoe collection is mostly made up of:
    a. Collectible designer sneakers
    b. Basic black and nude dress shoes and classic sneakers in basic white or navy blue
    c. Simple but modern boots and shoes with hidden closures
    d. Motorcycle boots or Converse
    e. Sandals, boots, Converse; an eclectic collection, some of which was purchased secondhand
    f. A collection of sneakers from all different price points; tasteful dress shoes purchased from a department store

7. If I could choose any one of these overnight bags for a short trip, I'd choose:
    a. A retro-inspired duffel bag with a modern twist, such as black leather and studs
    b. A piece of tweed Hartmann or Louis Vuitton luggage
    c. A black leather bag of great quality but no obvious labels attached to its outside
    d. A beat-up leather bag that you've had forever and is worn to perfection
    e. A vintage bag found at a thrift store
    f. A sporty duffel bag that might have a Nike or other sportswear logo on the outside

8. If I could wear my hair in any style, I would:
    a. Wear it in an asymmetrical style, shave lines into the side, or shave off part of my hair and leave the rest longer
    b. Keep the sides and back short, the top slightly longer, get it trimmed often, and wear it in a side part
    c. Wear it slightly long, perhaps slicked back with hair product

d. Wear it longer without obvious use of hair product; it would look natural and a little unkempt

e. Keep it natural, grow it long, or wear dreadlocks

f. Wear it very short and immaculately groomed

9. My ideal jewelry collection would consist of:

   a. Thick black leather cuffs, unusual necklace pendants

   b. A Rolex or Cartier watch with a stainless-steel, gold, or alligator-skin band; very few or no diamonds on face or band

   c. A classic watch but perhaps with a black instead of white face, or a streamlined watch

   d. Bracelets or necklaces that use leather cords

   e. Jewelry made of leather cords, woven thread

   f. Gold, platinum, and diamond bracelets, necklaces, and watches that are made to be noticed

10. If I had to include one of the following items or looks into my appearance every day for the next month, I'd choose:

    a. Skinny jeans

    b. A roomy white polo shirt with a designer emblem on the chest

    c. Monochromatic clothing from head to toe

    d. A leather cord necklace with a pendant

    e. A woven string bracelet

    f. A large gold-and-diamond watch

If you answered mostly:

A   you are mainly Creative Edgy.

B   you are mainly Modern Classic.

C   you are mainly Minimalist Modern.

D   you are mainly Rock 'n' Roll.

E   you are mainly Bohemian.

F   you are mainly Urban Sporty.

How to Interpret the Style Categories

Most people do not fall into a single style category, nor should they. Having more than one dimension to personal taste makes wardrobes more complex and interesting. For example, Rock 'n' Roll accessories can contrast nicely with Minimalist Modern clothing. It is not hard to dissect someone's closet and identify some sort of common theme in his or her clothing choices. If someone's style isn't evident in his or her closet, it might show in home decor. As mentioned earlier in this chapter, the initial consultation in the client's home is often enlightening for the stylist. When the stylist meets with the client, it might be useful to note which items of clothing are the client's favorite pieces in his or her closet because they often indicate what style categories the client prefers.

UNDERSTANDING COLOR

Color is another important element of design, and a thorough understanding of it, not to mention a keen eye, is essential for fashion stylists in all areas of the profession. It can make the wearer look invigorated and alive or, conversely, sick and exhausted. Most people have probably noticed examples of this on themselves or others. Some people might say, "I wish I could wear that color, but it makes me look awful." For example, when someone with strong yellow skin undertones wears a yellow green, his or her skin can appear pallid and sick. On the other hand, when the same person wears pumpkin orange or chocolate brown, the warmth of the skin tone is brought out and enhanced.

The Color Wheel and Pantone Color Chips

All creative professionals, no matter what their area of expertise, use the color wheel. The color wheel shows how colors relate to each other and how they are combined. Often if a person can wear one color, he or she can also wear a similar shade on the color wheel. By referring to one, the stylist might be able to better see all of a client's color options. The color wheel also makes a great teaching tool during client consultations because the client can see exactly what color the stylist is describing. (See Figure 4.6.) Pantone color chips are more comprehensive color references but are more expensive for a stylist to purchase. A personal stylist might want to purchase a Pantone Color Guide or Magic Palette Color Guide as he or she becomes more established.

["Whoever said orange was the new pink was seriously disturbed."
—*Elle Woods in* Legally Blonde]

Figure 4.6
The Pantone color numbering system allows a client to see the exact color a stylist is describing.

The Two Basic Color Families: Cool and Warm

Knowing the difference between cool and warm skin tones is integral to good styling. An experienced stylist should be able to look at someone and tell very quickly whether he or she has *warm* (yellow or orange) or *cool* (blue or green) undertones. Many people naturally gravitate to the palette that best suits them. A warm person looks great in autumnal rusts and browns. A cool person looks great in pastel pinks, blues, and mint greens.

There are an almost infinite number of cool and warm colors, ranging from bright to pastel to neutral. Although skin tone has either cool or warm undertones, some people can have both undertones on different areas of their bodies. For example, someone can have a warm or flushed look to his or her face but a cool skin tone on the body.

As a rule, the best way to choose correct clothing colors is to closely examine skin, eyes, and hair. (See Figure 4.7.) The colors people should wear are variations of what is found on their body. For example, a woman with golden skin like Beyoncé looks great in gold jewelry. A woman with pale rosy skin like Lady Gaga looks great in silver jewelry. Of course, these rules can be broken when people intentionally play with hair, makeup, and clothing color contrasts as Rihanna does. One person's skin, eyes, and hair can have a surprising array of colors from which to choose.

DOWNTIME: WHAT TO DO BETWEEN JOBS

Image management, like other areas of styling, is often a freelance job. Since freelancers aren't always on a job, downtime is frequent and needs to be used productively. As with any area of fashion styling, it is important to build personal relationships with retail managers and salespeople. A stylist should visit preferred vendors often enough to know what is in stock, know when new shipments are arriving, and maintain relationships with staff. When the staff and stylist's relationship is on a first-name basis, it may be more likely that the staff will call the stylist when new shipments arrive. Downtime is also a great opportunity to keep informed about the fashion world.

Figure 4.7
As a rule, the best way to choose correct clothing colors is to closely examine skin, eyes, and hair. One person's skin can have a surprising array of colors from which to choose. The same goes for eyes and hair.

DRESSING THE PART

Whether a stylist is shopping for a client or going to a meeting, appearance matters. Groomed hair and polished makeup is a must, as is a stylish and well-fitting outfit. Clothing doesn't need to be expensive, but it needs to fit correctly. In fact, affordable clothing that is altered to fit correctly often has a pricier look. A stylist shouldn't be afraid to dress with creative flair. This might entail a bold pair of eyeglasses, an edgy haircut, a funky pair of shoes, or a unique accessory.

Wardrobe Essentials

TWELVE STYLIST WARDROBE ESSENTIALS FOR WOMEN

Wardrobe essentials are the basic building blocks of a well-curated closet. The following list mostly applies to women, though some of it can be translated to men. A good wardrobe of basic pieces can be mixed and matched endlessly. They are basic building blocks that can be added to over time. When chosen and combined properly, these pieces can be casual but polished for a day on the job, or rendered sophisticated for a night out.

1. **Black trousers:** A mid- to high-rise waistband and a straight leg are versatile. This style is the most versatile for different body types and different occasions. Some body types don't look good in tapered or skinny-leg pants. There are going to be some occasions where a low-rise pant is too casual or unprofessional. A straight-leg pant with a mid to high waistband will take the wearer a lot of places.
2. **Medium- or dark-wash jeans:** These should also have a mid-rise waistband and straight leg.
3. **Basic black and white T-shirts:** These should be high-quality shirts. It is not necessary to spend $100 on a T-shirt; just make sure it is good-quality fabric that won't fade or pill. Also, steer clear of shirts that are too tight. Bulging, pulling, and clinging are signs that the shirt does not fit.
4. **White button-down shirt:** A white button-down shirt is a great investment piece. Some people are lucky enough to have a body shape and size that are easy to fit. Everyone else should count on using a tailor to adjust the fit. Length can be shortened for shorter torsos. People with broader shoulders and bigger chests should buy a size up and have the waist taken in if necessary.
5. **Black knee-length skirt:** This can be pencil, straight, or A-line. A-line is a universally flattering shape for every body type. However, if someone is lucky enough to look good in pencil skirts, he or she should go for it. Pencil skirts create a sharp, clean silhouette. Look for skirts with a flat front and side zip. A medium-weight material is most versatile.
6. **Cardigan sweater:** The best choice here is cashmere, although it is also more expensive. If possible, it is great to invest in cashmere because it is beautiful, durable, and timeless. If not, the next-best thing is merino wool. People who live in warmer climates might do better with good-quality cotton knit.
7. **Basic black or tan wool coat:** A black hip-length coat is a good basic coat to have. People who live in cold climates will need to invest in heavier winter wear as necessary.
8. **Trench coat:** A nylon trench is great for rainy days and always looks appropriate whether it's worn to work or on the weekend.
9. **Camisole:** This is a layering piece that can be worn under shirts or sweaters, so a bit of lace detail is nice. Choose a cut and fabric that can be worn alone as well for evening occasions.

10. **Neutral shoes:** These include nude-colored pointy or slightly round toe heels, nude sandals, and neutral knee-high boots. Quality shoes are worth the investment because they wear better and last longer. Leather is a classic material and a great choice unless there is a moral objection to wearing animal hides.

11. **Neutral bags:** These include a nude-colored day bag, small solid-color clutch, and neutral tote bag. A day bag like a satchel or a tote bag is perfect for everyday wear, but it should not be carried to evening events. A clutch is more appropriate for such events, and for a very formal affair, a small clutch or minaudiere is appropriate.

12. **Good shapewear and undergarments:** These include flesh-colored bras and underwear, slips, and shapewear. Well-fitting shapewear and undergarments smooth, slim, and lift the body, helping garments fit better and making fabric look better against the body. Good fit is essential with undergarments like panties, bras, and shapewear because otherwise they will cause noticeable flaws in a finished outfit like panty lines, bulges, and ripples.

Wardrobe Essentials

TWELVE STYLIST WARDROBE ESSENTIALS FOR MEN

Like the preceding list, this list is a useful guide for building a basic wardrobe.

1. **Black suit and gray or beige suit:** This basic two-suit wardrobe will suffice for the man who doesn't need to wear suits professionally. A good black suit can be worn to evening formal events, and a gray or beige suit is good for dressy daytime events. Reevaluate suits every few years to see whether they look outdated. Pleated pants with cuffed ankles might not look as current as flat-front pants. The suit can be broken up and the jacket and pants worn separately for a more casual look.

2. **Medium- or dark-wash jeans:** Different men look better in different jeans. For example, men with more muscular legs look better in relaxed-fit jeans than straight-leg jeans.

3. **Basic black and white T-shirts:** Never skimp on quality. It is not necessary to spend $100 on a T-shirt; just make sure it is good-quality fabric that won't fade or pill.

4. **White button-down shirt:** A white button-down shirt is a great investment piece.

5. **Variety of ties:** A good, basic tie wardrobe for someone who doesn't wear suits often is one striped tie and two solid ties. The solid ties are more versatile, and a red, brown, or black dark one is good for evening, while a gray, yellow, or light blue lighter one is good for daytime. A striped tie can be a good way to update a look without going to too much expense. Striped ties can be found in more current seasonal colors and widths.

6. **Collared polo-style shirt:** This can be worn alone for warm casual days or layered under sweaters on cooler days.

7. **Sweaters:** The best choice here is cashmere, although it is also more expensive. If possible, it is great to invest in cashmere because it is beautiful, durable, and timeless. If not, the next best thing is merino wool. People who live in warmer climates might do better with good-quality cotton knit. At least one pullover and one button or zip cardigan are good foundations. The pullover can be worn over a button-down shirt and under a suit jacket. The cardigan can be worn with jeans.

8. **Basic black or tan heavy lined wool coat:** A black hip-length coat is a good basic coat to have. People who live in cold climates will need to invest in heavier winter wear as necessary.

9. **Tan trench coat or windbreaker:** This is good for damp, cool days. Opt for a style that can be worn to both the office and out on weekends.

10. **Neutral shoes:** One pair of black dress shoes for evening and brown for daytime are good starting points. If there can only be one pair of sneakers, it should be a classic pair (such as Puma or Converse) that is stylish enough to be worn out to dinner with jeans.
11. **Neutral bag:** Whether it is a cross-body messenger style or handheld duffel, it should be large enough for all of the clothes needed for an overnight stay. Consider purchasing a tan color that will match both black and brown shoes and also coordinate with sneakers.
12. **Good white cotton undershirts and undershorts:** These can make a big difference in personal comfort.

INDUSTRY INTERVIEW

Interview with Preston Konrad

Preston Konrad is a celebrity stylist, creative consultant, and television personality based in New York City. Before launching his own creative consulting agency, Preston spent twelve years working for storied life brands, overseeing brand-creative styling, 3-d environments, visual marketing, and fashion direction. Preston served as style director for the iconic American Heritage brand American Eagle Outfitters, overseeing all styling and trends for domestic and international advertising campaigns, ecommerce, marketing initiatives, and multimedia.

Website: *www.PrestonKonrad.com*
Instagram: *@PrestonKonrad*
Twitter: *@PrestonKonrad*

What celebrities, companies, or high-profile clients have you worked with?

I'm lucky that I am able to juggle styling celebrities and as well as consulting for incredible brands. I love being able to elevate someone's individual look as well as evolving the image of a brand. I've worked with celebrities such as Chris Pine, Theo Rossi, [and] Ashley Thomas and have styled advertising and multimedia campaigns for Ralph Lauren, Belstaff, American Eagle, Original Penguin, and more.

How did you get into the fashion industry? Did you have formal training, or is it something that evolved or you fell into?

I never in a million years imagined working in the fashion industry. I grew up on a small farm in the quiet countryside of eastern Pennsylvania. One of my many jobs during my college years was working for the GAP in Boston. (I have to tell you, I was quite the denim folder!) One day while at work a gentleman came into the shop and mentioned he was interested in recruiting me to work for a new brand called Rugby, owned by Ralph Lauren. Me? You mean, me? I was shocked to say the least. I followed his lead and ended up working for Ralph Lauren in college, which snowballed into a corporate job on Madison Avenue the week I graduated school. The rest was history (and a hustle!).

Did you go straight into styling, or did you assist first?

After working for Ralph Lauren for eight years or so in creative services (window styling and visual merchandising) I was contacted internally about a role in the styling department. I was ready for my next move and this is where everything happened for me. I jumped right into styling, both advertising campaigns and digital marketing, albeit at a junior level. Of course, there were countless hours of packing trunks, hauling bags, and lugging accessories through the mud on location, but at the end of the day I didn't actually have to intern or assist anyone. I was learning from the best in the business.

Now that you are styling, what qualities do you look for in an assistant?

Organization and punctuality are two must-haves. Styling a shoot can be very chaotic. Hundreds of pairs of shoes, countless bags of accessories, thousands of dollars' worth of clothing, all with receipts, tags, and memo forms to keep track of. I really rely on my assistants as my right hand when styling a big shoot or celebrity for an event. I need them to show up on time (if not five minutes before me) and stay right until the end of the day, always asking "what else can I do?" … In our new world of tethered living, it's also super important that my assistants are not glued to their phones during work. Of course, I understand there are emails to be read and texts to answer, but selfies and snapchats while on set drive me crazier than anything!

What kinds of job duties did you do when you first started working?

There's a lot of manual labor involved in styling. Although the locations and final images are often gorgeous, there's not tons of glamour behind the scenes. Be prepared to pack and lift heavy trunks (filled with gorgeous shoes, however), tie a lot of shoes, carry heavy garments in crazy weather conditions, and burn yourself on steamers, all while keeping a positive attitude!

Do you have any funny or horror stories of when you first started?

I was styling a major celebrity for the Met Gala in 2010; I remember being so incredibly nervous to meet him in his hotel room. I found myself knocking on his door, holding half my body weight in tuxedo options for him, and he answered the door in his underwear . . . holding a bowl of spaghetti, with a script under his arm. Doesn't get more Hollywood than that, does it? Halfway through our session I realized the watch he was meant to wear did not make its way into the garment bags. I calmly told him I left it in the lobby and began to run all over the West Village in search of another option. We ended up with something fantastic and I left on the verge of tears . . . ; the fears of letting myself or him down weighed on me. I remember waking up the next morning, opening the *New York Post*, and seeing him marked as one of the best-dressed men of the night.

What's something you wish someone had told you before you started? What advice would you give your younger self about styling?

Don't take everything so personally. There is so much that is out of your control, and if you're trying your absolute hardest, it will reflect in the final image.

What do you feel is a common mistake that many people make when they first start out in the industry? Or a common misconception about what you do?

I think many people assume that the job is easy, glamorous, and fun and that because they are in "fashion" they can be rude to people. Don't get me wrong; the job is a blast, but more than anything it is hard work and you have to be kind. Your success lies on your reputation in this business.

What's your philosophy of styling or dressing a client?

Make the client feel their best while pushing their personal style limits. If a client was 100 percent comfortable in everything I dressed them in from the moment they tried it on, I'm not doing my best. My goal is to elevate their personal brand and take them to an exciting new place through their style expression.

Where do you like to shop?

I love a good department store. Selfridges in London is one of my absolute favorites and of course Bergdorf Goodman in New York. I also love a classic pair of Gap jeans . . . ; maybe that goes back to my days folding jeans in school?

What are some of your favorite men's designers?

I'm a fan of the classics. Ralph Lauren will always hold a special place in my heart. Right now, I am in love with what Todd Snyder is doing with menswear—elevating the everyday man.

What are some hidden gems or offbeat places where you pick up stuff for jobs?

Manhattan Wardrobe Supply off 6th Avenue is truly stylist heaven. This is the must-go place to stock up your kit or pick up something out of the box that a photographer is requesting you bring for a shoot. There is literally a floor-to-ceiling wall of just safety pins! (I just got excited when writing that.) I make sure to stop in with my assistant before every major shoot I go on.

How much of your own personal style can be influenced on a job?

I'm always slightly influenced by what job I'm working on. I remember styling a Holiday shoot on which we helicoptered to the top of a glacier in Alaska. When we got to the top, the photographer looked me up and down, assessing my outfit. . . . I realized I was in a head-to-toe glamour/rugged ski-bunny outfit complete with silver puffer jacket, metallic sunglasses, a giant pompom beanie, and almost knee-high snow boots. Hey, it's a fun part of the job!

Who are your muses? How or where do you find inspiration?

I've never really looked to anyone in particular for style inspiration, more to moments in time. The classic Robert Redford era of style always inspired me—the denim shirts, fantastic trousers, oversized topcoats, chunky turtlenecks, etc. I also take great style inspiration from travel. A business trip to London or Paris always injects me with fresh styling inspiration.

What's something that you don't like about being a stylist? If you could change something about the industry, what would it be?

The assumption that you can be rude to people. I try my hardest to be kind to everyone I meet. Shake hands, speak to people with a smile, send thank-you notes. Those little common courtesies are often forgotten in our business. And laugh—it's just fashion!

It can be difficult keeping track of so many items on a big job or when juggling a multitude of shoots. How do you keep organized? Do you have a special system, so to speak, that you like to use?

You must have a great team with you at all times! Even if it's just one other person. Nowadays it's also all about the iPhone. My assistants do a wonderful job of taking pictures of everything we pull for a shoot and sending records to me. Once everything is logged, I ask them to lay out everything on tables by color and category and hang all garments by color and type as well.

Name two styling tips for styling men.

For men, it is all about fit. Make sure pants are always tailored (even jeans). There is nothing worse than seeing photos of your client on the red carpet with a saggy pant. Blazers, suede, and even leather jackets should all get a review by a tailor before being worn by your client.

How does styling for male clients differ from working with female clients?

It's really about making your client feel comfortable. Your job is to help the client express themselves through clothing and to feel confident. Men perhaps are bit less risky when it comes to fashion, but in general, always make sure your client looks you in the eye and says, "I love it."

What do you think are some common mistakes men make when styling?

I think the biggest mistake men make is not tailoring each piece of clothing in a look. If my client is wearing jeans and a T-shirt for a "not so styled" look, everything is tailored, including the T-shirt!

Summary and Review

Image consulting is the only area of styling where the stylist works with real-life people. Because image consultants work with regular people who have regular body shapes, they have to be more cognizant of fit and flattering silhouettes. Celebrity styling, personal styling, and personal shopping are also included in this category. Personal styling is mainly a freelance job, and the stylist is self-employed. It is the only area of fashion styling where a stylist can be certified. Celebrity styling is a highly specialized area that involves styling famous people for special events. Celebrity stylists are self-employed and are usually hired by a movie studio or a publicist. Personal shoppers are on-staff at a retailer and provide one-on-one assistance to help their clients shop at that retailer.

Key Terms

- apple-shaped body type
- Association of Image Consultants International (AICI)
- Bohemian
- celebrity stylist
- Creative Edgy
- curved lines
- diagonal lines
- Glamazon
- hand
- horizontal lines
- hourglass-shaped body type
- image consultant
- image consulting
- line directions
- Minimalist Modern
- Modern Classic
- pear-shaped body type
- personal shopper
- personal stylist
- Rock 'n' Roll
- Romantic Vintage
- style categories
- style consultant
- Urban Sporty
- vanity sizing
- vertical lines
- wardrobe consultant

Review Questions

1. Describe two unique challenges that face personal stylists and celebrity stylists.
2. How does an image consultant decide what colors are best suited to a client?
3. List three best practices that personal shoppers should follow when billing a client for services.
4. List two ways a personal shopper can grow or maintain a client base.
5. Describe the differences between how horizontal, vertical, diagonal, and curved lines affect the wearer.
6. What silhouettes or styles are good for apple-shaped women?
7. What silhouettes or styles are good for pear-shaped women?
8. What silhouettes or styles are good for hourglass-shaped women?
9. List at least two differences between Creative Edgy style and Minimalist Modern.

10. List at least two differences between Romantic Vintage style and Bohemian.

11. Why is an image consultant's own image important?

LEARNING ACTIVITIES

Learning Activity 4.1: Conduct an Internet search for an image consultant in your area. If your area doesn't have anyone, look for an image consultant located in the closest large city. Look specifically for an image consultant with a well-developed personal website. If the website doesn't contain enough content to answer the following questions, then keep searching until you find one that does. Answer the following questions:

1. List the consultant's name, website, and location.
2. Describe the image consultant's appearance. Do you think he or she has an appealing personal style?
3. What services does the image consultant offer?
4. Describe the pricing or service packages available to potential clients.
5. Who are this stylist's target customers?

Learning Activity 4.2: Choose a favorite actor, actress, or musician to be a "client." On a piece of standard 8.5- x 11-inch blank white printer paper or using a website such as Polyvore, make a collage of two complete outfits that you would create for that client if you were a celebrity stylist. One outfit is to wear to an awards show that the client is attending; the other outfit is to wear when the client appears on a television talk show. For each outfit, be prepared to:

1. List what the client will be doing in the clothes (for example, does he or she need to be able to sit down or pose for photos?)
2. List the elements that would be provided to the client to wear
3. Identify where to pull or purchase these items
4. Describe two problems that could occur with each outfit and how to solve each problem

Learning Activity 4.2: Using online resources, including social media, find and print out an example of three different types of personal style described in this chapter and write a paragraph explaining why each look exemplifies the style.

RESOURCES

"About Image Consulting." Association of Image Consultants International. http://www.aici.org/?page=About ImageConsulting.

Binkley, Christina. "Inside a Department Store's Secret Shopping Service." *The Wall Street Journal.* August 11, 2011. https://www.wsj.com/articles/SB10001424053111904140604576498733634049992.

"Certification." Association of Image Consultants International. http://www.aici.org/Certification/Certification.htm.

Colon, Ana. "The Petite Girl's Guide to Stress-Free Shopping." Refinery29.com. March 29, 2015. http://www .refinery29.com/84286.

Cowles, Charlotte. "How Much It Costs to Send a Celebrity down the Red Carpet." *New York Magazine*. January 30, 2012. http://nymag.com/thecut/2012/01/cost-of-red-carpet-fashion.html?mid=pinterest-share-thecut.

Dariaux, Genevieve Antoine. *A Guide to Elegance: For Every Woman Who Wants to Be Well and Properly Dressed on All Occasions*. New York: William Morrow, 2004.

Dooley, Roger. "The Psychology of Vanity Sizing." *Forbes*. July 29, 2013. https://www.forbes.com/sites/roger dooley/2013/07/29/vanity-sizing/#4a41859b1e32.

Farr, Kendall. *The Pocket Stylist: Behind-the-Scenes Expertise from a Fashion Pro on Creating Your Own Look*. New York: Gotham, 2004.

France, Kim, and Andrea Linett. *The Lucky Guide to Mastering Any Style: How to Wear Iconic Looks and Make Them Your Own*. New York: Gotham, 2008.

France, Kim, and Andrea Linett. *The Lucky Shopping Manual: Building and Improving Your Wardrobe Piece by Piece*. New York: Gotham, 2003.

Grigoriadis, Vanessa. "Slaves of the Red Carpet." *Vanity Fair*. February 10, 2014. http://www.vanityfair.com/holly wood/2014/03/hollywood-fashion-stylists-rachel-zoe-leslie-fremar.

Halbreich, Betty. *I'll Drink to That: A Life in Style, with a Twist*. New York: Penguin Press, 2014.

"Image Consultation." My Image Expert. http://www.myimageexpert.com/image_consultation.html.

"Information on Design Lines." Joy of Clothes. http://www.joyofclothes.com/style-advice/magazine-articles/style -articles/design-lines.php.

Ingraham, Christopher. "The Absurdity of Women's Clothing Sizes, in One Chart." *The Washington Post*. August 14, 2015. https://www.washingtonpost.com/news/wonk/wp/2015/08/11/the-absurdity-of-womens-clothing-sizes -in-one-chart/?utm_term=.926af5ab935a.

King, Peter. "Personal Shoppers Find Clothes to Make the Man." *The Wall Street Journal*. August 12, 2010. https://www.wsj.com/articles/SB10001424052748704164904575421373622725304.

LaPorte, Danielle, and Carrie McCarthy. *Style Statement: Live by Your Own Design*. New York: Little, Brown, 2008.

Levin, Jenny. *Harper's Bazaar Great Style*. New York: Hearst Books, 2010.

Magsaysay, Melissa. "Hollywood's Top 25 Most Powerful Stylists Are Celebrated." *Los Angeles Times*. March 15, 2012. http://latimesblogs.latimes.com/alltherage/2012/03/hollywoods-top-25-most-powerful-stylists-are -celebrated-.html.

Mathis, Carla Mason, and Helen Villa Connor. *The Triumph of Individual Style: A Guide to Dressing Your Body, Your Beauty, Your Self*. Menlo Park, CA: Timeless Editions, 1993.

Morrison, Sasha Charnin. *Secrets of Stylists: An Insider's Guide to Styling the Stars*. San Francisco: Chronicle Books, 2011.

"Pantone Color Guide." Amazon. http://www.pantone.com

Sauers, Jenna. "Rachel Zoe's Exorbitant Styling Fees, Revealed." Jezebel.com. March 20, 2011. http://jezebel.com /5780546/rachel-zoes-exorbitant-styling-fees-revealed.

"Client Style Files." Alexandrastylist.com. https://alexandrastylist.com/category/client-style-files/.

Tejeda, Valerie. "How to Become a Celebrity Stylist, from Selena Gomez's Go-To Fashion Pro." *Teen Vogue*. July 25, 2014. http://www.teenvogue.com/story/how-to-be-celebrity-stylist.

Writing, Alexis. "Business Image Consultant Tips." *Houston Chronicle*. http://smallbusiness.chron.com/business -image-consultant-tips-300.html.

Zee, Joe. *Unbuttoned, Episode 1: "Oscar Red Carpet Politics."* February 27, 2015. https://www.yahoo.com/style /listen-to-unbuttoned-yahoo-styles-new-podcast-112220826833.html.

5 Careers in Styling

In this chapter you will learn:
- Why stylists diversify their skills
- About runway styling
- About off-figure clothing styling
- About prop and set styling
- About food styling
- About jewelry styling
- About visual merchandising
- About digital styling for ecommerce and social media

WHY FASHION STYLISTS DIVERSIFY

Many freelance stylists diversify their skill sets so that they can work more consistently. Others do it simply because they enjoy working with different teams of people and different types of merchandise, and they enjoy developing different skill sets. Building a diverse portfolio can be a great way to gain visibility, especially if stylists live in a smaller city. This opens them up for more jobs and might help to keep their **bookings** consistent. Bookings are committed jobs on a stylist's calendar. More work equals more pay, which is a welcome thing for most freelancers.

Even stylists who are on staff would be wise to develop their skills in a variety of different areas of styling. The more they can do, the more value they bring to their company and the fewer outside stylists a company has to bring in, which saves money. In tough economic times, versatility can also mean job security. For example, a retailer might want to save money on an advertisement by shooting clothing without using models (explored later in the "Off-Figure and On-Figure Styling" section). If a stylist doesn't know how to style this type of shoot, he or she may be out of a job.

Figure 5.1
Just like editorial styling, other areas of styling require the stylist to stay current, to be able to pick out the best, most relevant trends, and to distill them into key looks.

Just like editorial styling, other areas of styling require the stylist to stay current, to be able to pick out the best, most relevant trends, and to distill them into key looks. (See Figure 5.1.) Runway stylists might be inspired by street fashion. Prop and set stylists might be inspired by the latest in interior design. A stylist working on a social media campaign might draw inspiration from what colors and styles are trending at the moment. Stylists who know what is going on in all areas of art and design create the most lasting images, as we'll explore more in Chapter 8, "Fashion Lexicon: Terms, Icons, History, and Inspiration."

The areas of styling outlined in this chapter include runway styling, off-figure clothing styling, prop and/or set styling, food styling, jewelry styling, visual merchandising, and digital styling for websites and social media platforms. Even if a stylist doesn't plan to work in every area – and most stylists don't – it's always helpful to understand what other people in the styling industry do and everyone can work together to create effective images.

RUNWAY STYLING

Runway styling entails styling a designer's collection before a show. Design houses hire stylists to bring a fresh vision to a collection and to finish each look. Stylists work closely with designers to create what people see on the runway during Fashion Weeks. Runway stylists sometimes also work on a freelance basis for smaller-scale runway shows. They are sometimes referred to as fashion coordinators. A department store that organizes a fashion show might hire a fashion coordinator to pull and put together looks.

The runway show that the audience sees is a far cry from the chaos that happens backstage. On the runway, poised models walk at a certain pace and with a certain gait. Their timing has been practiced during rehearsals beforehand. (See Figure 5.2.) During the show, models rush backstage to get changed and line up for their next walk down the runway. **Dressers** work behind the scenes during a show to clothe models as quickly as possible. In some cases, the runway stylist might work double-duty as a dresser during the show. It's the dresser's job to keep clothing organized, unzipped, unfastened, and ready for quick changes. Dressers usually work on a volunteer basis. Opportunities can be found online or through local fashion schools. Being a dresser is a great way to break into runway styling. If the show has employed a stylist or fashion coordinator, he or she might be backstage overseeing the models as they dress.

Figure 5.2
On the runway, poised models walk at a certain pace and with a certain gait. Their timing has been practiced during rehearsals beforehand. During the show models are rushing backstage to get changed and line up for their next walk down the runway.

Recently, many designers have opted to forgo a runway show in favor of hosting a presentation, where models present a fashion collection without walking. Instead, they stay in the same place for an hour or two while the guests come in and out, look at what they're wearing, and take photos or video. Although the models are not moving or changing clothes, presentations still require many of the same styling responsibilities. The complexity of a presentation can vary from models simply standing in rows in an event space or on a stage to groups of models posing in elaborate sets. When a designer decides to create a set, a runway stylist may work with a prop stylist or rely on his or her own prop styling skills to bring the designer's vision to life.

Before a runway show, the stylist and the designer work together to put looks together. The designer conveys to the stylist the look that he or she is going for, and the stylist helps to translate that on the runway. The stylist and designer collaborate to create a cohesive runway collection, which depends as much on each head-to-toe look as on the order in which the looks are sent down the runway. This list of looks, which often is given to the guests attending the show, is called a **run of show**. Some examples of a stylist's influence could be using colorful tights with every look or adding specific handbags to complement each look. Stylists also work with the hair and makeup team to translate the designer's vibe into a modern beauty look that works on a variety of different models. On the day of the show, clothing, shoes, handbags, and other accessories need to be clustered together so that it is obvious how ensembles are meant to be arranged. Sometimes plastic bags with accessories are hung from the hangers of their corresponding outfits. Hangers are tagged with numbers that denote the ensemble's place in the show lineup. (See Figure 5.3.) The combining of clothing with accessories is usually a team effort between a designer's creative staff and the stylist, or the retail merchandiser and the stylist. Model casting is done through modeling agencies, and models are chosen based on their headshots, their look, and their walk.

During the show, the pace backstage is swift and precise. If everyone is not working together and the stylist and the dressers are not organized, it can go downhill fast. It's crucial to remain organized,

Figure 5.3
Sometimes plastic bags with accessories are hung from the hangers of their corresponding outfits. Hangers are tagged with numbers that denote the ensemble's place in the show lineup.

calm, cool, and collected. The average show lasts about 10 to 20 minutes, which may seem like a lot of work for such a short amount of time, but there's no telling how many people will be seeing the show. In addition to the audience in the venue, many shows are live-streamed around the world and posted on numerous websites. Wrapping the show involves breaking down the set and returning the clothing either to the designer's showroom or to the retailer's sales racks. In the days and weeks following the show, runway samples are made available to magazine editors, celebrity stylists, and for use during Market Week.

OFF-FIGURE AND ON-FIGURE STYLING

Off-figure and on-figure modeling are common ways of photographing items without using a model. They are used in both editorial and commercial styling. **Off-figure styling** involves showing clothing, shoes, or accessories in artful arrangements. This can mean that items are folded, draped, stacked, or tacked to a board. **On-figure styling** involves fitting clothing onto a mannequin. Common types of mannequins include **dress forms** (headless mannequins), traditional mannequins, and ghost mannequins. Also called invisible mannequins, a ghost mannequin has modular, removable pieces that correspond to openings in clothing, like the "V" between the lapels of a jacket when it's buttoned up. When these pieces are removed, it gives clothing a hollow, 3D look, as if it's being worn by a ghost. This can be particularly effective when styling for ecommerce.

Off-figure clothing usually requires a little help to get it to look good for the camera. It doesn't have the benefit of the model wearing it to give it shape. (See Figure 5.4.) If it is not shown on a form, it might be stuffed with **batting**, the polyester fiberfill used in quilts or pillows, or with thick paper to give it structure. The purpose of tacking clothing to a board is to be able to photograph it in flat form, so the background is not important. A stylist for a catalogue or online retailer carefully styles and photographs each piece that appears on the website. (See Figure 5.5.) Off-figure shooting may not seem as creative for a stylist as editorial styling, but it can be a great way to learn useful styling techniques. This type of styling still requires steaming and folding and an intense attention to detail, along with an understanding of proportion, photo composition, and fabric.

PROP STYLING

Prop styling entails styling small objects, such as housewares, and larger objects, such as furniture, rugs, or drapes. Another name for this position is **set designing** or **set styling**. This type of styling is used in still images, such as catalogues and advertisements, and in moving images, such as television productions, and work can be divided into editorial and commercial categories.

Editorial shoots are typically done for magazines or magazine-style websites. Even when a magazine photographer shoots someone's home, there is always styling that takes place. That's because what looks good in real life doesn't always translate into the best photograph. To create that effective image, prop stylists must remove clutter and other elements of everyday life like TV remotes, stacks of mail, or kids' toys. They make sure everything is clean, including windows, and they steam or wipe down fabrics like drapes and pillows. Once the area is prepped, they begin to bring things in: fresh flowers, colorful throw pillows, decorative boxes, and coffee-table books. Sometimes they even replace a homeowner's art or area rugs. When the shoot is over, of course, it all must go back, either to its place in the house or to the store or showroom where it was purchased or pulled.

Commercial set styling involves creating interior spaces used in advertising. Television advertisements are often set inside realistic-looking homes. Prop stylists are responsible for this, and they think about all

Figure 5.4
Off-figure clothing usually requires a little help to get it to look good for the camera. It doesn't have the benefit of the model wearing it to give it shape.

Figure 5.5
An online retailer carefully styles and photographs each piece that appears on the website.

the details that make interiors look like real spaces. Furniture, drapes, rugs, and decorative accents are curated to reflect the commercials' themes and to appeal to target customers.

As in other areas of styling, a prop stylist needs to be able to source materials and also has to maintain a stylist kit. A prop stylist's kit is similar to a fashion stylist's kit. For example, both kits usually include a steamer, tape, and pins, but a prop stylist will need some additional items, including a hammer and nails and floral wire for helping flowers to stand up straight.

Sometimes the prop stylist is called on to create custom props for a shoot. If the storyboard calls for a hard-to-find object, the prop stylist needs to create it from scratch. (See Figure 5.6.) For example, perhaps a television commercial has a historical masquerade theme but the masks are hard to find. The prop stylist would research masks and source the materials from a craft or fabric store. He or she would then create the masks specifically for the shoot. In this case it is useful to have a talent for sculpture, painting, and drawing. An educational background in fine art is useful as well.

Most prop stylists are freelancers. The best ways to get into prop styling is to work at a magazine like *Martha Stewart Living* or to assist an established prop or set stylist. Prop stylists are paid rates ranging from $150 to $350 a day, and as with photo styling, most jobs will include shopping and return days.

Figure 5.6
Sometimes the prop stylist is called on to create custom props for a shoot. If the storyboard calls for a hard-to-find object, the prop stylist needs to create it from scratch.

"When a job is prepped and you are ready to send everything out for the shoot day, I always do a 'run-through' with my list; usually with a second set of eyes from my assistant. For example, I'm sending my walls out with a job; I run through the steps of putting a wall together: size of screws, how many jacks are needed, screw gun, cross boards, staples for the canvas, etc. I do that with every aspect of what is going on the job and what tools are needed. I've learned some hard lessons of having to run out during the job and get a tool that is needed."
—Sara Foldenauer, prop stylist. "Tips for Prop/Set Styling," www.setsbysara.com.

FOOD STYLING

Food styling is often seen in food advertisements, cookbooks, and menus. Often the food is not palatable in real life; it is styled to look appetizing for the camera. There are many tricks of the trade to making food look good for the camera lens. The "Food Stylist's Kit Checklist" provides a handy list of the basic tools of the trade that every food stylist must bring to the table.

Aspiring food stylists have a lot of resources to draw from. There are numerous books and workshops for learning the trade (see "Educational Resources for Food Stylists"). Unlike fashion styling, food styling has certain tricks of the trade. It's not like fashion styling, where what people see on the magazine page is interpretive. Food styling has a science to it and uses visual composition. (See Figure 5.7.)

The practice of doing **mock-ups** is unique to food styling. Mock-ups are test runs using similar food, and they are done before a shoot to check composition and lighting. Photography studio lights are hot, the food is very perishable, and the stylist and photographer might only have a short window of time before the food starts looking less appetizing. Therefore, ironing out kinks beforehand is a must. Photo shoots are done in photographers' studios, private kitchens, or **test kitchens**. Test kitchens are independently owned, owned by publications, or owned by food companies. Chefs might go to them to refine recipes for cookbooks, or food companies might test recipes using their products.

Some food stylists belong to the **International Association of Culinary Professionals (IACP)** (www .iacp.com). IACP offers an annual conference for professional food photographers and stylists.

Food Stylist's Kit Checklist

Food stylists buy the tools for their kits at supermarkets and tool stores. Their tools are often easier to find than fashion styling tools. The following items can be found in a food stylist's kit:

- ☐ Tweezers—to grab small objects
- ☐ Glue—to patch or hold things together

Figure 5.7
Food styling is not like fashion styling, where what people see on the magazine page is interpretive. Food styling has a science to it and uses visual composition.

- [ ] Paintbrushes—to apply oil or other liquids to food as needed
- [ ] Small bowls—to hold oil, water, glue, paint, or anything else that might be useful
- [ ] Large and small scissors
- [ ] Wooden skewers and pins—to hold things together
- [ ] Cotton swabs and paper towels—to clean surfaces
- [ ] Glycerin and eyedropper—to mix glycerin with water to make droplets that stay in place
- [ ] Spray bottles and squeeze bottles—to apply oil or other liquid as needed
- [ ] All-purpose cleaning solution

Educational Resources for Food Stylists

There are many resources for food stylists, including books, workshops, and classes. In addition, the blogosphere is full of tips and minicourses from successful food bloggers. If you are thinking about investing in a workshop, it may be worthwhile to invest in a food styling book and trying a few projects first.

The wonderful thing about food styling is that if a stylist is a decent photographer, he or she can build a test portfolio without outside collaboration. Unlike fashion, food styling doesn't require a model, hair stylist, or makeup stylist. Some popular food styling books include:

- *Food Styling: The Art of Preparing Food for the Camera* by Delores Custer
- *The Food Stylist's Handbook* by Denise Vivaldo
- *Food Styling for Photographers & Stylists* by Linda Bellingham, Jean Ann Bybee, and Brad G. Rogers
- *Plate to Pixel: Digital Food Photography & Styling* by Helene Dujardin

"Don't fall in love with your sandwich. You can spend a long time styling and tweaking a product and you can feel really proud of the results. And more often than not, you'll be asked by an Agency Art Director, Client, or the Director to completely change it. First you sigh, internalize your pain, and then, move on and make a new one. This is a team project, and you have to be willing to play well with others.
—Alyssa Sarfity, food stylist. "Tips About Food Styling," www.alyssasarfity.com.

JEWELRY STYLING

Photographing jewelry is difficult because pieces are small and reflective and require very precise lighting. Photographers often work with stylists when jewelry is photographed off-model, either by itself against a neutral background or with props. Because these photographs are often tight, close-up, and precise shots, it is the stylist's job to minimize any dirt, dust, or debris on the set and make sure the jewelry itself starts clean and stays clean. Common styling responsibilities include removing price tags (and cleaning off any adhesive residue left behind) and arranging the pieces so the photographer can capture important details. For example, a brooch or a ring might be placed in a standing position, which can be done by using a small amount of prop wax. To keep jewelry clean, a stylist often wears gloves and uses tools like chopsticks or dentist tools to nudge items together or remove any excess wax from underneath pieces.

Visual Merchandising

Visual merchandising involves creating retail displays. This area of styling can involve fashion, furniture, cosmetics, or whatever the retailer is selling. This profession is one of the few areas of styling that offers full-time salaried positions. A visual merchandiser can work at the corporate level or in a store.

Visual merchandising can be similar to prop styling in that the stylist creates displays. Visual merchandisers often use a wide variety of props when styling. In fact, prop ideas are limitless and sometimes surprising. Some common props are rocks, fruit, and fresh flowers. For example, an accessory might be placed on a bed of shiny rocks. Fresh flowers might be placed on a table at a store entrance. (See Figure 5.8a–b.)

Department stores have prop rooms that also might double as the visual merchandisers' office spaces. In addition to props, there might be one or more places in the room where trend or inspiration pictures are posted. Just like other fashion stylists, merchandisers stay current on trends and clip photos for future reference.

Prop rooms store everything from mannequins, wigs, seasonal decorations, vases, signage, and **risers**, the platforms or pedestals on which merchandisers set items to display. Shoes and handbags are commonly found sitting on risers. Department stores use different props for each department. For example, the risers in the men's department might be made of dark wood, whereas women's department risers might be white. Prop rooms are typically very full and need to be cleaned and organized regularly.

Visual merchandisers' jobs include fashion styling on mannequins and dress forms, but also much more. Among other duties, they may have to help put new shipments out onto the sales floor, install signage to denote special events in the store, set up seasonal decorations, and source new props from unexpected places, such as flea markets or thrift stores.

Fashion Styling Using Digital Media

Styling for digital media has varied meanings. It can entail professionally styling clothing for an online retailer. It also can involve styling for websites such as Polyvore and for apps such as Stylebook, and creating looks on and off a virtual model or creating original photos, videos, and live feeds for social media sites like Instagram and Snapchat.

Most major retailers have apps that make accessing their stores easier. The most notable characteristic of retail websites and fashion apps is the direct interaction between the viewer and the screen. Viewers are able to interact with fashion in ways that aren't possible with print styling. They can zoom in on design details, view the front and back of a garment, and in some cases click and drag different pieces together to help visualize an outfit. The user/customer can also give feedback to other customers and the retailer instantly. In addition, apps allow users to set up profiles and select favorite garments from as many retailers as they wish.

Companies who hire online photo stylists usually look for candidates with an associate's or bachelor's degree in a fashion-related field and/or some styling experience. Styling for an online retailer has a very direct impact on sales because online shoppers depend on proper styling to determine the fit, drape, and proportion of garments. Online photo stylists usually work in very fast-paced environments. A single website can sell women's, men's, and children's apparel, not to mention shoes and accessories. Retailers also constantly introduce new styles while reducing prices on older ones. Each piece needs to

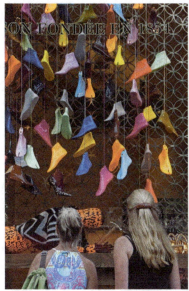

Figure 5.8a–b
Visual merchandisers often use a wide variety of props when styling; in fact, prop ideas are limitless and sometimes surprising.

be photographed from a variety of angles and therefore needs to be properly and meticulously prepared. Styling a high volume of merchandise takes organization and stamina.

The way that the subject is styled and shot is determined by the company's protocol. Some companies use models that have certain hair and makeup looks that reflect their brand, and others might use standard prop outfit pieces, such as nude pumps or black slacks, to help create complete outfits. Online retailers send out staff initiatives to communicate current trends and give direction on how they should be conveyed or styled online.

Virtual fitting rooms allow users to try clothing on models or on uploaded photos of themselves. A good example of an online retailer's use of this technology is the Hugo Boss Virtual Fitting Room (store-us .hugoboss.com). Various apps for handheld devices also give the user the ability to put clothing on a model or collage pieces together to see how they coordinate. For example, the Fashiolista app for the iPhone allows a user to create a profile and put together items from different retailers. If users like one another's style, they can follow one another. Users can also see what is **trending**, or gaining in popularity at any moment, and plan their shopping or outfits accordingly.

"Working in E-commerce is fast fashion. It's creative and inspiring but you have targets and high pressure. We have to shoot at least sixty products and 600 videos each day. The hair, makeup and styling has to be perfect and brand specific and not a blanket treatment for all."
—*Lauren Amps, studio and video manager at ASOS-UK*

FLATLAY STYLING

A **flatlay** is a type of product shot that is popular on social media sites like Instagram. It is usually a square-shaped image that mixes different objects positioned on a flat surface and taken from a bird's-eye view. Flatlays are used in both editorial and commercial realms.

What is included in a flatlay is dictated by the job. For example, if the shoot is for a magazine's Instagram feed, it may follow a theme like "popular beauty products," or if it is for a designer's Instagram feed, the theme might be items from that designer's collection. A flatlay can be styled like a puzzle, with pieces placed simply with space between them, or styled to convey a mood, with layers and more design details.

Here are five guidelines for styling an effective flatlay:

1. Keep the background basic; choose a solid-color floor or table or a white bedsheet.
2. Follow a specific color palette: for example, only black and white, only blush tones, or only a single color.
3. Limit items to three primary products and then accent with a few well-chosen smaller pieces.
4. Vary texture and height to create visual interest.
5. Use filters and apps like Facetune to sharpen, edit, and filter.

INDUSTRY INTERVIEW

Interview with Rebekah Roy

Rebekah Roy is one of London's top fashion stylists and creative consultants. For more information, visit http://www.fashion-stylist.net/blog/about-rebekah-roy-fashion-stylist-creative-director/.

Website: *www.Fashion-Stylist.net*
Instagram: *@Rebekahroy*
Twitter: *@styliststuff*

What celebrities, companies, or high-profile clients have you worked with?
Visa, Nintendo, Harvey Nichols, John Lewis, and Virgin to celebrity clients including Kate Nash, Becca Dudley, Nero, The Feeling, Sarah Brightman, and Billy Idol and top models Kate Moss, Erin O'Connor, and Rosie Huntington-Whiteley. [I've] styled commercial catwalk shows for Harrods, Royal Ascot, Bjorn Borg, Clarks, and The Ford Supermodel of the World competition. [I've] consulted for the brands Sarah Angold, Mimpikita, Wonderluk, and Azza Fahmy, as well as for larger brands such as Kate Spade and Wella.

How did you get into the fashion industry? Did you have formal training, or is it something that evolved or you fell into?
I didn't have anyone in my family who worked in the fashion industry. I think I just loved clothes and understood from quite a young age how powerful they could be, that fashion was a language. I'd worked in retail from when I was sixteen, and at university I studied women's studies and theatre. I became more interested in costumes and my work evolved from there.

Did you go straight into styling, or did you assist first?
I'd done lots of different jobs in the fashion industry, from retail, personal shopping, and working as a buyer, but it was only when I did an internship at British Vogue did I realize that what I wanted to do was styling; back then, not too many people knew about styling as a profession. After my internship I did everything I possibly could to build up my portfolio. I was meeting hair and makeup artists and researching photographers. I was just trying to meet people I could work with, and I was testing two to three times per week. It was crazy busy. I would even help my friends organize their closets or take them shopping; I wanted to do anything creative and productive just to keep learning.

Now that you are styling, what qualities do you look for in an assistant?
I look for assistants that have lots of common sense, are respectful, who are insightful, kind, and enthusiastic. You spend a lot of time with your team, so I really want us to work well together but to also have a lot of fun together too.

What kinds of job duties did you do when you first started working?
Everything I did when I first started I still do now, from making tea at a shoot, going to PR appointments, and doing returns. I don't ask anyone to do something that I wouldn't do myself.

What do you feel is a common misconception about what you do?
I think there's a lot of misconception about what a stylist really does. It's a great job, but it's not as glamorous as people think. I don't think most people, even within the industry, know all the logistics that are involved from running errands, doing carnets [customs documents], and dealing with luggage. I spend more of my time researching, planning, and preparing for the shoot than on actual shoot days.

What's your philosophy of styling or dressing a client?
I do lots of research before I meet a new client; I want to know as much about them as possible. When we meet, we bounce ideas back and forth in terms of developing their signature aesthetic. Then, I go off

to do more research and start curating a selection of looks and accessories that meet their needs; then I plan to take them to the next level, to anticipate their needs and the direction they are going so they can be their best selves!

Where do you like to shop?
This is the part where I'm quite lucky, and I think the more glamorous part of my job, as I often choose my favorites pieces from the designers that I work with. I like to wear things from people I know. It's important that my clothes and accessories mean something to me, to have a memories attached to them. My favorite time to shop is when I'm traveling, and I have some great pieces that I got in Pakistan and in Jakarta.

What are some of your favorite designers?
There are so many designers that I really like, and I love accessories and hats! I love Theo Fennell, and over the years I now have a wonderful little collection of hats from Steven Jones.

What are some hidden gems or offbeat places where you pick up stuff for jobs?
I love to pick up things when I travel. I love going to markets and finding fabric, haberdashery, and jewelry.

How much of your own personal style can be influenced on a job?
I'm not really interested in my own personal style on a job. I think a job is more fun; I love the dream of fashion, and the stories that you get to tell when you do a shoot, the things that you wouldn't and couldn't do in real life.

Who are your muses? How or where do you find inspiration?
I try to look for inspiration in everyday life. I don't think you have to look far to find inspirations. I feel like I'm a perpetual tourist. If I'm in between meetings and have 15 minutes, I'll try to pop into one of the museums. I love watching films and pop culture, and people watching is one of my favorite things to do, especially when I travel.

It can be difficult keeping track of so many items on a big job or when juggling a multitude of shoots. How do you keep organized? Do you have a special system, so to speak, that you like to use?
We have a checklist of all the garments and accessories; we know exactly what items are coming to a shoot. On the shoot, once everything is all set up, we check it against our list and we photograph it.

You've worked a lot with designers on their fashion shows for things like London Fashion Week. How is styling for runway different from working on an editorial or photo shoot?
Styling fashion shows is a completely different job from doing editorials, and it comes with different stresses. Some designers I work with months before the show and others only a few weeks before the show, so even those jobs have different requirements. If you're involved from the early stage, you might be doing mood-boards or trend reports, consulting on the designs, and then you'll work on the castings, the hair and makeup looks, and the accessories for the show. Show styling has so many different elements to it. I was recently doing a show; we booked sixteen models, and 30 minutes to show time we were

still missing six models. We weren't sure if the show was going to happen. At the last minute the show producer pulled six girls from another show that had just finished. We did the fittings and then hair and makeup, were doing everything while the girls were in the lineup, ready to go on the catwalk. It was manic but in a calm, focused way; the show ran a bit late, but no one knew it almost didn't happen. You never know what problems you're going to encounter; a fashion show is live; it's happening right now, and editorial you have all day.

You also work a lot with new, emerging designers. Is there any difference between working with someone new on the scene and working with a well-known brand or big fashion house?
In many ways there are huge differences and no difference at all. Emerging designers are building their brand; they might have a clear idea of who they are, but it's really early days and they still have a long way to go. Usually if I'm doing a show, I'm working directly with the designers, new or established. The difference, of course, is money and all the things you can do with money. No matter how big or established a designer you are, you're always working within a budget and have to justify it to someone in the end.

Summary and Review

Freelance stylists often diversify or broaden their skill sets so that they can work more consistently. Fashion stylists can also find work as runway stylists, on- and off-figure stylists, prop stylists, food stylists, jewelry stylists, or visual merchandisers. Runway stylists, sometimes called fashion coordinators, work for designers and retailers. On- and off-figure stylists, also called digital stylists, often work for online retailers to style products for ecommerce. Prop stylists and set stylists style objects on both small and large scales. They can style settings as small as tabletops or as large as entire rooms or houses. Food stylists work to make food look appetizing for the camera lens. Their work can be found in advertisements, menus, and cookbooks. Visual merchandisers create displays in retail settings, and they often use props to showcase retail products. Visual merchandising shares some similarities with prop styling.

Stylists don't necessarily have to pigeonhole themselves into one discipline. Sometimes freelance stylists with broader skill sets can earn a more consistent income, especially in smaller cities. There are many educational resources, such as books and workshops, for stylists looking to diversify their portfolios.

Key Terms

- batting
- bookings
- dress form
- dresser
- flatlay
- food styling
- International Association of Culinary Professionals (IACP)
- mock-up
- off-figure styling
- on-figure styling
- prop styling
- risers
- run of show
- set designing
- set styling
- test kitchen
- trending
- visual merchandising

REVIEW QUESTIONS

1. Why do stylists branch out into other areas of styling?

2. Describe how a fashion stylist and a prop stylist work together on a fashion show.

3. A client wants to sell a jacket. Describe the best way to style this jacket for a print advertisement, an ecommerce listing, and a social media post.

4. List three responsibilities of a prop stylist when photographing a home for an editorial shoot.

5. What is a mock-up?

6. Why is jewelry styling challenging?

7. What is the difference between prop styling and visual merchandising?

8. List three retailers where a stylist can find work in visual merchandising.

9. What is a flatlay?

LEARNING ACTIVITIES

Learning Activity 5.1: Find a catalogue from a retailer that sells home furnishings. Find one picture that shows multiple items for sale. It could be a picture of a room or table setting, for example. Cut out the picture and attach it to paper. On a separate piece of paper, write at least a half-page paragraph about the styling in the photo and what you might have done differently if you were the stylist.

Learning Activity 5.2: Find two different examples of each of the following items that show two different styling specialties (digital styling, runway styling, food styling, prop styling, etc.). For each image, tell where the image came from, what styling specialty was involved, and whether the image is commercial or editorial.

1. A man's sport coat
2. A pair of socks
3. A watch
4. A taco
5. A couch

Learning Activity 5.3: You are hired by a mobile phone company to create two different flatlays to promote its mobile phone to two different types of customer: a fashion lover and an athlete. Create a flatlay to appeal to each target audience, and for each image, describe why you chose each piece and what filter you used and why.

RESOURCES

"About Us." International Association of Culinary Professionals. https://www.iacp.com/about/.

Achitoff-Gray, Niki. "Food Styling 101: Pro-Tips to Step Up your Game." Serious Eats. October 2015. http://www.seriouseats.com/2015/10/food-styling-tips-for-home-cooks.html.

Dolkas, Peter. "What's in a Prop Stylist's Set Kit? You'll Be Surprised." MyDomaine. October 1, 2014. http://www.mydomaine.com/prop-stylist-kit?utm_campaign=article-share&utm_source.

"Fashion Stylist Jobs." Indeed. http://www.indeed.com/q-Fashion-Stylist-jobs.html.

Flanagan, Lauren. "10 Things Prop Stylists Do Before a Photo Shoot." Spruce. May 9, 2016. https://www.thespruce.com/things-prop-stylists-do-before-photo-shoot-4044786.

Freeman, Hadley. "Just What Does a Stylist Do?" *The Guardian.* March 7, 2003. https://www.theguardian.com/lifeandstyle/2003/mar/07/shopping.fashion1.

Henderson, Emily. "How to Become a Prop Stylist." Emily Henderson. December 11, 2012. https://stylebyemilyhenderson.com/blog/how-to-become-a-prop-stylist.

"How to Style Still Life/Beauty Products and Off Figure Clothing for Photoshoots?" The Fashion Spot. January 4, 2008. http://forums.thefashionspot.com/f90/how-style-still-life-beauty-products-off-figure-clothing-photoshoots-66946.html.

"How to Use a Ghost Mannequin for eCommerce Product Photography." StyleShoots. May 9, 2016. http://styleshoots.com/product-photography-tutorial/2016/4/how-to-use-an-invisible-mannequin-for-ecommerce-product-photography.

Kissling, Kim. "Food Styling: Tools of the Trade." Chef's Blade. http://chefsblade.monster.com/training/articles/1783-food-styling-tools-of-the-trade.

Mabel, Amanda. "Five Tips for Taking the Perfect Flat Lay Instagram Photo." *Vogue* Australia. April 22, 2015. http://www.vogue.com.au/blogs/spy+style/five+tips+for+taking+the+perfect+flat+lay+instagram+photo+,30509.

McKinney, Ellen C. "Teaching Fashion: Off-Figure Fashion Styling Assignment." *Worn Through.* March 25, 2011. http://www.wornthrough.com/2011/07/from-the-archive-teaching-fashion-off-figure-fashion-styling-assignment/.

"Online Fashion Stylist Jobs." Simply Hired. http://www.simplyhired.com/a/jobs/list/q-online+fashion+stylist.

Prop Closet. http://www.propcloset.com.

Roslund, Tony. "How to Photograph Jewelry for Catalogs." Fstoppers. September 5, 2013. https://fstoppers.com/commercial/how-photograph-jewelry-catalogs-35913.

Scott, Drew. "How To: The Perfect Flat Lay Photo + Editing // Instagram." YouTube. March 26, 2016. https://www.youtube.com/watch?v=w1rybaZ3U5U&t=13s.

Soo Hoo, Fawnia. "Fashion Week 101: What It Is and Why It Matters." *Teen Vogue.* February 13, 2015. http://www.teenvogue.com/story/what-is-fashion-week.

Retail Design Blog. https://retaildesignblog.net/category/visual-merchandising/.

Getting Established as a Fashion Stylist

6 Portfolio Building, Branding, and Networking

CHAPTER TOPICS CALL SHEET

In this chapter you will learn:
* What to include in a portfolio
* How to create a digital and a hardcopy portfolio
* Marketing tools for freelancers
* Proper professional etiquette
* About fashion internships and assisting opportunities
* Building and leveraging social media marketing

TOOLS OF THE TRADE

Many stylists work on a freelance basis. They are self-employed and are responsible for finding their own jobs, billing clients, and maintaining their own businesses. Being a business owner comes with big responsibilities, including finding ways to stay profitable, staying organized, and preparing income taxes. To effectively market themselves, do their jobs successfully, and drive their own businesses, freelancers employ certain tools. Maintaining one's business, once the stylist has it up and running, is the topic of Chapter 7, "Business 101 for Freelance Stylists." This chapter deals with what it takes to get the stylist's business started.

There are two types of tools that a stylist uses in his or her business: marketing tools and professional tools. Marketing tools are what stylists use to promote themselves: *portfolios*, *websites*, *business cards*, *comp cards*, and *social media profiles*. Professional tools are the technical tools that help stylists do their jobs: equipment such as garment steamers, clothing-care items, computers, and printers. This chapter outlines the basic rules for portfolios and how to build them, as well as other marketing tools.

Marketing Tools

A portfolio, a website, a business card, a comp card, and social media profiles are the most important marketing tools for stylists. These can provide visual examples of a stylist's best work, and various versions can be made for different audiences. They are important tools for networking and gaining name recognition. (See Figure 6.1.) They are also vital tools for spur-of-the-moment encounters with potential professional contacts.

PORTFOLIO BASICS

A **portfolio** is a stylist's primary marketing tool. Also called a Book or a Port, it is a collection of the stylist's work that conveys to the client that the stylist has the experience, the talent, and the work ethic to accomplish a client's goals. A portfolio can be in a digital or a hardcopy format, but regardless of the format, it must showcase a stylist's best, most marketable, and most memorable work. Creating a portfolio is the first task of an aspiring stylist and the lifework of a professional stylist. It is never finished and is constantly being added to and edited. In fact, some savvy stylists even change up their portfolio to appeal to a specific client if they know they are being considered for an important job with that client.

Every stylist's portfolio will be different, but the goal of every portfolio is the same: to showcase the stylist's skill. The best way to do this is through *quality, diversity*, and *timeliness*. Quality speaks for itself: all photos included in a portfolio must be professional-grade, using real models wearing the most perfectly styled clothing and accessories possible.

A portfolio must also include a diverse range of photographs so the client can see that the stylist can handle any type of job. A portfolio should include indoor and outdoor shoots, studio shoots, and on-location shoots. It should reflect a diversity of different types of items and also showcase a stylist's creativity in working with these items. For example, a fashion stylist's portfolio should include gowns but also swimsuits, active wear, everyday clothing, and even an accessories-only shoot. A successful portfolio must also include a range of different models. This does not mean nonprofessional models; rather, it means showing work that includes men and women, models of different ethnicities, and even children of different ages.

Finally, a portfolio should be timely, meaning a stylist should strive to include his or her most recent work. This is why **test shoots** are important for stylists: to ensure that their portfolios always have a diverse mix of new photos. Test shoots are discussed in detail in Chapter 9.

Figure 6.1
A website provides a visual example of a stylist's work and is a valuable marketing tool.

For a professional stylist who gets paid to style editorial or commercial shoots, the most highly prized portfolio photos are **tear sheets**. These are images that have been published, either in print or online, in a fashion magazine, advertisements, catalogues, or other similar types of media platforms. A tear sheet is like a job listing on a résumé: it shows that the stylist was paid to do a job and that the client was so satisfied with the result that the image was published. The difference between a tear sheet and a photo is that the tear sheet generally has some sort of printed indication that it was published, such as a page number or a caption. A tear sheet can be digital, downloaded from an online version of the printed material, or a printout of the original web page if it is digital-only. Whenever possible, it is preferable to obtain a high-resolution photo because this will be the highest quality. The higher the quality, the easier it is for the stylist to enlarge the image if it's very small, or for the stylist to print the images on a comp card or business card, as will be explained in more detail later in this chapter. If the image is digital, a higher-quality photograph also allows a client to zoom in to see detail without it looking fuzzy.

When tear sheets are actual pieces of paper, they should be carefully cut out of magazines with a blade and straight ruler. They are then neatly mounted in acetate page protectors within the portfolio. (See Figure 6.2.)

When using tear sheets from an editorial shoot, a stylist should include the entire series of published images. This shows the client that the stylist can consistently deliver quality styling across many photos, not just in a single image.

Creating a Hardcopy Portfolio

There may be times when a stylist is asked to bring an actual hardcopy portfolio to a meeting with an agency or a prospective client. If this happens, there are some rules to follow when choosing a portfolio and compiling the photos inside it. (See Figure 6.3.)

Figure 6.2
Tear sheets.

Rule 1: Buy and Maintain Two Identical Hardcopy Portfolios

This is essential in case one portfolio gets damaged or lost. Also, if a stylist has agency representation, his or her agent might ask the stylist to keep a portfolio at the agency. Portfolios and portfolio covers should be purchased from a professional supplier. There are a variety of different portfolios, from leather-bound to stainless steel. The one a stylist chooses should reflect his or her professional identity. Soft-sided portfolios can permanently bend images inside if improperly stored. Hard-sided portfolios are best because the outer case doesn't bend. Purchasing a portfolio cover for each one will also help protect this investment. Seeing a portfolio in person before purchasing is always preferable, but if no local stores carry a good selection, purchasing from online and catalogue portfolio sources is a great alternative.

Rule 2: Restrict Paper Size on Printed Photographs

A good rule of thumb is that images should be either 9 × 12 or 11 × 14 inches. These are the industry standards. A larger portfolio, like those used by photographers and artists, can be unruly to handle, and an image that is too large can make portfolio pages difficult to turn. A stylist never knows where or how a portfolio might be viewed; for example, it might have to sit on someone's lap in a crowded space while he or she flips through the pages. For this reason, it should be as convenient to browse through as possible. Also make sure paper size is uniform throughout for continuity and neatness. (See Figure 6.4.)

Rule 3: Use Good-Quality Images

Most of the images in the portfolio should be in color. Black-and-white images tend to have a vintage feel. If there is a black-and-white image, it should be an intentional color choice that matches the theme of the shoot. Images should also

Figure 6.3
This is a bound portfolio with images held together by the spine in the middle of the pages. A bound portfolio basically means that it is in book form. Tear sheets are neatly presented in acetate page protectors. It is a manageable size that is easy to browse.

Figure 6.4
These photographs are being presented in large-format, loose-leaf form. This works well for fine artists but is not the industry standard for stylists. The images look beautiful when presented in this way, but they receive more wear and tear from handling. A stylist usually has only a limited number of tear sheets and needs to protect them. A photographer can always make more prints from negatives.

be printed using a good printer on good paper, so a basic home or school printer might not be sufficient. If financially possible, professional printing is the best way to go. The choice of paper should also be a conscious one. An image printed on glossy paper will have a different look and feel than one printed on matte paper. Also, photographs should be presented as **bleeds**, meaning that the image extends all the way to the edges of the page. White borders should be professionally cut away with a paper cutter, unless they are intentional design elements of the image.

Rule 4: Mount Photographs Securely
Securely mount one printed photo per slipcover page. A page with one image that is neatly presented has more perceived value than a page of collaged images. Each image should be presented as a thing of value and an example of technical skill. When photographs fall off their mounts and slide around inside the portfolio, it detracts from their value. Also beware when choosing a portfolio in which images are presented in a loose-leaf fashion because it will be subject to more wear and tear during handling. A bound portfolio with sheet protectors makes a cleaner presentation.

Rule 5: Choose One Orientation and Stick with It
Try not to change page orientation from portrait (vertical) to landscape (horizontal). Switching positions to look at a portfolio is inconvenient for the viewer. Again, a stylist never knows where a portfolio might be viewed.

Rule 6: Store a Portfolio with Care

Store the portfolio flat in a cool, dry place so that it remains in optimal condition. Heat can warp pages, so hot cars are not the ideal place to keep portfolios. When a portfolio is stored upright, the flimsy acetate pages inside can bend and become permanently distorted. Laying it flat prevents this.

Rule 7: Give the Portfolio a Unified Look

Portfolios should have a cohesive overall appearance. That means that any cover pages or section dividers should look like they belong together. Use the same fonts and paper for each typed page. A cover page should simply have the stylist's name, what type of stylist he or she is, and his or her contact information. Divider pages can be used to divide sections if necessary. Examples of sections are editorial, lifestyle, food styling, and prop styling. Text should be thoughtfully placed on the page. If it is centered on the page, it will have a more traditional look than off-center text. Text placement should be in the same area of each page for continuity. Any bullet points or other formatting characteristics should also be the same from page to page.

Digital Portfolios

A stylist today must have a portfolio available digitally. There are four primary ways to host a portfolio on a digital platform, and a stylist must determine the best method or combination of methods that works best for his or her business.

1. **Professional website:** The details of hosting and creating will be discussed later in this chapter, but a professional website is a perfect place to post portfolio photos. Separate different categories of styling jobs using menu tabs such as *off-figure styling*, *on-figure styling*, and *prop styling*, and be sure to arrange photos within each section in a cohesive, attractive manner.
2. **Portfolio-hosting website:** There are myriad websites that specialize in hosting portfolios across a range of creative professions, like ArtsThread.com, Kredo.com, and Behance.com, and many of them can be used for free. Not only do these websites work for portfolio hosting, but if they allow portfolios to be made public and have searchability and interactivity capabilities, they can be helpful for networking and marketing, too.
3. **Portfolio app:** A portfolio app allows a stylist to create an attractive, organized digital portfolio that can be accessed offline. This is important because if a stylist meets with an agency, potential client, or a creative team, he or she can bring an iPad loaded with his or her portfolio without risking WiFi connection issues or having to access the client's network. Also, a digital portfolio easily can be shared with others via email or social media. There are a variety of portfolio apps available, and this function also is available through portfolio-hosting websites like Behance.com, SquareSpace.com, Foliolink.com, and Kredo.com.
4. **Social media and blogs:** Sites like Instagram, Facebook, and WordPress are the least effective platforms for something as important as a professional portfolio. If a stylist's work is only visible on a free social media account or blog, it makes that stylist look like an amateur. Although social media accounts and blogs are important for a stylist to have, they work better for marketing and promotion; this will be explored more later in the chapter.

"There's never been a better time to consider fashion styling as a career path. It's true that the industry is changing, but for those that know how, there are more tools available to you so you can create more of the work you love, showcase your creative process and get yourself noticed."

—Sam Southern, expert producer at Mastered, www.mastered.com

EXPERIENCE: THE WAY TO BUILD A PORTFOLIO

Testing and assisting are the two most common ways that an aspiring stylist can build a portfolio. Internships also provide opportunities for portfolio-building experience. Testing is an unpaid collaborative effort among people who want to create photos for their portfolios (it is explored in more detail in Chapter 9, "Preparing for a Test Shoot"). **Assisting** is the process of helping a professional stylist before (prep), during (set), and after (wrap) a shoot. It can be unpaid or sometimes pay a small fee. Both testing and assisting require networking to find opportunities. A beginning stylist should start networking as soon as possible, and the best people to connect with are those involved in setting up test shoots: models, photographers, and hair and makeup artists.

Assisting for Job Experience

As an assistant you should expect to do anything that is asked of you, from steaming clothes to fetching coffee for the crew. Assisting can be a great way to learn the ropes and build your professional contacts. It is best not to expect to be paid and instead treat it as a free learning experience. Any money made is just a bonus. Sometimes an assistant stylist can get his or her name listed on the credits of an editorial shoot, which means the stylist can get "credit" for the shoot and include it in his or her portfolio. This is far more valuable to a beginning stylist's career than any small paycheck.

If there is no credit or no money, do not get discouraged. Assisting should be approached simply as a learning experience, and there really is no better way to learn the ropes. Often a stylist will expect certain behavior from an assistant and sometimes even print out a sheet of rules for the shoot, including rules surrounding the use of social media and how, when, or whether photos taken on set can be posted. It is best for the assistant not to be offended if this happens. This is an opportunity that should be approached with humility and an open mind.

How to Find Assisting Opportunities

The best way to find assisting jobs is by networking to find a good local stylist who can use some free assistance. Past classmates and internship contacts can be helpful in finding networking contacts. Another good place to start looking is local fashion and lifestyle magazines. Often these stylists source and shoot locally with local talent. Look for a magazine that runs **fashion editorials**: published photographic fashion stories that are centered on a central idea or theme.

Among the shoot participants, names that should be listed in the credits include the photographer, fashion stylist, hair and makeup stylist, and model. A quick internet search can sometimes yield the stylist's website, through which he or she can be contacted. If the stylist is listed as a style or fashion editor, then he or she can be contacted through the magazine's offices. Networking is not the time to be shy. It is about being assertive in order to meet people in the professional community.

Assisting 101

Stylists who are assisting don't need to bring their own full kit; the lead stylist takes care of that. However, a stylist assistant should bring a tool belt stocked with small items such as a stain-remover pen, a lint roller, clips, a pen, hand wipes, hand sanitizer, and small scissors. Arrive early to the shoot, or at least at the same time as the lead stylist, if not a little before. Be sure to turn off the cell phone ringer along with any notifications, and it's best to keep the cell phone put away while on set. Nothing irritates a leads stylist more than seeing an assistant distracted by a screen when there's work to be done.

The assistant should be ready to help set up and prep for the shoot as soon as the lead stylist gets there. During the shoot, the assistant should be busy organizing, unpacking, steaming or ironing, taping shoes, removing or reattaching tags, and basically being proactive in finding any way, large or small, to assist the lead stylist. The assistant should also plan to stay after the shoot is over to help the lead stylist wrap up and repack. The lead stylist might also request some help with returning merchandise to retailers in the days after the shoot. Be sure to keep all receipts and paperwork to give back to the lead stylist for his or her records. It also never hurts to follow up with a hand-written thank-you note in the days following the shoot.

Places to Find Testing and Assisting Opportunities

The following list gives some places to meet aspiring photographers, stylists, hair and makeup artists, and models. It is always important to use discretion with professional networking websites. Never agree to set up a meeting at someone's home, because these people have not been subject to background checks. Always choose a public place when meeting with a potential professional contact, and take care when giving out personal contact information; no one needs to know your home address. Also use good judgment when choosing a photographer from the websites listed. Those who are shooting adult material should be avoided.

- Craigslist (craigslist.com)
- Instagram (instagram.com)
- Model Mayhem (modelmayhem.com)
- Muse Cube (musecube.com)
- Local modeling schools or agencies (such as Barbizon; others vary by city)
- Local beauty schools (such as Aveda, Toni & Guy, and Paul Mitchell; others vary by city)
- Local photography schools (often found in art colleges and fine arts departments within universities; vary by city)

The Etiquette of Assisting

When an aspiring stylist assists a lead stylist, certain rules of etiquette apply. If the assistant follows these rules, the lead stylist will be happy and the shoot will run smoothly.

- Don't try to strike up conversation with others at the shoot—be there to work for the lead stylist only.
- Don't try to socialize with the client—that connection belongs to the lead stylist.

- Don't give feedback unless asked.
- Stay on the sidelines or in the background of the shoot unless invited to jump in.
- Be prepared to do a lot of grunt work and to help the stylist the entire time, including with prep work and returning clothing afterward, if asked.
- Keep cell phones silenced and out of sight while on set.
- Always ask about social media policies and about whether it's appropriate to photograph anything on set, including any of the merchandise.
- When posting anything related to the shoot or the creative team on public social media sites, remember to be professional, be respectful, follow any rules set down by the client or team, and be sure to tag all people on the team so that they can use the posts for marketing, too.
- Never engage in gossip: the styling world is small, even in a big city.

"Every job is an audition for the next one. You need to stay two or three steps ahead of the stylist you're working for. Anticipate their needs to keep the set flowing smoothly."
—Rap Sarmiento, fashion and wardrobe stylist, www.rap-sarmiento.com

Internships

Internships can provide valuable contacts. Good places to look for internships are PR firms, fashion magazines, local newspapers, and high-end retailers. These internships might put the intern in contact with fashion stylists, photographers, merchandisers, designers, editors, journalists, publicists, and hair and makeup artists. All of these people will potentially know a stylist who is looking for an assistant. It may be useful to connect on social media with new contacts or jot down their names and information right after meeting them and add them to a contact list or database later.

"Work your a— off and make sure that you're giving it 150 percent. An internship is not just an internship."
—Marissa Webb, fashion designer. "8 Invaluable Fashion Career Tips from Industry Professionals," Fashionista, http://fashionista.com/2016/10/best-fashion-career-advice.

WEBSITES, BUSINESS CARDS, COMP CARDS, AND SOCIAL MEDIA PROFILES

Aside from the portfolio, a stylist's other main marketing materials are a website, business card, comp card, and social media profiles. These marketing materials work together to create a strong professional networking package, often referred to as a **brand**. To create a strong brand, it is critical to be cohesive: use the same or similar colors, phrases, hashtags, or content across all platforms. For example, a website with a bright background and loud font will not match a business card with a beige background and subdued font and an Instagram feed that just showcases photos of flowers or cute dogs. Think of a major corporation, such as McDonald's. The logo is the same on everything, from the cups to the signs to the employee uniforms. The logo would not have nearly as much impact if it were not exactly replicated. A stylist, or any small-business owner for that matter, should strive for the same brand continuity. The visual goal of good marketing materials is to reflect the stylist's aesthetic point of view and professional image in one cohesive package.

Websites

Websites are a must for all freelance stylists, as they facilitate marketing and make it easy for clients to contact a stylist and see his or her work. This is where stylists publish their portfolios online. A good website should have a clean, uncluttered design that's easy to navigate. Users shouldn't have to go through too many steps to view a portfolio. (See Figure 6.5.)

The best-case scenario for a stylist is if he or she has a personal self-named website. Devoting a URL specifically to a portfolio and résumé is an unbeatable marketing tool. Although there are expenses involved in establishing a website, one of a beginning stylist's main goals should be to launch a dedicated site as soon as possible.

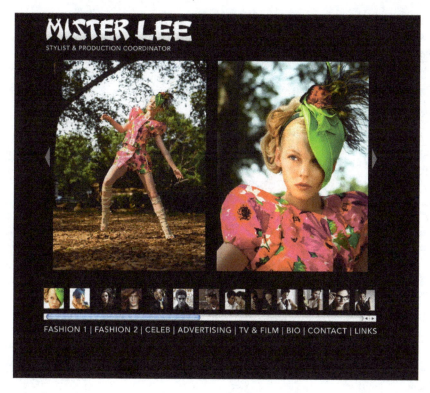

Figure 6.5
A good website should be easy to navigate. Users shouldn't have to go through too many steps to view a portfolio.

A stylist should be choosy about a domain name. The goal is a web address that is easy to remember, easy to spell, and thoroughly professional. The best and easiest domain name is often the stylist's name. If that isn't available, consider adding a word like *stylist* or *Style* to the domain name: for example, "www.JohnSmithStyle.com." Avoid anything too cutesy or gimmicky; never use a *z* in the place of an *s* or a *k* instead of a *c*. If a stylist has a name that is difficult to pronounce or spell, consider using initials only.

Do-It-Yourself Website Design Sources

As a beginning stylist, it can be expensive to hire a Web designer to design a personal website. Yet a stylist needs a personal website for marketing purposes and to show his or her portfolio.

Using a self-design service to build and publish a website can be a good option. With these services, users can build their own websites and publish them for a reasonable price. Many of these services cater especially to creative professionals who are showcasing portfolios.

The user builds a website by choosing from different design templates. It is best to create a website that visually coordinates with other marketing materials, such as the comp card and business card. This way, the marketing materials can be designed to have a brand identity. It's also important to make sure that the site is easy to navigate on the back end and that it is not complicated to change photos or text or to upload photos or video from a mobile phone or from websites or social media. Here are some services that offer web pages for creative professionals.

- sitewelder.com
- pixpa.com
- wix.com
- wordpress.com
- bigblackbag.com
- foliolink.com
- foliosnap.com
- squarespace.com

Business Cards

Although they may seem quaint in this increasingly digital world, business cards still can be helpful to have. They are fast and easy to hand out, and an attractive business card can be an important component of a complete brand. A stylist may be tempted to whip up a card and print it out at home, but this should be avoided. There are so many inexpensive ways to get quality business cards with quality graphics on thick cardstock paper (check out Moo.com and Vistaprint.com) that there really is no reason to settle for a DIY approach. These days, all that's necessary to print on a business card is the stylist's name, a business name if applicable, a cell phone number, a Web address, an email address, and social media handles like Instagram, Snapchat, Twitter, or Facebook.

Comp Cards

Comp cards, like business cards, can seem old-fashioned, but they can be helpful if a stylist has the resources to create them. If a stylist is represented by an agency, sometimes they can be required. A comp card is similar to a postcard, and it is given away to prospective clients, photographers, and fashion editors. It is meant to provide recipients with a visual reminder of the stylist's work.

Comp cards can vary greatly in size. They are generally either 4 × 6 or 5 × 7 inches, the standard photograph sizes, and have printed examples of a stylist's work and his or her contact information. Some comp cards have one picture, while others have six or more pictures collaged on the surface. It is up to the stylist how many images he or she wants to include. Sometimes it is tempting to add a lot of images to the card because it shows the scope of the stylist's abilities. However, a cluttered comp card can detract from the overall quality of the work. Also, comp cards can be double-sided. It often makes a beautiful statement to have one great image on one side of the card and a few images collaged on the other side. The stylist's name and contact information must be clearly printed on the card as well. If the stylist's agency requires comp cards, the agency name will also need to be included on the card.

Social Media

A social media presence is a requirement in fashion. Social media incorporates still images, moving images, disappearing images, direct messaging, public messaging, live-streaming, and even selling, and it's accessible to anyone with an internet connection, almost anywhere in the world. Social media may be the only marketing tool that allows a stylist to promote work on a big photo shoot alongside what he or she ate for breakfast and have the messages be equally impactful. If it's used well, social media can bring a wealth of opportunities to an aspiring stylist. If it's used badly, however, it holds the potential to harm a stylist's career, so it is imperative to approach every post with a professional attitude and a commitment to stay on-brand.

The global social media landscape is always changing, and there may be a new must-have social media site that pops up after this book is published. What follows is a list of the most popular social media sites in the fashion industry as of press time, including tips on how best to leverage each one.

Instagram

For stylists and others in visual media, Instagram is the gold standard. While there are legions of bloggers and "influencers" who make their living using their Instagram feed for sales and promotion, the value of Instagram for stylists lies in its marketing potential. This is where stylists can show off behind-the-scenes snaps, selfies with models, and racks of fabulous clothes, all of which shows that they are working, in demand, and successful. This is also where stylists can curate images of things they love, conveying to the world that they have fabulous taste. Ultimately, a stylist must curate a feed that, taken together, reflects his or her brand. Here are some quick tips on how to do that:

1. **Master basic Instagram photography techniques:** The key to making a photo shine on Instagram is to take a good photo in the first place (for example, morning or afternoon light works best for outdoor shoots) and then to use the right filter to optimize the image. There are countless filter apps available in addition to the stock Instagram filters, many of which are free, that allow a user to pop colors, remove shadows and lines from faces, and manipulate images in a variety of ways. It's also helpful to learn how to look good in a selfie. A good rule of thumb is for a stylist to use

the hand on the same side as his or her "good side." Remember to watch backgrounds in photos, since no one wants to see a stylist's messy bathroom counter, and be mindful of too many party pictures, even if they're fashion parties. After all, working stylists spend most of their time working, not going out.

2. **Keep posts on-message and on-brand:** If a stylist specializes in fashion, to suddenly start posting photo after photo of buildings or puppies is counter to the brand message. Not only will the stylist lose followers, but if a potential client goes to the feed to get a sense of the stylist's aesthetic, it won't be there, which wastes a marketing opportunity.

3. **Tag strategically:** When posting photos of colleagues, it's good netiquette to tag everyone pictured along with brands featured, especially if items are pulled or on loan. This also increases the chances that the photo will be re-grammed, which can bring new eyes to a stylist's feed. Spend some time investigating what types of hashtags well-known stylists use on their feeds, and use those, too, when appropriate. Also, keep an eye out for opportunities to get posts published thanks to the inclusion of a specific hashtag.

4. **Be realistic about followers:** It is validating to have a lot of followers, but Instagram's changing algorithms make building a huge following very difficult, especially when it's not one's primary business. Stylists should keep in mind that the goal of their feed is not to get more followers than Kendall Jenner; it is to network among fashion industry types like editors, retailers, stylists, and designers and to impress them, maybe even enough to land a job.

5. **Network, connect, and converse:** Instagram is not a one-sided bulletin board; it is a social network that can be an unparalleled resource for networking and connecting with brands, designers, and other creative professionals. Take time to create a community, not just through follows, but by leaving positive comments and compliments and even reaching out with a direct message to an admired designer or with a question for a successful stylist. After all, it is fast and free, and the worst that can happen is nothing at all.

"It's possible in today's world to be instantly famous, whether it's through Instagram or what-ever platform it may be, but it's a very different matter to be successful financially and in the long-term."
    —Anna Wintour, editor-in-chief, Vogue. "Anna Wintour Has Some Harsh Advice for Fashion Students," Dazed, http://www.dazeddigital.com/fashion/article/20439/1/anna-wintour-has-some-harsh-advice-for-fashion-students.

Snapchat

Although this smart phone-only app has more users than Instagram, it is not as valuable for fashion industry marketing because its images and videos are not permanent. One way a stylist can utilize Snapchat is through Stories. For example, if a stylist is going shopping, going to a fashion show, or prepping for a test shoot, he or she could bring followers and fans along for the ride, walking through a shop or a set and narrating the experience. Whether or not a stylist actually creates content on Snapchat, it is still important to know what is going on there. Burberry has used Snapchat exclusively to promote events and even to launch a fragrance, and the Valentino Snapchat account has taken followers on tours of its showrooms, providing an invaluable opportunity to see a space that might otherwise be inaccessible.

Facebook

A fashion stylist can extend his or her marketing presence by using Pages to create an online presence for his or her business. This is a great, free resource and allows the stylist to keep his or her private Facebook page truly private so that business contacts don't have to see personal photos of friends, family, pets, and baked goods. Here you can post interesting articles, link to fashion spreads, or cross-post photos from Instagram.

Polyvore, Stylebook, and Other Wardrobing Apps

These sites are valuable tools for personal stylists to showcase their skills in styling outfits and curating collections of clothing and accessories for specific clients or types of clients. Stylists can post their own OOTD snaps, or they can create categorized collections like "Great for Apple Body Types" or "GNO Must-Haves" to show off their skills.

[
"I've always been about what the 'next big thing' is. Please, I was the one that would help my grandmother put the VCR together when I was little and got a Tivo 15 years ago. People fear what they don't understand, but trust me, magazines, designers and retailers are getting to understand what social media is faster than they can say 'that's fabulous.'"
—Joe Zee, editor-in-chief and executive creative officer of Yahoo! Style. Hitha Prabhakar, "How the Fashion Industry Is Embracing Social Media," Mashable, http://mashable .com/2010/02/13/fashion-industry-social-media/#5Ztc7ES1f5qJ.
]

Interview with Alexandra Lipps

My family calls me Sasha as it's a shorter version of Alexandra and a common name in the Russian culture. I am nineteen years old, a first-generation American from Long Island, New York. My parents came to the United States from Ukraine at a young age. Growing up, I played tennis for nine years on a competitive level, until I got an injury. It wasn't until high school that I started exploring my entrepreneurial instincts, which was when I started my own handmade jewelry business at fourteen, selling on Etsy as well as in local flea markets. Eager to begin work, I started my first internship going into freshman year of college and have had one every semester except for my current fourth semester. I decided to take this semester off for interning to explore the opportunities that come along with blogging.

Website: *www.alexandrachloe.com*
Instagram: *@alexandra_chloe*
Twitter: *@alexandra_lipps*

What are some celebrities, companies, or high-profile clients whose style you admire and why?
Celebrities: None really. I find myself to be more inspired by just your everyday person. I was never really into "Hollywood," but a celebrity that I admire personality-wise is Salma Hayek. To me, she is just so

feminine, classic, and confident. I also really admire Carolina Herrera. I ran into her on Madison Avenue and was in just complete amazement of her elegance, gracefulness, and sophistication, especially for her age. Being in the mid-sixties, she looks AMAZING, in a natural, non-Botox way!

Companies: Chloé, Valentino, Alexis. I would say Chanel, but that's a given for almost everybody!

I admire Chloé for their delicate and airy pieces; I find their collections to always have that touch of bohemian spirit mixed with classic, yet modern and feminine silhouettes. For a luxury company, they target a younger female, I would say in the twenties to thirties, which is hard to do considering your average female can't really afford their pieces at that age. I love Valentino for their beautiful gowns. There is really nothing like them, their intricate detailing and uniqueness.

You are currently studying at FIT (Fashion Institute of Technology). What are you studying?
I am studying Advertising and Marketing Communications.

What's the main purpose of your style blog? How did you start it? How has it grown?
I started my blog last year as a freshman at FIT with the purpose of using it as an outlet for sharing my personal style as well as other thoughts and ideas. I never really understood how much time *actually* has to go into it (a lot!) until I got myself into a VERY saturated marketplace. There is also a big money investment. In October 2016 I started experimenting with a photographer to get consistency and quality throughout my content. This curated how I was going to stand out and is helping me figure out my blog's purpose. Like any creative strategy, it takes time to "hit the jackpot"; I'm nowhere close to where I would like to be, growthwise. It also takes time to truly understand the logistics of the "blogging industry." Now I take it much more seriously and professionally.

My blog's purpose now is to inspire girls from the ages of seventeen to twenty-four, an age where girls try to find themselves and their style. I aim to be authentic and transparent with all my followers. I never try to dress or style myself in a way that I normally wouldn't. What I have found is that most bloggers are in their mid-twenties to early thirties, and it's hard for this particular demographic to relate to them. So I feel starting out now I have this advantage of relating to my own age group. It is the reason why many looking for styling advice turn to bloggers, to see relatable fashion.

What's your philosophy of styling or dressing?
Be yourself! Yes, it's a great idea as a fashion lover to keep up with trends, but that doesn't necessarily mean you *have* to follow them or dress yourself in them. Just because it's "in" doesn't mean it will suit you. For example, I love the overall trend and the bomber jacket trend, but the bomber jacket doesn't fit with my personal style, and overalls make my petite frame look even smaller! You have to find what works for you. Also, when buying clothes, splurge on classic pieces such as a handbag or a nice pair of shoes. I strongly believe that either of these pieces can make a $20 outfit look just as expensive as the bag or shoes you wear.

Where do you like to shop?

I love to shop anywhere where I can get a deal or steal! Century 21 is one place I love to shop, BUT it's always a hit or miss. I love Intermix because they always have the best-curated and unique pieces. I also love Bergdorf's and Neimans to see what the designers are doing. They also have AMAZING sales where I score most of my designer shoes and clothing for 50–60 percent off. I'm not much of an online shopper, but I recently started to buy online if there are free returns. Some of my favorite online sites include ASOS, Revolve, and ShopBop.

What are some of your favorite designers?

Genuinely, I don't have an ultimate favorite designer I stick to; I always find myself finding something I love in every designer/brand. Of course I love the classics (Chanel, Valentino, Brunello Cuccinelli), but I'm not at the age or maturity to really afford to dress in those pieces just yet.

Where do you look to find jobs and internships?

Fashionista.com career section is a great place to look for starter positions. I found my second internship through them for Cami NYC. Also, if you're in college, take advantage of your university's Facebook "Group" where kids post various relevant information. I found my first internship through a post of a girl who was a prior intern for the PR agency. Also, take advantage of any connections you have: high school teachers, family friends, friends of friends, etc. You'd be shocked how many people are willing to help you. Also, don't be afraid to CALL that company or agency you want to intern for and see if they have any positions. I did that with my last internship at a luxury menswear company and got the internship.

How much of your own personal style can be influenced on your blog, or do you collaborate with brands to showcase their pieces?

One hundred percent of my personal style is reflected in my blog. I only collaborate with companies that I feel I would use or reflect upon my style. I've had a bunch of companies/brands reach out to collaborate, but I had to kindly reject and explain to them that I wouldn't be the best fit for them because their products don't reflect my style. If I don't truly love the brand, their products, or see a use for it in my life, I wouldn't want to promote something I don't believe in. As I've stated before, my aim is to be 100 percent authentic and transparent with my followers. Those who view my Insta-stories on Instagram know this to be true. I learnt my lesson once by collaborating with a store I have been shopping at since a baby. The outfits I was shot in were not outfits I would ever personally put together or wear. In the end, I never posted those photos because they didn't represent me. So going forward, when collaborating with a clothing brand, the collaboration must represent my personal style reflecting upon their products. I'm not a model; I'm an influencer, but it was a good lesson to learn regarding my brand.

Who are your muses? How or where do you find inspiration?

As corny as this sounds, I owe it to my mom for style. She always let me experiment with different styles until I was able to find what works for me. It's okay for your style to change; mine definitely has since last year. Apart from that, I love browsing through Instagram's various bloggers. I think it's important to not limit yourself to where you seek ideas and inspirations. My absolute favorite influencers include @SongofStyle and @somethingnavy. Out of all the bloggers/influencers/stylists, both Arielle and Ami showcase pieces that my personal style relates to or aims to be.

A few styling tips—
Dress for yourself, no one else.

Just because it's in, doesn't mean it suits you.

Own your body. Find styles and pieces that highlight you. If you're petite (like me), I try to stay away from anything that will make me look even smaller than I already am. I know a super big trend right now are the jeans that are flared at ankle length; I tried on a pair and it made me look at least three inches shorter than I actually am!

My go-to casual and comfortable outfit consists of a pair of comfortable jeans, a T-shirt, and a leather jacket with sneakers. Looks chic, but is simple and easy to wear all day.

How does social media shape what you do for your blog? Any advice on posting for fashion on social media?
Social media plays such an important role in daily life now. It's my outlet for creativity. Since I've started to post with my blog and also following people on social media, seeing what they are up to, my personal style and outlook have changed for the better. I have more confidence and the ability to talk with people. I get so excited when a girl messages me asking for advice or a tip on styling. Social media has really inspired me stylewise, and I hope that my fashion blog has helped me to inspire others, so a full circle is how I look at it.

In terms of posting, Instagram keeps changing its algorithms, so it can be tricky to figure out when the best time to upload is. It really depends on your own following to find what is perfect for you. I find my followers respond best to early in the morning or later in the evening, so that's when I choose to post.

Do you have any advice for anyone wanting to start up a style/fashion blog? Do you sell off your blog? What was helpful to you when starting your blog?
I am connected with LIKEtoKNOW.it and ShopStyle, so my followers can purchase what I'm wearing. When starting a blog, you just have to go for it. A lot of girls message me saying things like, I don't have time, I'm nervous, I'm not sure what I should talk about. I tell them, "just blog" and do it for the sole purpose to make yourself happy. Don't do it to get free products or collaborations. I didn't start my blog from a business perspective; I started it because I had so many creative ideas going on in my head. It was my way of getting my scattered thoughts out there. Luckily it's been something a lot of girls my age can relate to. My tip would be, find your niche; do it because it is something you have a passion for.

If you create with passion, people will naturally gravitate towards it. Don't be afraid of being yourself. Some blogs lose this if they are doing it for the sole purpose of making money. They start to feel like ads and [can seem] less authentic. Your followers will notice this.

Where do you see yourself in the next five to ten years regarding the fashion industry?
That's hard to say! I definitely want to get a master's in Luxury Brand Management. I'm still in the process of finding the perfect career fit for me, but I know it can't be a 9–5 desk job. I want it to combine my love for business with creativity. It's a long shot, but I want to have my own boutique company. Right now, what I'm really interested in exploring is branding/brand consulting, Brand Strategy, Special Events Marketing, something along those lines. My ideal career would be something that can combine all of the above. I love strategizing and finding a solution to a problem. I love helping others find their USP [unique selling point], and I love seeing an idea go from conceptualization to delivery. When someone gives me an idea or problem they have, my brain won't turn itself off until I can come up with a solution or strategy for them to tackle the problem.

SUMMARY AND REVIEW

Marketing tools are essential for stylists to get their names out and build a solid professional reputation. The five main marketing tools are portfolios, websites, business cards, comp cards, and social media sites. A stylist's marketing message must look and feel similar across all of these platforms to create a cohesive brand, and every aspect of a stylist's marketing platform must fall within acceptable professional standards.

A portfolio is a stylist's primary marketing tool, and this can be hosted digitally or prepared in a hardcopy format. A portfolio showcases a stylist's skill, style, and body of work. It is important that all photos in a portfolio be high quality, diverse, and recent. There are two ways for a beginning stylist to build a portfolio: testing and assisting. Testing is unpaid collaboration between a photographer, fashion stylist, and hair and makeup artist. Aspiring professionals and established professionals alike participate in test shoots to keep portfolios current and to practice skills in other areas. Assisting a lead stylist is another great way to build a portfolio and gain professional experience.

It is important for a stylist to have his or her own website, and it can be useful, too, to have business cards and comp cards. A stylist also must maintain a social media presence, for both promotion and net-working. Instagram is the most important social media platform, and a stylist should spend time to ensure that his or her feed is optimized. Other social media sites like Snapchat can be helpful, and personal stylists might want to utilize wardrobing apps.

KEY TERMS

- assisting
- bleeds
- brand
- fashion editorial
- portfolio
- tear sheets
- test shoots
- testing

REVIEW QUESTIONS

1. Why is it important that stylists think of themselves as a brand?

2. List three rules for creating a professional portfolio.

3. Why is it important to have a digital portfolio that can be viewed without having to access the internet?

4. List five tasks an assistant can do for a stylist to assist on set.

5. If an assistant stylist is given a choice of earning money or earning an editorial credit, which should he or she choose and why?

6. Why is it important for a stylist to have a personal website?

7. Describe a situation where it could be helpful to have business cards.

8. What are three things a stylist can accomplish on Instagram?

9. What does the Snapchat Stories tool allow a user to do?

10. How can a personal stylist use a wardrobing app to market his or her skills?

LEARNING ACTIVITIES

Learning Activity 6.1: It is time for a portfolio update. Find ten images from at least four different editorial fashion shoots, put them together in a cohesive manner, and for each image, describe the skill being presented and list the ways in which the image reflects diversity in models, themes, merchandise, or location.

Learning Activity 6.2: Conduct an internet search for a fashion stylist's website, a prop stylist's website, and a celebrity stylist's website. For each website, write the name of the stylist, the Web address, his or her styling specialty, and a brief description of what the website includes. For example, does it link to the stylist's social media feeds or an online portfolio? In your opinion, has that stylist successfully created a cohesive brand? Why or why not?

Learning Activity 6.3: The live feed is an important part of creating original content on social media. Using a cell phone, create a mock live feed by creating a video that lasts between five and seven minutes. Take the viewer somewhere related to fashion—a shop, an art exhibit, or even inside a closet or a dressing room during a staged personal styling session. The stylist must be well groomed and must speak clearly and enthusiastically, and the content must be interesting and make the viewer want to start watching and continue watching.

RESOURCES

Alexandra. "10 Tips to a Great Fashion Portfolio." Searching for Style. November 6, 2012. http://searchingforstyle .com/2012/11/10-tips-to-a-great-fashion-portfolio/.

"All About Becoming a Fashion/Wardrobe Stylist." The Fashion Spot. December 16, 2003. http://forums.the fashionspot.com/f90/all-about-becoming-fashion-wardrobe-stylist-25956-69.html.

Bellucco, Amanda. "How to Create an iPad Portfolio, for Photographers." Explora. https://www.bhphotovideo.com /explora/photography/tips-and-solutions/how-create-ipad-portfolio-photographers.

Hall, Melissa. "5 Instagram Tips to Strengthen Your Network." The Emerging Designer. http://theemergingdesigner .com/5-instagram-tips-to-strengthen-your-network/.

Imogen. "7 Popular Wardrobe and Outfit Planning Apps Reviewed." Inside Out Style. March 24, 2016. https://insideoutstyleblog.com/2016/03/readers-favourite-style-and-wardrobe-apps.html.

Indvik, Lauren. "How Fashion and Retail Brands Are Using Snapchat." Fashionista. May 10, 2016. http://fashionista .com/2016/05/snapchat-fashion-brands.

Matthews, Erika. "How to Build the Perfect Fashion Portfolio!" YouTube. September 13, 2016. https://www.youtube .com/watch?v=sCWd2_s8YQg&t=46s.

"What Does a Stylist's Portfolio Look Like?" School of Style. March 11, 2016. https://www.youtube.com/watch?v =bz2cGWsG8rY&t=73s.

Wilson, Yvette. "My Top 5 Marketing Tips for Instagram." The Stylist Splash. June 7, 2016. http://thestylistsplash .com.au/top-5-marketing-tips-instagram/.

Yankovich, Gyan. "16 Life-Changing Instagram Tips from Fashion Blogger Margaret Zhang." BuzzFeed. July 17, 2015. https://www.buzzfeed.com/gyanyankovich/teach-us-how-to-flat-lay?utm_term=.gfA18xBWv8#.eeknDNZwmD.

7 Business 101 for Freelance Stylists

Chapter Topics Call Sheet

In this chapter you will learn:
- What beginning stylists need to know
- Essential business documentation
- Agency representation vs. freelance
- How to build a freelance business plan
- Studio, office, and financial basics

What Beginning Stylists Need to Know

A freelance stylist is responsible for networking, finding work, and collecting payments for completed jobs. (See Figure 7.1.) It is important to know the terms of a job before committing to and preparing for it. Stylists can set themselves up for disappointment if they find out the job wasn't what they hoped for. For this reason, having the terms of a job spelled out in writing is protection for everyone involved, from the stylist to the client. This written documentation ensures beforehand that the stylist will get paid, spells out the shoot budget, allows the stylist to borrow clothing from retailers, and helps the stylist collect payment afterward.

Figure 7.1
A freelance stylist is responsible for networking, finding work, and collecting payments for completed jobs.

Essential Business Documents

Freelance stylists create their own business documents. If a stylist is represented by an agency, the agency takes care of all of this paperwork. The terms and forms are explained below on the assumption that the stylist is working freelance. (See "Checklist of Business Documents.")

Confirmation, Contract, or Booking Agreement

A **confirmation** (sometimes called a **contract** or **booking agreement**) is the initial form that a stylist drafts and submits to the client. It spells out the terms of the job, such as dates, job description, and rate of pay. This is an important protection for stylists, because they can definitively mark off their calendars and turn down any other job offers that might conflict with those dates. It also assures them that they will be paid. (See Figure 7.2.)

Pull Letter or Letter of Responsibility

A **pull letter** (also called a **letter of responsibility (LOR)**) is a letter or PDF of a letter that is issued or endorsed by the client or by an editor at an assigning publication. A stylist provides it to a retailer, designer, or showroom when getting permission to pull, or borrow, clothes. The pull letter gives assurance to the holder of the merchandise that the stylist is not solely liable for any damaged merchandise. It states that in the event of damages, the client will cover expenses. Many retailers require this because they want to know that a company with deeper pockets than the stylist will be able to pay for any damaged goods. (See Figure 7.3.)

Pull List

A "pull list" can come in handy when pulling clothing. The list might be divided into categories, such as department stores, boutiques, and showrooms. Each store's profile can list the name, phone number, address, and contact person. A list like this takes time to build, and getting the name and email address of the contact person can take time. These contacts can be established during the stylist's downtime.

Invoice

An **invoice** is submitted to the client after a job is completed. It summarizes all charges that are being billed to the client. Expenses can include hourly rates, miscellaneous charges like buying last-minute supplies, and reimbursement for travel. An invoice is submitted to the client promptly after the job or booking is over because billing should occur while the details of the job are still fresh in memory. There are many invoicing apps and services like Invoice2go and Square.com, which work on computers, iPads, and any mobile device. Invoices can be customized with logos, emailed instantly to clients, and printed on wireless printers, and clients also can pay the stylist electronically. Charges range from a monthly fee to a small percentage of all money collected via credit card payments.

Joe Stylist

123 Main Street, Suite 123, Anytown, USA, 12345
(555) 555-1212
www.joestyle.com | joe@joestyle.com

Booking Agreement

This booking for styling services between Joe Stylist and (*client name*) is described below in the following terms and conditions:

1. Joe Stylist will be lead stylist, with the following stylist assistant(s) at $____/day rate each:

_____

2. Shoot location: _____

3. Shoot date and call time: _____

4. Job description: _____

5. Shoot budget and items that the stylist will source/provide: _____

6. Client contact information: _____

7. Art director name and contact information: _____

8. Photographer name and contact information: _____

9. Rate of agreed-upon pay for styling fees: _____

10. Advance payment for job (balance is due upon job completion): $_____

This contract is a binding agreement between the stylist and client. The stylist will provide all necessary supplies to complete the job. The stylist agrees to arrive on time, execute the agreed-upon creative vision, and give the client final approval of all looks. The stylist will complete the job barring a major illness or other catastrophic event. If by some extreme circumstance the stylist cannot complete the job, the stylist will provide referrals for a replacement. The stylist's fee is due, paid in full, within 10 days after completion of the job.

Stylist signature:_____ Date: _____

Client signature: _____ Date: _____

Figure 7.2
A confirmation or booking agreement spells out the terms of the job, such as dates, job description, and rate of pay.

Figure 7.3
A pull letter states that in the event of damages, the client will cover expenses.

STYLED BY JANE: Personal Styling Services

1122 Main Street, Suite 123, Anytown, USA 12345
(555) 555-1212
www.stylbyjane.com | jane@stylebyjane.com

INVOICE

Invoice #: (*Use a consecutive numbering system here for easy reference when doing taxes or if a client needs to have the invoice reissued.*)

Date of issue:(*Important because the stylist needs to know how long it takes the client to pay the invoice, and if further action needs to be taken in order to collect late payments.*)

Client name:

Job date:

Job description:

Rate of pay: (*Depends on the job. An editorial shoot for a small local fashion magazine might only pay $200 for the entire job, whereas personal-styling services might run $50-$75 an hour. All rates vary by city and type of job.*)

Duration of job: (*Insert number of hours or days here.*)

Total amount owed: (*This amount shouldn't be a surprise to the client. The client should know how much the stylist's services will cost at the onset of the job.*)

Checks can be mailed to the address above. Please call or e-mail me to request information about bank deposit or PayPal payment arrangements.

(*Some stylists open PayPal, Venmo, or other electronic payment services accounts that allow them to e-mail money requests to clients. Some clients might prefer to deposit money directly into the stylist's bank account and need routing/account numbers.*)

Figure 7.4
An invoice summarizes all charges that are being billed to the client.

Voucher

A **voucher** has two different meanings. For freelancers working as personal stylists or image consultants, a voucher is a kind of gift certificate for services such as personal shopping, wardrobe consultation, or closet organization. Vouchers such as these can be useful for attracting new clients and can be given out as special promotions or purchased by people who want to give them as gifts.

For freelance stylists working for an agency, however, a voucher is something totally different: a form, usually printed in triplicate, that gives the client, the stylist, and the agency a receipt showing the time the stylist was actually on set. The stylist must turn in a voucher to his or her agency following a job in order to get paid. Vouchers come in pads, and each voucher includes three carbon copy pages, often in white, pink, and yellow. The top copy is white: the stylist fills this out with the time he or she arrived and the time the shoot wrapped (which can be different from the time frame set at the time of booking), the stylist's rate, and the address and contact information for the client. Typically, the client's representative and the stylist sign the voucher; the stylist gives the top copy to the client, and the stylist keeps a copy and gives the third copy to the agency. Most agency-represented talent use vouchers, including models and hair and makeup artists. (See Figure 7.5.)

Checklist of Business Documents

☐ Confirmation/contract/booking agreement

☐ Pull letter/letter of responsibility

☐ Pull list

☐ Invoice

☐ Voucher

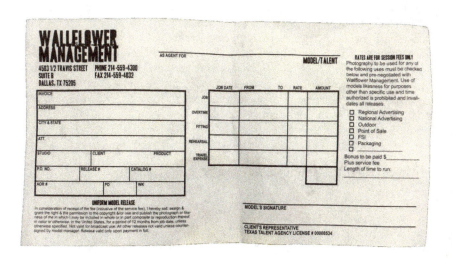

Figure 7.5
A voucher is a more detailed breakdown of the information included in the invoice. It is an itemized list of job expenses that the stylist give to the client to verify and sign.

Figure 7.6
Agency representation can allow a stylist to focus more on the creative side of the job.

AGENCY REPRESENTATION VS. FREELANCE

A **talent agency** acts as an intermediary between the stylist and the client, taking care of scheduling, hiring, and payment paperwork and collecting payment in exchange for a percentage of the profit. Different agencies represent different types of talent. Some represent models or actors, some represent photographers, and some represent hair and makeup artists. Agencies usually add a percentage to the top of the billed rate, usually about 20 percent. In addition, some agencies require stylists to pay them a lesser fee than the standard 20 percent when they work with existing clients, even though the agency didn't book the job.

Working through an agency can sound great, but most larger agencies will not accept a beginning stylist. They want established stylists who bring a strong book, a solid reputation, and professional contacts to the agency. If an agency does accept newer stylists, it will book them out as junior stylists or as assistants only until they gain enough experience to handle a job on their own.

Agencies aren't for everyone; some stylists prefer to have complete control over their bookings and to not give a percentage of their fee to the agency. They feel that they have good contacts and can handle their own invoicing without an agency. Other stylists will gladly hand over the task of booking jobs and invoicing because they see it as a chore. This frees up the stylist to focus more on the creative side of a job and to spend any extra time on marketing, networking, and testing. (See Figure 7.6.) It is simply a matter of personal preference for the established stylist.

Major Talent Agencies That Represent Stylists

- Art + Commerce
- Jed Root
- See Management

- Starworks Artists
- Stilista Agency
- The Wall Group
- Zenobia

BUILDING A FREELANCE BUSINESS PLAN

Freelance stylists are their own agents and managers. Starting a new business venture requires a concrete plan, called a **business plan**. Writing a business plan forces the stylist to think out the small details of the freelance business before jumping in. Some commercial small-business plans can be as long as a book and are designed to get loan funding from a bank. Freelance stylists don't usually need to have business plans quite so lengthy and detailed, since they're probably not getting bank funding to launch. However, a stylist's business plan should cover some critical information so that everything is thought out and the stylist can mark his or her progress and update it accordingly. (See Figure 7.7.)

Elements of a Stylist's Business Plan

1. Summary or Mission Statement
This section explains the business and identifies the target clients. This is the paragraph that explains a stylist's areas of specialty, such as print, commercial, or film. Although this section is the introduction to the plan, it might have to be rewritten after the Location and Market Analysis section.

2. Owner Profile and Skill Set
This section is for listing educational background and skills pertinent to the job, such as related college courses or degrees, past fashion-related job experience, and past management or administrative experience, since the stylist needs these skills as well. Thinking these things out from the start helps with self-promotion. It also can help the stylist see if there are any areas that need improvement. For example, if a novice stylist has had schooling but has not worked in the fashion industry, there might be some room for growth. He or she might start looking for some local opportunities to make industry contacts. Local fashion shows often hire unpaid backstage dressers to dress the models, and this is a good place to get some experience without committing to a job. Retail sales or merchandising experience also might be helpful.

3. Location and Market Analysis
This section should consider the stylist's city. This is a good place to analyze the market and figure out whether it will support a freelance stylist. Sometimes a stylist will start out thinking he or she will specialize in print work and find jobs with magazines or catalogues. However, closer analysis of the city's market might show that such a narrow area of specialty won't provide consistent, well-paying work. It is important to research potential clients in an area so that stylists know if they need to market themselves in other areas of styling. Perhaps there might be local catalogue companies, fashion show producers, or magazines that hire stylists.

Business Plan for Style by Jane, Inc.

(Incorporating is a business option that gives the owner some financial advantages. It can allow the owner's credit history to be independent of his or her company, and can also have tax advantages.)

Mission Statement *(Example: Style by Jane is a multifaceted fashion styling company that provides services to a wide variety of clients. These include print publications, corporate advertisers, fashion-event producers, public relations firms, and individuals. Services include sourcing and styling clothes for shoots, styling runway shows, styling personal wardrobes, and personal shopping.)*

Owner Profile List relevant educational background and professional experience here.

Skill Set List relevant skill sets here.

Location and Market Analysis *This section and the one below are especially important. This is where the stylist examines where the business is based and if the city can support it. A complete market analysis includes the following points:*

- *Define the target market: Who are the target customers who would use these services? Can they afford these services, and is there enough of a population to support the business?*
- *Identify competitors: Are there other similar businesses in the area? If so, where are they located and how long have they been in business? Do they have a high degree of customer loyalty? If starting an image-consulting business, for example, also consider boutiques where employees act as style consultants.*
- *Is there a need or growing need for the business? What factors might contribute to this? Is the city growing? Are large companies relocating their headquarters there? Are new neighborhoods being built? Is real estate selling quickly? Slow commercial and residential sales can indicate stagnant economies.*
- *Research from local business listings, the department of city planning, and real estate websites should support all of the above information.*

Plan for Business Growth *Are there opportunities for advertising and promotion in this city? If so, what are they? Research local newspapers and magazines that might be good places to advertise, and find out how much ad space costs. Are there charity functions that you could participate in to gain visibility? Can you offer gift certificates for services to attract customers? Would it be helpful to diversify into other areas of styling outside of fashion?*

Rates and Fees *How will you pay bills for the initial months before the business becomes profitable? What bills need to be paid to keep the business afloat? How long do you anticipate until the business becomes profitable? Do you have enough money set aside to*

Figure 7.7
To achieve the level of detail required in the many sections of a comprehensive business plan, a stylist can utilize an informal list of questions or a more formal worksheet like the one shown in this sample questionnaire.

Freelancers can look at the possibility of marketing themselves in neighboring cities as well. Start by thinking about some larger urban areas within a day's drive. Perhaps there are even friends or family who can provide a room for the night during a booking.

Another option for increased marketability is the possibility of broadening a skill set and building other books/portfolios. For example, clothing stylists can branch out into personal shopping or prop styling so that they can market themselves to more clients.

Sometimes photographers or clients ask fashion stylists if they can do hair and makeup in addition to styling for a booking. This often is an attempt to save money in the overall budget, since it is cheaper to hire one stylist to do three jobs than to hire two to three stylists. The fashion stylist has to make this decision. Many stylists say that this is unfair to hair and makeup stylists. They might also say that it makes the shoot too hectic, and it's too difficult to do everything and still do a good job. Other stylists, especially those in smaller cities, choose to get hair and makeup training as well as fashion-styling experience to increase their marketability. A more common practice is that the models are simply asked to come to the booking with their hair and makeup already done. Sometimes retailers even tell them how to style their hair and which makeup shades are on-brand.

This part of the business plan is also a good place to highlight standard fees and rates set by competing stylists in the area.

4. Plan for Business Growth

An important goal for the stylist starting out is to acquire steady clients. These are the clients who will hire repeatedly and somewhat regularly. Having a roster of steady clients allows freelance stylists to have a relatively steady source of income. A stylist also should leave room in his or her schedule for less regular clients and interesting jobs because those interesting jobs are great ways to build a creative portfolio. (See Figure 7.8.) In the plan for business growth, a beginning stylist can set a goal of having one regular client in six months to a year and build from there. He or she can keep adding to the client list until a good balance of consistent work and less regular bookings is achieved.

5. Rates and Fees

Stylists usually charge a **day rate**: the rate for a standard day's worth of professional service. An analysis of the area's market and competition will give a good idea of what to charge. If a beginning stylist is still building a

Figure 7.8
An important goal for a stylist is to acquire steady clients.

book, he or she might want to charge lower rates in the beginning. This will make him or her more competitive with experienced stylists in the area and provide jobs to fill a book. Eventual increases in rates might be projected into the plan.

This section is also a good place to project the time it might take between billing a client and actually getting paid. Often clients don't pay right away. It might take some time to be reimbursed. This is also a good time to consider ways to collect delinquent payments.

Billable Hours and Scheduling

When charging a day rate, billable time includes **prep work** such as shopping for the shoot. Prep work is all of the work stylists do beforehand to prepare for the shoot. Billable time also includes **wrap work**: everything that is done after shooting ends. It is often done the day after the shoot. Wrap work includes returning the borrowed clothing and writing and submitting editorial credits taken from the cheat sheet. It is important to do all of these things as quickly and efficiently as possible.

Sometimes a client will want to negotiate a flat rate for the job, which includes prep and wrap work. Other times, if the shoot is going to last a while, the client might try to negotiate a flat rate and have the stylist on call for weeks at a time, since chances are the stylist will have to turn down other jobs. If a shoot is on location, a stylist must also negotiate payment for travel time plus the actual expense of the travel such as an airplane ticket or mileage and lodging, as well as a per diem for food costs and incidentals. Stylists don't necessarily have to take a job just because it's offered. Sometimes the disadvantages outweigh the advantages, and a job has to be turned down. Stylists aren't getting paid consistently, so there might be days or even weeks when they aren't earning any pay. This might be a consideration when deciding whether or not to take a job.

Holds

When a client tentatively books a stylist for a job, it is called a **hold**. A hold means that the stylist is first in the client's mind for a job. It does not guarantee a job, though. A job is not set in stone unless it is **confirmed**, which means the client has agreed to hire and pay the stylist. If another client requests the stylist during hold dates, the stylist does not have to automatically turn down the job. At this time, the stylist can issue a "second hold" and then call the first client to see if it is ready to confirm. If the answer is no, the stylist can certainly decide to take the second job, providing this client is prepared to confirm. In fact, it is often in the stylist's best interest to take the first job that confirms. Above all, freelance stylists must protect themselves and their income.

6. Office, Work Space, and Overhead

An analysis of office and overhead expenses is a big factor in profit because these expenses must be deducted from any pay received. Many freelance stylists work from home and don't rent office or studio space. (See Figure 7.9.) This cuts down significantly on overhead. Also, home office space can be tax deductible.

Renting space in a coworking environment can be an economical way to have a professional space to meet with high-net-worth or celebrity clients. Often the rent includes things like internet access, access to a copy machine, and a small kitchen, which cuts down on expenses and hassle for the stylist. It also can

Figure 7.9
A home office doesn't always need to take up an entire room. Having a lot of space is ideal but not necessary.

be ideal for stylists who regularly receive packages and deliveries, because there usually is a receptionist who can sign for items and a secure storage area. A stylist's studio might also be a climate-controlled storage unit. While this is not usable work space, storage can be very important for a stylist. Over the course of many stylists' careers, it is inevitable that they accumulate clothing, accessories, and props for various jobs. Some of these might have been purchased for test shoots from secondhand stores. Others might simply be items stumbled upon and purchased for future use. If a stylist has enough space at home or can afford to rent space, either area can be designated as a studio. Storage space is especially necessary for prop stylists, who work with and tend to accumulate larger objects.

Office-Supply Checklist
Setting up a home office requires office supplies. A home office doesn't always need to take up an entire room. Having a lot of space is ideal but not necessary. A desk and some wall space in the corner of a room can make an efficient home office space.

Hardware
- Personal computer with both wired and wireless internet connections and a color printer for client presentations and research. So much of what a stylist does involves Web surfing and emailing, so it is not practical to rely solely on an iPad or a phone.
- Filing cabinet, a handy place to store paperwork and tear sheets. Often paperwork such as invoices and pull letters can be stored electronically to reduce clutter. However, tear sheets are very important for visual communication and creating storyboards. They can be filed by theme, such as "Historical Decade," "Mood," or "Dominant Color."
- A day planner or calendar. Whether it's paper or electronic, a stylist must be able to access his or her calendar at all times. A planner is also a handy place to keep track of mileage.
- Bulletin board for posting fashion/trend information or upcoming job information.
- Inspiration wall for posting pictures of current runway looks and other important images unique to each stylist. It is important for stylists to read and interpret trends.
- A garment rack for hanging merchandise.
- A bookcase for storing fashion books; a stylist can never have too many!
- An alarm system to safeguard merchandise stored in the studio, preferably one that can be monitored from a phone.

Software
- Cloud-based business service or services (like Quickbooks and Square) that can send (and resend) invoices, accept online payments, run metrics such as what months are the busiest and which clients book most frequently, record expenses, record payments received, maintain client lists, and keep track of any inventory a stylist might carry, in the case of personal stylists.
- Time-tracking software. This can be helpful for hourly jobs and for measuring productivity.
- Online inventory system for keeping track of merchandise that's coming and going.
- Online and offline backup systems for all digital documents, records, photos, and files.
- An account with a service used for sharing and sending large digital files.
- An Adobe creative suite account if the stylist wants to work in Photoshop, Illustrator, or Indesign.
- The stylist's own internet service. It can be tempting to rely on a neighbor's open network, but relying on chance and charity is never wise, and a stylist's luck might just run out at the most inopportune time.

7. Analysis of Living Expenses and Supplemental Income

Sometimes, especially in the beginning, bookings may not be consistent. It is important to have enough money to cover basic needs, such as food, shelter, insurance, car expenses, and taxes. Some stylists have another job in the beginning out of necessity, but there are downsides. A "day job" or "side hustle" is a great way to supplement styling income, but it also can get in the way of potential bookings. The best-case scenario for a beginning stylist is to save enough money to be able to devote undivided attention toward building a business. Another decent scenario is to have a freelance job with flexible hours that can be done from home. Both of these may be unrealistic for many, however, so fitting two careers into one schedule takes thought and planning.

8. Uses for Downtime

Once a stylist starts billing for his or her time, it is important to think of all downtime as time that could make money. Therefore, it is important not to waste it. Downtime should be spent as productively as possible. That may mean anything from looking up potential new contacts and networking opportunities, to conducting industry research. Another good use of downtime is forging local retail contacts. It might be helpful for beginning stylists to make a list of local retailers with whom they want to build relationships. The list can also include a store phone number and contact person.

Stylists frequently have to buy things for shoots that they cannot return, and sometimes they may receive gifts or promotional items that they cannot use or wear. Downtime is a great opportunity to throw items up for sale on websites like eBay or Tradesy. On the flip side, stylists often are on the hunt for specific items for their kit, their styling wardrobe, or prop styling jobs. Downtime is the perfect time to shop for deals without the stress of a looming deadline.

Business Requirements: Finances and Expenses

There are many financial and legal decisions involved in starting one's own business. A stylist is encouraged to seek help via a lawyer, accountant, or comprehensive research. The following information is general and informative in nature; it is not meant to be specific advice or a complete overview of all of the possibilities.

Entity Formation

An important first step for an aspiring stylist is to decide how he or she would like that business to be treated under state and federal law, especially at tax time. The stylist must decide which business entity he or she would like to form. For example, a stylist could run his or her business as a "sole proprietorship." There is no paperwork to fill out or file for this designation, and the business name is the person's name. If the stylist wants to do business under a company name, he or she will need to file a DBA form, which stands for Doing Business As, with the appropriate government office. While a sole proprietorship is the easiest of business structures, it does not protect the stylist against personal liability from debts or lawsuits. A stylist instead may opt to create a limited liability company. This option shields the stylist from being held personally responsible for the debts of the business, but there are filing and record-keeping requirements and costs that can result from forming an LLC.

Employer Identification Number

A stylist who runs a business must register with the federal government for a unique, nine-digit number that is used for paying taxes. This number also can be used instead of a social security number for sole proprietors.

Insurance

Stylists who are self-employed are responsible for purchasing health insurance and also insurance to cover their business. A good policy or bundle of policies can be purchased to cover property damage, loss of office contents, including merchandise in the office, and even the cost of any damage to a stylist's kit or equipment that is on the road with the stylist on a job.

A Business Bank Account and Credit Card

If a stylist would like to be considered a business, he or she needs his or her own business bank account. This way, a stylist can keep expenses and liabilities separate from his or her personal funds, expenses, and liabilities. With a business bank account, a stylist also can get business checks and also a credit card in the name of his or her business to cover expenses. Some stores require a credit card number as security for loans, and it's always wise to submit a business rather than a personal card.

Capital

It is recommended that a stylist have enough money in the bank to cover at least six months of operating expenses. Launching a business is expensive, and even successful stylists don't have money flowing in during the first few months and days of their new business.

IRS Rules

Most freelance stylists file with the IRS as self-employed individuals. This means that they are responsible for setting aside money for the IRS from their income. There is no employer in this situation that withholds taxes from paychecks. Self-employed individuals should have a solid knowledge of their tax-related responsibilities before they start their businesses. All individual taxpayers must submit the basic Form 1040 each year. Self-employed individuals must also submit a Schedule C or Schedule C-EZ. These individuals file differently than business owners and do not have employees. Some self-employed individuals hire CPAs to handle taxes and financial records, while others opt to do it themselves.

Following is a list of financial documents that freelance stylists need to save for taxes. A good way to keep them organized throughout the year is to purchase an accordion file for receipts, with one section for each month of the year. As receipts accumulate, they can be placed in the folder. During quiet times in the office, try to scan as many of these receipts as you can and upload them into budget-making programs like Quicken. Dedicating a little bit of time each week or so will make filing taxes a snap come April.

Gross Receipts

Gross receipts record any income made, and they can include bank deposit slips and invoices. These need to be saved because they are added up to determine annual income. A monthly accordion file for invoices is helpful for organizing invoices, deposit slips, and copies of payment checks received. If invoices have been sent electronically and paid online, there will already be an electronic record that is integrated with billing and budgeting software.

Expenses

Expenses can be documented with sales receipts, invoices, canceled checks, or account statements. Expenses are any overhead costs that relate to running the business. This can include office supplies, utility bills, and rent, among other things.

Travel Expenses

Sometimes if a job requires travel, the client will pay a partial day rate for travel time and all travel expenses. In that case, because the stylist makes money on the days he or she travels, that profit is included in gross income. However, if the client is not going to pay for travel, the expenses can be deducted from income taxes. Gas, lodging, airfare, and public transportation all qualify as travel costs.

Assets

Assets include furniture and property that are used in the business. It is important to keep records of when these assets were purchased. If they are sold or improved upon, the profit or cost must be reported to the IRS.

Investment and Retirement Plans

Because a stylist is self-employed, there is no company-funded retirement plan or pension. It is up to the stylist to prepare for his or her own retirement. It is never too early to start investing money for retirement; even just a few dollars a week when a stylist is starting out can grow into a substantial amount over time. There are numerous ways to save and invest for retirement; a good place to start is with one's bank or simply do a Google search and begin researching to find the best plan.

[
"Keeping your money in order is key for running a thriving prop/set styling business."
—*Sara Foldenauer, prop stylist, www.setsbysara.com.*
]

Interview with Joseph A. Delate

Joseph Delate is a New York City–based fashion stylist and consultant. He started his career working for top national and international media publications. Joseph's eclectic style and professionalism have placed him in high demand in the industry. He spends his free time restoring his family's fourth-generation home in Trenton, New Jersey's historic district. Joseph's greatest inspiration has always come from his family friends and the forever-changing streets of New York City.

Website: *Josephdelatenyc.com*
Instagram: *@joeydnyc*

What celebrities, companies, or high-profile clients have you worked with?
Niki Taylor, Iman, Sally Field, Gloria Steinem, Andy Cohen, Tyson Beckford, Matthew Broderick, Téa Leoni, Anna Paquin.

Nike, Ralph Lauren, Coca-Cola, Macy's, Apple, Mary Kay, Cover Girl, Sprint, Neiman Marcus, The Gap, Tommy Hilfiger, Royal Caribbean.

How did you get into the fashion industry? Did you have formal training, or is it something that evolved or you fell into?
I always loved clothing shopping and New York City. I remember being a small child in the fitting rooms of Bonwit Teller with my mother and aunt telling them what looked great and what they had to keep. At the end of my grandmother's favorite soap opera *The Guiding Light*, the announcer used to say, "All

clothing provided by Barney's and Bergdorf Goodman." I used to say to myself, "I've been to those places and I can certainly dress those people."

After graduating college with a degree in fine arts and education to make my family happy, I moved into the East Village. My first job in fashion was working for a major NYC hair salon. I was hired as a receptionist but quickly learned who all the top fashion editors were that came in and worked closely with the creative directors and PR team on special events and dressed the models for hair shows. This is how I first decided I could make a living styling. I began to reach out via fax to all the top NYC stylists for assisting opportunities. I knew I needed much to learn and that by assisting I would gain invaluable on-the-job training and experience. I assisted two of the top fashion and music celebrity stylists for three years before I was offered my first magazine job. I learned what to do, what to say, how do I act, what to expect, and how much to ask for and exactly how to get it. I was taught that the clients came first and I was supposed to be an invisible cheerleader with a never-ending supply of unlimited fabulous options.

I have many funny stories and luckily not too many horror stories. I remember one time looking at my watch and realizing I had less than an hour and a half to be at Newark airport. I just got a call that there was a pickup ready at Cartier and Bvlgari for the job I was working on. I literally grabbed my overnight bag—all the shoot clothes had been sent FedEx—and hopped on the train. I did both pickups, over 4 million dollars of jewelry, and stuffed it into my puffy coat's interior pockets. I somehow jumped in a cab and made it to Newark airport with seconds to spare. I literally banged on the plane's door to let me in. This was long before security checks and regulations post 9/11.

Do you have any funny or horror stories of when you first started?
One night I decided to wear a white leather French designer jacket fresh off the runway to a dinner party. Of course, six hours later at a club someone spilled an entire glass of red wine on me and it. It was 2 a.m. and my drycleaner, Exquisite [Cleaners] on 1st Avenue, opened at 8 a.m. I stuffed it in a plastic bag to stop the stain from drying and waited until they opened. Looking more a mess than the jacket, I was told to go to bed and come back at 4 p.m. Yes, miracles do happen. Abe, the owner, is a genius and the only person I trust to dryclean anything. He is honest and fair. (And it did not cost $1,000 like a supposedly top fashion drycleaners would have charged.)

Now that you are styling, what qualities do you look for in an assistant?
I tend not to employ the typical fashion assistant. I need someone with me that is a real honest hard-working individual that understands my personality and quirks. I shop every job myself, and I only use assistants as a second set of hands. Sometimes that is frustrating for them; however, by being privy to the behind-the-scenes details of my business and life, what an up-and-coming fashion stylist can learn is my perfected style of working and streamlined sensibility after working twenty-plus years in this business.

What's something you wish someone had told you before you started? What advice would you give your younger self about styling?
Be nice to everyone. You never know what corner they were going to be around or where they might

pop up again. They might need you or you might need them. Kindness goes a long way and is never forgotten. Always be available to lend five minutes of support whether it be physical or emotional. Many lives have changed in less than five minutes.

When many young stylists start out, they think that it is all about being super fabulous; they don't realize all the logistics that are involved . . . such as the business end of it and the importance of having an agent. Being in business for ourselves, we take on many responsibilities, legally binding ones. We are ultimately responsible for any item we are lent, have borrowed, rented, or purchased for a production. We are also responsible for the actions of our assistants or interns. Any mistakes made are ours alone. No finger-pointing cry babies are rehired. No one really understands how physically challenging it can be to move twenty trunks of clothes for a fitting, then a shoot. Or how especially unglamorous one can feel after being sent up in the same elevator as the garbage to a particular client's offices or apartment because you're not allowed with all the trunks and the normal passenger elevators.

What's your philosophy of styling or dressing a client?

Every job I have ever been on I am not utilized in the same capacity. It is like I start fresh every time. Every big job, every small job, I am the same person on. Never let one client think they are lesser than another; we have to be thankful for everyone and treat them with equal respect.

I love working with people's personal style and pumping it up to the maximum. I like a little bit of glamour and luxury. However, after years of doing commercial jobs, I have also gotten into period and character dressing.

Where do you like to shop?

My favorite place to shop for a job, a personal client, or gift is Bloomingdale's flagship on Lexington Avenue, New York City.

Bloomingdale's studio service department is unmatched. They set the standard in the industry for servicing a fashion stylist.

Who are some of your favorite designers?

I have had a lifelong obsession with Gucci. I love mixing very high-end designer pieces with athletic wear. It has been my personal style signature my entire career.

I have a soft spot for New York designers. I love Norma Kamali. Her entire aesthetic is a true New Yorker's dream.

I also have a great appreciation for Michael Kors. He has managed to build an amazing business based on classic American style and stay on top of his game. When I was a very young stylist leaving for a shoot on location, he personally waited in his office and handed me my requested dresses packed for the shoot way after showroom closing hours. I'll never forget that work ethic.

What are some hidden gems or offbeat places where you pick up stuff for jobs?

I rent all my shoes for all my shoots from *Montanarader.com*. Montana's collection of pristine designer shoes is a stylist's best bet to get rebooked on a job. When clients see her high-end shoes lined up like fashion soldiers, they all know you have the taste level that it takes to be considered a top fashion stylist.

Another tip is when vintage clothing is requested of the everyday variety to lend real mess or a hipster vibe to a look, I love No Relation Vintage on 1st Avenue in the East Village. They have a huge selection of 50s through 90s vintage clothing at amazing inexpensive pricing. One of the last great stores of its kind.

How much of your own personal style can be influenced on a job?

My personal style tends to be a bit eclectic and "street." I have to be sensitive with clients to their needs. I do personalized presentations and mood boards for every client so we are on the same page. My presentations speak louder than my personal wardrobe, which is hugely important.

The flipside of this is I have been hired for many projects based on my personal styling and sensibility. Everyone always wants to know where I get my sneakers. I think it is a real New York thing.

Who are your muses? How or where do you find inspiration?

I am very lucky my muses are my best friends Kim Williams the model, Leah Levin the stylist/fashion archivist, and Melissa Burns the model/NYC nightlife promoter. These three women I have been blessed with in life. Friendship means everything to me.

I really love being a stylist; I love working with different people every day; I love to shop; I love to constantly find new and exciting things to make life more interesting and comfortable.

I am super organized and find great satisfaction in that special talent. Every item that I rent or purchase for a shoot is returned in the original packaging it was sent to me in or better. I have over twenty collapsible nylon trunks that are supposed to be for hockey equipment that have wheels on them. Every single item that leaves my storage is placed in one of these bags for a shoot. They are my saving grace and help me keep track of everything.

How do you network?

As a stylist I have always had an agent. They know the legal ins and outs of the business as well as handle all my billing estimates and travel arrangements. I have my latest and greatest work posted on the agency website and my personal website. I love telling people, just google me. Always makes me smile and it is impressive (to me at least). I really have firsthand seen the power of Instagram. I don't have 1 million followers, but I have important ones.

I still have portfolios, but they are rarely used and not as up-to-date as my websites due to all the advances in technology over the past twenty years. I force myself to become computer savvy so I can do my presentations and send them quickly and efficiently to clients.

Technology has its downfalls. I feel that certain elements of surprise are harder to come by. That little bit of magic, that special something you find for a shoot, has become harder to keep secret. On many jobs, I message to an Amuse board (a shopping board) and then supply images of the shopping to let the clients feel comfortable that I have the exact item in here; many times I have to refer them back to the shopping board to remind them what it looks like on figure.

It is super important to build relationships within the industry.

Finally, I would like to end this with saying all talent should have representation and an agent behind them to help them deal with setting their rates, invoicing, collecting, and making sure contracts are signed off on. This is not a business where a "gentleman's handshake" can be trusted. Make sure you set up an LLC or incorporate yourself. Health insurance, renter's insurance, workman's comp insurance are all necessary and, luckily at this time, affordable.

Be cool. Don't overwhelm your clients with your availability. Let them know you enjoy working for them and you hope to hear from them soon. When new work comes in, share it because you're proud of it. Some of my best clients I've built a strong longtime relationship with. You need to be realistic; you can't do every single job with your favorite clients that they are working on, for various reasons and factors. Just be grateful for what you do get to work with them on and always work at 200 percent capacity; make them miss you and want you. Set the bar for others to live up to. Never make any situation their problem; it is always your problem; fit it. Don't get jealous or mad; just work harder.

SUMMARY AND REVIEW

Stylists run businesses like any other business owner does. This means that certain professional tools are required to run the business smoothly, like a computer, software, a business plan, office space, and office supplies.

Paperwork includes documents such as contracts and invoices. Software designed for invoicing and accounting makes keeping track of financials a lot easier. A business plan is advisable for beginning stylists so that they can think out all of the details relating to their businesses. It is also essential for stylists to have well-stocked work spaces so that they can complete the administrative side of the job and also store merchandise and equipment between jobs.

Styling can be fun and inspiring, but there also is an administrative side of the job that is equally important. When essential details such as proper financial planning, income taxes, and organization are handled carefully, then a business has a greater likelihood for success, and more time can be spent pursuing the creative activities that can lead to a thriving career in fashion styling.

KEY TERMS

- assets
- book
- booking agreement
- business plan
- confirmation
- confirmed job
- contract
- day rate

- expenses
- gross receipts
- holds
- invoice
- letter of responsibility (LOR)
- prep work
- pull letter
- talent agency
- voucher
- wrap work

REVIEW QUESTIONS

1. List three details that must be agreed upon before a booking can be confirmed.

2. What are some advantages for stylists to be represented by agencies?

3. A company wants to hire you for a three-day styling job in a town that's a six-hour drive or a two-hour flight away. You will need to pull and return merchandise and bring it with you. Think about the time commitment involved and the expenses you would incur being out of town, plus the costs of transporting yourself and your merchandise to the location. Make a list of all of the expenses that you would want to ask the client to cover.

4. List three points included in a freelance stylist's business plan.

5. What are three things a stylist can do during his or her downtime?

6. Why is it important to have both a cloud-based backup system and an external hard drive?

7. Why is business insurance important for a freelance stylist? List two situations in which a stylist would be able to file a claim to cover loss or damage.

8. List one benefit of a sole proprietor business structure and one benefit of being a limited liability company.

9. What types of things can be included in expenses?

10. What types of things can be included in assets?

LEARNING ACTIVITIES

Learning Activity 7.1: You are a freelance stylist working without an agency. Yesterday, a magazine editor emailed you about styling a shoot from Monday through Wednesday. You replied and said you were available. The magazine editor did not confirm. Today, an art director at a clothing company asked you if you were available to style a catalogue shoot on Tuesday and Wednesday. How do you handle this situation? Draft an email to both the magazine editor and the art director.

Learning Activity 7.2: Congratulations! You just leased a studio space for your freelance styling business. You have a lot to do before your grand opening. Answer the following questions:

1. List the Web address for the business internet provider in your area and find out how much it costs for installation and a service contract.
2. Find two business service companies that offer online invoicing, contact management, and expense tracking. Make a table, and use the columns and rows to list and compare the services offered by each and the prices they charge. Which is the better deal for your business and why?
3. Where can you buy a rolling rack, and how much does it cost?
4. How much does a desk and desk chair cost? Find what you'd like and price it out. Remember to include tax and shipping or delivery expenses.

Learning Activity 7.3: You are setting up a freelance business as a limited liability company, and you need to register your business with federal, state, and local authorities. Decide on a name for your business, research the following information, and answer these questions:

1. Employee Identification Number: What is it? Can the paperwork be found online? Can the paperwork be submitted online? If so, what is the Web address? If not, where do you need to go? How much does it cost?
2. Limited Liability Company: What is it? Can the paperwork be found online? Can the paperwork be submitted online? If so, what is the website? If not, where do you need to go? How much does it cost?
3. DBA: What is it? Can the paperwork be found online? Can the paperwork be submitted online? If so, what is the Web address? If not, where do you need to go? How much does it cost?

RESOURCES

"All About Becoming a Fashion/Wardrobe Stylist." The Fashion Spot. December 16, 2003. http://forums.thefashion spot.com/f90/all-about-becoming-fashion-wardrobe-stylist-25956.html.

"Business Plans: A Step-by-Step Guide." Entrepreneur. http://www.entrepreneur.com/businessplan/index.html.

"Checklist for Starting a Business." IRS. https://www.irs.gov/businesses/small-businesses-self-employed/checklist-for -starting-a-business.

"Choose Your Business Structure." SBA. https://www.sba.gov/starting-business/choose-your-business-structure.

Cox, Susan Linnet. *Photo Styling: How to Build Your Career and Succeed.* New York: Allworth Press, 2006.

"Gift Voucher Wardrobe Makeover." Delilah Fashion Stylist. http://delilahfashionstylist.bigcartel.com/product/gift -voucher-150.

"Invoice Advice." Model Mayhem. August 29, 2008. http://forum.modelmayhem.com/po.php?thread_id=337700.

"Pulling, Pull Letters, Asking Designers for Clothes." The Fashion Spot. May 15, 2005. http://forums.thefashionspot .com/f90/pulling-pull-letters-asking-designers-clothes-27744.html.

"Small Business and Self-Employed Tax Center." IRS. http://www.irs.gov/businesses/small/index.html.

Whitman, Michael. "What Is a Modeling Voucher and Why Do I Need One?" BusinessofModeling.com. August 31, 2015. https://www.businessofmodeling.com/modeling-industry/what-is-a-modeling-voucher-and-why-do-i-need-one/.

Wright, Crystal. *The Hair, Makeup & Styling Career Guide.* Los Angeles: Motivational Media Productions, 2007.

Zahorsky, Darrell. "Accounting Tips for Small Business Startups." The Balance. http://sbinformation.about.com/od /taxaccounting/a/accountingstart.htm.

8 Fashion Lexicon: Terms, Icons, History, and Inspiration

CHAPTER TOPICS CALL SHEET

In this chapter you will learn:
* Why stylists need to be fluent in fashion
* The anatomy of apparel
* The language of fashion
* Fashion icons and timeless garments
* Screen classics and other cultural inspirations

WHY IT IS IMPORTANT TO BE FLUENT IN FASHION

Communication within the fashion industry is constant and often fast-paced. Buyers communicate with showrooms. Designers communicate with suppliers. Stylists communicate with clients, showrooms, editors, and photographers, and once the image is published, they communicate with the public. Stylists and photographers are often a designer's liaisons to the public. They communicate visually through imagery, but to get to that point they must have a verbal discussion beforehand.

Most professional interactions include some degree of friendly chit-chat, and there's nothing fashion people love talking about more than what's going on in their industry. It's critical for an aspiring stylist to keep abreast of headline-making news within the business of fashion as well as who wore what from whom at important events like the Oscars, the Golden Globes, and the Met Ball. When a stylist is interesting, engaging, and friendly, it's easier to build the professional relationships—and even friendships—that are essential to success.

It's a given that a stylist must be able to properly pronounce the names of important fashion designers and fashion houses. There are many online resources and even YouTube videos that can help you navigate such easy-to-mangle names like Demna Gvasalia, Alessandro Michele, and Hermès.

A productive and effective discussion also must include the right vocabulary. Most stylists write their own editorial credits and therefore need to know how to accurately describe clothing. They need to know the names of collars, seams, cuffs, fabrics, and garments, and the list goes on. It's also critical to understand important fashion reference points, because often these movies, musicians, and famous fashion icons are used as shorthand for an entire look. For example, if an editor wanted to commission a photo shoot that utilized baby doll dresses and models with vacant expressions, he or she need only say "Valley of the Dolls" to the creative team, and everyone would have a complete understanding of the desired vibe.

This chapter will highlight some key points in the styling-industry lexicon and cover some common sources of inspiration for designers, stylists, and virtually every creative person involved in a fashion shoot.

Keeping Up with the World of Fashion

Life, work, and school's demands often leave little time for staying abreast of fashion trends, but people in the industry are expected to stay current on what's going on, not only with style trends but also within the world of fashion. For example, they must know who tops the masthead at prominent magazines and whether or not an editor has left or gone to another publication. They need to know the must-watch bloggers and Instagrammers and should keep up with fashion news headlines to know if a fashion house has hired a new designer, if a department store is going out of business, or who is collaborating with whom on a major capsule collection. The internet is usually the best way to keep up with breaking fashion news. Following social media feeds from connected fashion personalities is another way to keep up, but going straight to the news source is always preferable. One of the most influential and comprehensive fashion news aggregation websites as of press time is BusinessofFashion.com, or BOF. Also good are *Vogue.com*, New York Magazine's The Cut blog, Racked.com, Refinery29.com, and the style section of NewYorkTimes.com. It is by no means necessary to become a walking encyclopedia. However, it is essential to establish a frame of reference for inspiration. (See Figure 8.1.) This frame of reference can include past and present fashion as well as predictions for the coming seasons.

Figure 8.1
It is essential to establish a frame of reference for inspiration. This frame of reference can include past and present fashion as well as predictions for the coming seasons.

Modern-Day Fashionistas and Fashionistos

These men and women are models, social media stars, actors, musicians, designers, and famous personalities who are known for their inspirational style. While many of them don't have one specific style that they are known for, they always are at the fashion forefront, taking risks, changing directions, rocking new trends, supporting emerging designers, and wearing clothing in new and innovative ways. They influence designers, stylists, and the public through their clothing choices. Aspiring stylists should make every effort to follow these style innovators and influencers on Instagram and to stay up-to-date on their latest looks:

- Alexa Chung
- A$AP Rocky
- Bella and Gigi Hadid
- Beyoncé
- Chiara Ferragni
- Justin O'Shea
- Kanye West
- Kate Moss
- Lady Gaga
- Pharrell Williams
- Rihanna
- Sarah Jessica Parker
- Veronika Heilbrunner
- Bryan Grey Yambao
- Solange Knowles
- Nicolette Mason
- Shala Monroque

"You should always be looking at blogs and following Instagrams of people you are inspired by fashion-wise. You should know what's happening in the industry and read all the trade publications like WWD. Get familiar with the major editorials and the collections, learn about designers, and study up-and-coming designers—these are all very valuable assets."
—Nicole Chavez, celebrity stylist. "So You Want to be a Stylist? Nicole Chavez's 5 Tips for Making It." The Fashion Spot. http://www.thefashionspot.com/runway-news/180143-how-to-be-a-fashion-stylist/

STARTING WITH THE BASICS: THE ANATOMY OF APPAREL

The anatomy of a garment includes fabric, buttons, pockets, zippers, and all of the things that can make a piece of clothing fabulous. **Clothing-construction terminology** is a general term to describe the vocabulary of garment details. It is imperative to understand these details so that effective communication can take place. If a stylist is describing garments to a photographer over the phone or in an email, specific images come to mind based on the stylist's descriptions. If the garments are not what were described when the photographer sees them, the stylist looks incompetent and the shoot might have a different outcome than expected. A stylist's fluency in clothing terminology not only makes him or her look better but is essential to the job and keeps communication running smoothly. Important areas to be fluent in include fabric, tops, bottoms, undergarments, and accessories.

Anatomy of Fabric

Knowledge of fabric is essential for anyone in the styling industry. (See Figure 8.2.) It can mean the difference between describing silk chiffon and silk jersey, or cable knit and rib knit. Basic knowledge includes knowing the difference between a natural and synthetic fabric, and knowing the difference between a knit and a woven. From there, stylists need to know about the hand of a fabric, or how it feels, and the names of specific weaves and knit stitches. Fibers are the smallest building blocks of fabric and come from a variety of natural and man-made sources. Yarns are made from fibers, and fabrics are knit or woven from yarns. This basic information will enable you to know how the fabric moves and how it will look.

Natural Fibers vs. Synthetic Fibers

Natural fibers are from natural plant, animal, or mineral sources. The primary natural fibers are cotton, wool, and silk. Some other plant-based fibers include jute, ramie, bamboo, and hemp. Other than wool, some examples of animal-sourced fibers are cashmere and alpaca. Mineral fibers result in materials with metallic sheens, like lame and lurex. **Synthetic fibers** are derived from liquid chemical mixtures that are extruded through small holes in showerhead-like devices called *spinnerets* to form fibers, and then hardened to maintain their shape. The primary synthetic fibers are polyester, nylon, rayon, and acrylic. There are many other synthetic fibers, and new ones constantly are being developed.

Figure 8.2
Knowledge of fabric is essential for anyone in the styling industry.

Knit Fabrics vs. Woven Fabrics

All fabrics are made of yarns. Yarns can be very thick and bulky or very fine and silky. Yarns are for making fabric, while thread is for sewing fabric. **Knit fabrics** are made of continuous strands of yarn that are looped together row by row. Knits can sometimes be unraveled as one long string of yarn. **Woven fabrics** are made of two different sets of yarns that intersect and interlace. The looped construction of a knit fabric gives it more stretch than a woven fabric.

The Hand of a Fabric

A fabric's **hand** is a simple concept. It describes whether the fabric is soft or rough, and thin and fluid or thick and bulky. The hand of a fabric imparts mood to an outfit and determines whether a garment will have very little structure or a lot of structure. This is important to a stylist because structure sometimes adds bulk to the wearer's appearance, so it needs to be used wisely.

Specific Weaves

In general, woven fabrics are known to be more durable than knits, so they are used in bottoms, where they receive more wear and tear. Fabrics are almost universally woven on machines. Hand weaving is usually only seen in couture, not in ready-to-wear clothing. The basic weaves are *plain*, *twill*, and *satin*. The plain weave, the most basic of weaves, is found in fabrics such as cotton muslin and broadcloth. The twill weave is known for its durability. It has diagonal lines on its surface that are formed by the weaving pattern. Denim is the most popular example of a twill weave. The satin weave often is seen in formal and intimate apparel. The weaving technique gives it a natural sheen but also makes it susceptible to snagging. Many people get confused by satin and think that it is a type of fabric. It is actually a type of weave that is often made of silk or polyester. Silk satin is found on more expensive clothing, and polyester satin is more affordable.

Specific Knit Stitches

Knit stitches are varied and can be creative and intricate. Laces are examples of intricate knit stitches that can be made on machines or handmade by skilled craftspeople. The basic knit stitches are courses and wales. Courses run vertically, while wales run horizontally. The knit stitches seen most in clothing are *jersey*, *rib*, *weft*, and *cable knit*. These knit stitches can make anything from the sheerest top to the thickest sweater, depending on the thickness of the yarn. Jersey is the most common knit and is often seen in T-shirts. Jersey knits have courses on the front and wales on the back. When they are cut, they don't unravel, but their edges roll up. Rib knits have courses on the front and back and are commonly found in tank tops. They are a durable type of knit, and they do not roll on cut edges. Weft knits are less common and are seen in thinner sweaters. They have courses on the front and back. Cable knits tend to be chunkier and are found in thick winter sweaters.

Anatomy of Tops

Tops are composed of two basic families: blouses and shirts. Blouses are constructed for women, tend to be dressier, and are often made of woven fabrics. Shirts can be constructed for women and men. For women they are more casual and often made of knit fabrics. Some knit shirts can be as dressy as a blouse. For men, shirts can indicate anything from a dressy button-down to a casual tee. The terminology used to describe tops covers everything from the collar, to the neckline, to the armhole, to the sleeve. Unless otherwise denoted, the following clothing-construction terms can be applied to both men's and women's apparel.

Types of Collars

Collars can affect how the wearer is perceived. A collar can portray the wearer as conservative, funky, prim and proper, young, or old. Common collars are *basic shirt*, *cowl-neck* (women only), *turtleneck*, and *notched*.

Types of Necklines

Necklines vary greatly and can have a big influence on the wearer's appearance. Common necklines include *crew*, *V-neck*, *bateau* or *boatneck*, and *scoop neck*.

Types of Armholes

The most common types of armholes are *inset* and *dropped shoulder*. Other types include *raglan* and, for women, *dolman*.

Types of Sleeves

Sleeves can run the gamut from cap sleeved to long sleeved. Some popular types of sleeves are *cap* (women only), *banded*, *cuffed*, and *batwing* (women only).

Anatomy of Bottoms

Bottoms range from shorts, to pants, to jeans, and, for women, skirts. Unless otherwise noted, the following terms for bottoms describe both men's and women's apparel.

Types of Shorts

Basic types of shorts include *cargo*, *plain front*, *Bermuda*, and *athletic*.

Types of Skirts and Dresses (Women Only)

These skirt terms can also be used to describe dresses. Some basic types of skirts include *A-line*, *bubble*, *drop-waist*, and *fitted*.

Types of Pants

Pants can come in a variety of shapes, but trousers are more specific. A trouser is dressier and usually has a full leg and a higher rise. Basic types of pants include *cargo*, *boot cut*, *skinny leg*, and *trousers*. For men, pants can be described by their appearance from the front: flat-front or pleated. Both are common, but flat-fronted pants are considered more modern.

Anatomy of Undergarments

Basic women's undergarments, which are also called foundation garments, are bras, underwear, and shapewear. Basic men's undergarments are underwear, including boxers, briefs, and boxer briefs.

Types of Bras (Women Only)

Bra sizes run by two size indicators: a number size and a letter size. The number size indicates the circumference of the rib cage, and the letter indicates cup size. Some basic bra types include *strapless*, *demi-cup*, *full-coverage*, and *sports bras*.

Types of Underwear

The most basic piece of underwear is briefs. For women they are bikini briefs, and for men they are basic waist-high briefs. Other basic types of underwear are *boxers*, *boy shorts* (women only), and *thongs* (women only).

Types of Shapewear

Shapewear is anything that can be worn under an outfit to smooth and trim body lines. Shapewear is also improperly referred to as Spanx, but this is a brand name, not a category. At the very least, shapewear is made of a control-stretch knit that holds the body in. Stronger figure control is achieved through a combination of boning and layered control-stretch fabrics. Shapewear is made to control the appearance of lumps and bumps from all parts of the body between the shoulders and the knees, and it is available for both men and women.

Anatomy of Accessories

For women, accessories can make the simplest outfit pop. They can add pizzazz to a plain black outfit and are the fastest way to make a quick change. An outfit worn to work can be ready for a dinner date with a quick jewelry, handbag, and shoe change. (See Figure 8.4.) Basic types of women's accessories (not including jewelry and eyewear) are handbags, shoes, and hats. Men might not wear accessories as frequently as women, but they are still influential buyers in the marketplace. The basic men's accessories are bags (for business or travel), shoes, and hats. Unless otherwise noted, the following terms cover men's and women's apparel.

Figure 8.3
Proper undergarments are the foundation of a seamless outfit. Unwelcome bra straps, panty lines, and bulges can undermine the best ensemble.

Figure 8.4
Accessories can make the
simplest outfit pop.

Types of Bags

Some basic bag shapes include *clutch* (women only), *messenger, tote, satchel, top-handle, hobo, cross-body, bucket,* and *duffel.*

Types of Shoes

Basic shoe shapes include *ballet flat* (women only), *stiletto* (women only), *flatform, sneaker, platform heel, sandal,* and *loafer.*

Types of Hats

Hats traditionally worn by men in the past are now available for women. Basic types of hats include *fedora, baseball cap, snap back, beret, wide-brimmed, cowboy, military,* and *sun visor.*

Jewelry and Eyewear

For a stylist, jewelry and eyewear complete an outfit. Jewelry is typically divided into two categories: *fine,* meaning jewelry made from precious metals and precious or semiprecious stones, and *costume, fashion,* or *bijoux,* meaning jewelry made of nonprecious materials. Depending on the designer and the size, the price of costume jewelry can rival that of fine jewelry. When writing editorial credits for fine jewelry, the stylist should be prepared to list such details as the type of silver (usually sterling), the type of gold (yellow, white, or rose), the karat weight of the gold (K), the carat weight of gemstones (ct or tcw for multiple gemstones), and the specific type of pearl, because this directly affects value. Eyewear is classified either as *glasses*, worn during the day to correct vision impairments, or as *sunglasses*, worn outside during the day to shield the eyes from the sun and by a certain famous fashion editor all the time.

Types of Wristwatches

Watch or *wristwatch* is a common term for a timepiece worn on the wrist, but if a watch is called a chronograph, it usually is a higher-end watch. Common wristwatch styles include *tank*, *digital*, *bracelet* (for women), *military*, *dive*, *sport*, and *smart*. Watch bands can be categorized as *bracelet*, *rubber*, *leather*, *alligator*, or *grosgrain ribbon*.

Types of Necklaces

Common necklace styles include *lariat*, *pendant*, *statement*, *choker*, *bib*, and *chain*.

Types of Rings

Rings can be described as *cocktail*, *statement*, *signet*, *engagement*, *wedding*, and *pinkie*. When a ring features a gemstone, common setting styles are *prong*, *pave*, *channel*, and *bezel*. Popular gemstone cuts include *cabochon*, *princess*, *marquise*, *cushion*, *baguette*, *emerald*, and *solitaire*. A statement ring commonly is worn on the middle or index finger. Men and women wear wedding rings on the left ring finger, and women wear engagement rings on their left ring finger. If they are engaged but not yet married, the engagement ring is worn alone; after the wedding, it is worn on top of the wedding ring.

Types of Bracelets

Bracelet styles for both men and women can be described as *wrap*, *cord*, *cuff*, and *i.d.*; a *bangle* is usually an exclusively women's style.

Types of Earrings

If an earring fits through a hole in the earlobe, it is called a *pierced* earring, and its component parts include the *post*, which goes through the hole, and the *jacket*, which slides onto the end to secure it to the ear. When ears are not pierced, the earring is called a *clip-on*, and it affixes to the ear with a clip. Both styles can be classified as *chandelier*, *drop*, *dangle*, *hoop*, or *stud*. Two styles of ear jewelry that are worn along the ear but not on the lobe are the *ear cuff* and the *ear crawler*.

Types of Glasses and Sunglasses

Common styles of eyeglasses and sunglasses include *aviator*, *cat eye*, *wire rim*, *tortoiseshell*, *horn-rimmed*, and *retro*.

Putting It All Together: Design Terms

While clothing-construction terminology forms the fundamentals of the "fashion speak" every stylist must be able to do, it's also worth noting that fashion fluency involves being able to talk about how they all come together in design: specifically, the **design terminology** listed in Chapter 4: *line, form, shape, space, texture, pattern,* and *color,* as well as *balance, emphasis, rhythm, proportion,* and *unity.*

One instance in which a stylist needs to know about design terminology is when speaking about specific fashion designers. Stylists need to know about the influential designers of past and present and how their visual trademarks often distinguish them from others. One example is Pierre Cardin's circles and curved lines in his sixties designs. (See Figure 8.5.) Another example is the signature Chanel bouclé suit. These textured suits that she began designing later in her career have become iconic staples of the label today.

Another instance of when a stylist needs to know about design terminology and principles is when looking at editorial layouts for magazines. Stylists may not get to provide much input on most jobs, but they can certainly critique what they see. Editorials should have a certain rhythm and unity from page to page. These principles might be helpful when selecting strong portfolio pieces or creating a portfolio or website to showcase work. Line, color, unity, and balance are among the many considerations for stylists when creating any marketing materials.

These are the elements that often distinguish one designer from another; thus, it follows that a stylist should be ready to converse in the language of design. (See "The ABCs of Fashion Design.")

Figure 8.5
Stylists need to know about the influential designers of past and present and how their visual trademarks often distinguish them from others. One example is Pierre Cardin's circles and curved lines in his sixties designs.

The ABCs of Fashion Design

Following is a list of well-known designers of past and present. These are great names for aspiring stylists to acquaint themselves with.

A Acne Studios, Alaïa (Azzedine), Altuzarra, Armani (Giorgio), Azrouël (Yigal)

B Badgley Mischka, Balenciaga, Balmain, BCBG, Beckham (Victoria), Beene (Geoffrey), Blass (Bill), Bottega Veneta, Burberry

C Callot Soeurs, Cardin (Pierre), Cashin (Bonnie), Cavalli (Roberto), Céline, Chanel, Chloé, Comme des Garçons, Courreges

D de la Renta (Oscar), Delpozo, Demeulemeester (Ann), Dior, Dolce & Gabbana

E Etro, Erdun

F Fath (Jacques), Ferragamo, Ford (Tom), Fortuny

G Galliano (John), Gaultier (Jean Paul), Ghesquiere (Nicolas), Givenchy, Grès (Madame), Gucci, Gurung (Prabal)

H Halston, Herrera (Carolina), Hermès

I Imitation of Christ, Issa

J Jacobs (Marc), Johnson (Betsey)

K Kamali (Norma), Karan (Donna), Kenzo, Khan (Naeem), Klein (Anne), Klein (Calvin), Kors (Michael)

L Lagerfeld (Karl), Lam (Derek), Lang (Helmut), Lanvin, Lauren (Ralph), Lim (Phillip)

M Marant (Isabel) Maison Margiela, Marni, McCardell (Claire), McCartney (Stella), McQueen (Alexander), Missoni, Miu Miu, Miyake (Issey), Mizrahi (Isaac), Moschino, Mouret (Roland)

N Norrell, Novis

O Opening Ceremony, Olawu (Duro), Owens (Rick), Public School

P Poiret, Posen (Zac), Prada, Proenza Schouler

Q Quant (Mary)

R Rabanne (Paco), Reese (Tracy), Ricci (Nina), Rodarte, Rodriguez (Narciso), Rykiel (Sonia)

S Saint Laurent, Sander (Jil), Schiapparelli (Elsa), Scott (Jeremy), Sui (Anna)

T Tam (Vivienne), Temperley London, Thakoon, The Row

U Ungaro

V Valentino, Vanderbilt, Van Noten (Dries), Versace, Viktor & Rolf, Vionnet, von Furstenberg (Diane), Vuitton (Louis)

W Wang (Alexander), Watanabe (Junya), Westwood (Vivienne)

X X. Q. Zhang, Xiomara (Kitty)

Y Yamamoto (Yohji)

Z Zadig & Voltaire, Zegna (Ermenegildo), Zoe (Rachel)

"Getting a little fashion history under your belt can really help when a client is making references to a period of time, photographer or designer, this way you can understand their vision and know what they are talking about."

—Chiara Solloa, celebrity stylist. "Interview: Life Lessons and Styling Advice with Celebrity Stylist, Chiara Solloa." Huffington Post. http://www.huffingtonpost.com/christina-scribner/interview-life-lessons-an_b_5684939.html.

The Classics: Fashion Icons and Timeless Garments

Communication in the fashion world relies heavily on common reference points, which include the fashion terminology as already described. They also might entail a specific designer's work. Very frequently reference points entail a specific fashion icon, an era in history, or simply a ubiquitous garment.

Fashion icons are people who inspire others through their style. These are often high-profile people—actors, models, musicians, and socialites—and they don't just have memorable personal style, but their identities actually are synonymous with a specific style. For stylists, this means that the mere mention of a fashion icon's name is enough to communicate a complete style direction.

Historical eras are also commonly inspirational to designers and stylists alike. Eras from the twentieth century are the most commonly referenced, but other older eras are referenced too. Some of these eras have provided us with ubiquitous garments that have become classic wardrobe staples. (See Figure 8.6.)

Timeless Garments and Their Origins

Fashion design is always pulling inspiration from the past, and some of the items we wear every day date back tens, hundreds, and even thousands of years ago, such as the toga-style gown, the corset belt, and the drawstring purse. The designs have been modified over time, but the basic concept has remained the same. For the fashion stylist or personal shopper, there are five **iconic styles** that are continually reissued and reinterpreted season after season. These are classic pieces that are wardrobe building blocks, and yet they can add modernity and style to even the most envelope-pushing editorial piece.

1. **The Trench Coat:** The fabric and style of this raincoat date back to the 1850s, but it caught on with the masses when British and French army officers wore it in the trenches during World War I. Hallmarks of the trench style are a khaki-colored waterproof fabric, a double-breasted button front, and a belt at the waist, and two of its most famous makers are Burberry and Aquascutum.

2. **The Motorcycle Jacket:** The first motorcycle jacket was designed and made by Irving Schott in 1928 and sold at Harley Davidson in New York. (Schott also designed the bomber jacket for the Air Force in World War II.) Schott named his jacket after his favorite cigar, The Perfecto, and it was the

Figure 8.6
Timeless Garments and Their Origins

first leather jacket made specifically for riding motorcycles. The style, made from black leather with silver zippers and silver stud detailing, became iconic when worn in the fifties and sixties by bad boy movie stars James Dean and Marlon Brando.

3. **The Wrap Dress**: Belgian-born Diane von Furstenberg invented this universally flattering cross-tie jersey dress in 1974, and more than 5 million were sold in just two years. *Vogue* magazine called von Furstenberg's wrap dress a "sartorial symbol of women's sexual liberation," and it has become a beloved classic.

4. **The LBD**: Coco Chanel is credited with inventing in the 1920s the short, simple little black sheath called the Little Black Dress (known now only by its initials). It was the Givenchy version worn by Audrey Hepburn in *Breakfast at Tiffany's*, however, that helped vault this simple style from popular to iconic.

5. **Le Smoking**: When Yves Saint Laurent sent a woman down the runway in 1966 wearing a tuxedo jacket in a style he called "Le Smoking," it sent shock waves across the fashion world. Women couldn't get enough of it, and they still can't. Often cited as a symbol of empowerment and gender fluidity, it remains the pinnacle of evening chic.

["Style is very personal. It has nothing to do with fashion. Fashion is over quickly. Style is forever."
    —Ralph Lauren, fashion designer]

SCREEN CLASSICS AND OTHER CULTURAL INSPIRATIONS

Within each historical era, including our own, art, literature, music, and other aspects of culture thrive. Social groups—and notably those outside current social norms—set the trends of their times. Just like fashion itself, ever-evolving sociopolitical and popular movements influence history's trendsetters and can provide cultural references and creative inspiration for the fashion stylist. (See Figures 8.7 and 8.8a–e; Tables 8.1, 8.2, and 8.3; and "Must-See Movies" and "Subcultures That Influence [or Have Influenced] Style.")

Figure 8.7
Movies often inspire stylists and designers, whose work in turn inspires countless filmgoers to follow a new fashion.

Subcultures That Influence (or Have Influenced) Style

- Bikers
- Greasers
- Emo
- Goths
- Hippies
- Nerds
- Jocks
- Rap and hip-hop
- Skate rats

- Surfers
- Preppy
- Alternative
- Drag queens; drag kings
- Mods
- New romantics
- Beatniks
- S&M and bondage

TABLE 8.1 Art Movements and How They Relate to Style

Art Movement	Relationship to Style
Impressionism (last half of 1800s)	Monet, Renoir, and Degas have been a continuing influence at the House of Dior.
Cubism (early 1900s)	Oscar de la Renta's Resort 2012 collection, inspired by Picasso's Cubist period
Art Deco (1920s–30s)	Gucci's Spring 2012 collection marked the ninetieth anniversary of the house.
Surrealism (1920s–30s)	Elsa Schiaparelli's collaboration with Salvador Dalí on the "Lobster Dress" in 1937
Neo-Plasticism (1920s–30s)	Yves Saint Laurent's "Mondrian" dress in 1965, inspired by paintings by Piet Mondrian, and Lisa Perry's spring 2016 line also included Mondrian references.
Abstract Expressionism (1940s)	Yves Saint Laurent's 2007 paint-splatter dress was inspired by Jackson Pollock's paintings from the 1940s and 1950s
Pop Art (1960s)	Famous Campbell's Soup paper dress inspired by Andy Warhol's silk-screened prints from the 1960s; designer Lisa Perry's entire line incorporates pop art references.
Graffiti and Cartoons (as high art in 1980s–present)	Vivienne Westwood collaborated with artist Keith Haring in the early 1980s; Marc Jacobs collaborated with Stephen Sprouse in 2001; Jeremy Scott incorporated Sponge Bob Square Pants and the Power Puff Girls.
Computer-Generated Art (present)	Alexander McQueen's Spring 2010 collection is an example; British designer Mary Katrantzou is known for her photo-realistic computer-generated prints.

TABLE 8.2 Music Genres and Their Influences on Styling

Genre	Influence
Jazz	The Jazz Age started in the 1920s and continued into the 1930s; Count Basie and Benny Goodman were famous names; beaded glitzy dresses, cloche hats and turbans, fur stoles, zoot suits
Country	Originated in first half of twentieth century but became more popular in the 1940s and 1950s with Johnny Cash, Patsy Cline, and Hank Williams; cowboy hats, jeans, Western-style shirts
Rock 'n' Roll	Originated in the 1950s; leather jackets, jeans, long hair; vintage styled à la 1950s Elvis Presley or alternatively styled in a more modern way; women rockers in the 1980s like Joan Jett and the Blackhearts embraced the black-leather look
Folk	Started in the 1970s with artists like Bob Dylan and Melanie; blends with rock 'n' roll style of the late 1960s; tie-dye, bell bottoms, smock dresses, army surplus clothing
Glam Rock	Started in the early 1970s; androgynous style seen by David Bowie and Iggy Pop; feathered hair, bright makeup, body-hugging silhouettes
Punk	Originated in 1970s; bands include The Clash and the Sex Pistols; brought to high fashion by Vivienne Westwood; fitted leather pants, spikes, cuffs, ripped jeans and shirts
Disco	A late 1970s phenomenon; artists include the Bee Gees and Donna Summer; polyester suits, butterfly collars, fluid knit dresses with a lot of movement in the skirt for dancing
Pop	Originated in 1980s; seen more recently in Lady Gaga, Rihanna, Harry Styles, and Katy Perry; outrageous, sometimes couture looks
New Wave	Became popular in the late 1970s and early 1980s; seen in bands such as The Cure, Depeche Mode, and Joy Division; dramatic eye makeup, bold hair colors, a more muted and sometimes more romantic version of punk style
Rap and Hip Hop	Originated in 1980s with groups such as Run-DMC and Fab 5 Freddy; baggy jeans, oversize tees, prominent logos ranging from couture to streetwear, over-sized and layered gold jewelry, limited edition sneakers
Heavy Metal	Took place in the mid to late 1980s; typified by bands such as Van Halen and Mötley Crüe; tight pants, ripped tees, leather boots, big hair
Grunge/ Alternative	Originated in 1990s with bands such as Nirvana and Pearl Jam; baggy jeans, army surplus clothing, thrift-store clothing

TABLE 8.3 Key Elements of Society and Style

A. 1900–1929

	1900–1909	1910–1919	1920–1929
Key Elements of Society	Edwardian era; industrialization; automobiles; Western settlers; tenement housing	World War I from 1914–1918; suffragettes; silent films	Roaring Twenties; women granted right to vote in 1920; prohibition; flappers; talking films
Silhouettes	S-shaped with stiff corsetry; dress hems at ankle; waistlines at the natural waist or slightly higher	Cocoon-shaped; narrow hems forced wearer to take small steps; waistlines above natural waist	Straight with tunic-shaped dresses; hemlines up at knees; waistlines drop down to hip
Eminent Fashion Designers and Labels	Doucet; Worth	Callot Soeurs; Fortuny; Lanvin; Paquin; Poiret	Chanel; Erté; Patou; Vionnet
Key Elements of Fashion	Huge picture hats; kimono sleeves; parasols; delicate embroidery and lace; heavily embellished clothing	Turbans; harem pants; Asian-influenced motifs on fabrics; beaded embellishments; Fortuny's Delphos dress	Little black dress; cloche hat; embellished shoes; costume jewelry; bias-cut clothing; continued Asian influence

B. 1930–1959

	1930–1939	1940–1949	1950–1959
Key Elements of Society	Great Depression; mass poverty; transition from agricultural to manufacturing economy	World War II from 1939–1945; patriotism; war rationing; women go to work; men overseas	Atomic Age; the "New Look"; disenfranchised youth
Silhouettes	Fitted with economical use of fabrics; hemlines at knee and lower; waistlines up to natural waist; emphasis on the back	Broad shoulders; narrow waist; shoulder pads; hemlines at knee and lower; waistlines at the natural waist	Nipped-in waist; hemlines at knee and lower; waistlines at natural waist; hourglass
Eminent Fashion Designers and Labels	Salvatore Ferragamo; Elsa Schiaparelli; Madeleine Vionnet	Madame Grès; Claire McCardell	Cristóbal Balenciaga; Pierre Balmain; Christian Dior; Jacques Fath
Key Elements of Fashion	Backless dresses and ankle-length hemlines for evening; women start wearing trousers more frequently	Sportswear; halter tops; bare midriff; short shorts; turbans; sleek skirt and pantsuits	Gloves with hats; matching shoes and bags; grand ball gowns; return to nostalgic corseted waists with full skirts

C. 1960–1989

	1960–1969	1970–1979	1980–1989
Key Elements of Society	Youth culture; mod look; counterculture; Vietnam; Space Age	Recession; the birth of punk; disco; Studio 54	Glass ceiling; pop and rap music; AIDS
Silhouettes	A-line and straight; miniskirts and maxi skirts; waistlines above, at, and below natural waist; hippie dresses	Diverse range; hemlines at the knee or lower; waistlines at the natural waist	Diverse range; hemlines all lengths from mini to maxi; waistlines at or below the natural waist
Eminent Fashion Designers and Labels	Pierre Cardin; André Courrèges; Paco Rabanne; Yves Saint Laurent; Mary Quant	Halston; Sonia Rykiel; Vivienne Westwood; Diane von Fürstenberg	Armani; Donna Karan; Calvin Klein; Ralph Lauren; Versace; Moschino
Key Elements of Fashion	1950s styles continue through first half of sixties; mod Space Age inspiration; hippie movement in late sixties	1960s styles continue through first half of seventies; leisure suits; high-waist pants; women's career wear; glitz of disco	Body-hugging clothing; athletic clothing worn as regular clothing; power suits; bold patterns and colors; Japanese designers

D. 1990–Present

	1990–1999	2000–Present
Key Elements of Society	Clinton era; grunge; Lollapalooza; mainstreaming of rap and hip-hop from urban to suburban; spread of Internet	Influence of street fashion; growing worldwide disenchantment with establishment; Coachella; cult of celebrity and reality TV; social media stars; growing acceptance of gender fluidity and mainstreaming of LGBTQ subcultures; rise of fast fashion; domination of athleisure; downfall of the mainstream department store chain and the mall
Silhouettes	Diverse range; hemlines all lengths from mini to maxi; waistlines above, at, and below natural waist	Diverse range; hemlines all lengths from mini to maxi; waistlines above, at, and below natural waist
Eminent Fashion Designers and Labels	John Galliano; Marc Jacobs; Isaac Mizrahi; Prada; Tom Ford	Alber Elbaz; Sarah Burton; Tom Ford; Nicolas Ghesquière; Stella McCartney; Alexander McQueen; Jeremy Scott; Vetements; Alessandro Michele; Alexander Wang
Key Elements of Fashion	Monochromatic neutral clothing; body-hugging silhouettes; thrift store chic; deconstruction	"It" bags; high-low fashion; capsule collections and designer collaborations across creative genres; unlikely clothing combinations; influence from many historic eras at same time; androgyny; geek chic; athleisure

Must-See Movies

Some movies have inspired stylists and designers alike. The movies on the list are all post-1940, though there were many great movies made before that year. It is worthwhile to view these and take note of the wardrobes as well as the set design, art direction, and overall mise-en-scène of each film.

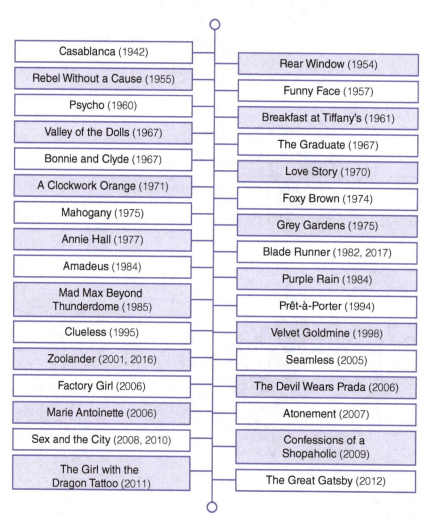

Casablanca (1942)

Rebel Without a Cause (1955)

Psycho (1960)

Valley of the Dolls (1967)

Bonnie and Clyde (1967)

A Clockwork Orange (1971)

Mahogany (1975)

Annie Hall (1977)

Amadeus (1984)

Mad Max Beyond Thunderdome (1985)

Clueless (1995)

Zoolander (2001, 2016)

Factory Girl (2006)

Marie Antoinette (2006)

Sex and the City (2008, 2010)

The Girl with the Dragon Tattoo (2011)

Rear Window (1954)

Funny Face (1957)

Breakfast at Tiffany's (1961)

The Graduate (1967)

Love Story (1970)

Foxy Brown (1974)

Grey Gardens (1975)

Blade Runner (1982, 2017)

Purple Rain (1984)

Prêt-à-Porter (1994)

Velvet Goldmine (1998)

Seamless (2005)

The Devil Wears Prada (2006)

Atonement (2007)

Confessions of a Shopaholic (2009)

The Great Gatsby (2012)

A Short List of Historic Fashion Icons

These men and women of the past and present are considered fashion icons, and they continue to inspire designers and stylists today. They are listed below chronologically by year of birth.

Figure 8.8a
Diana Vreeland

Figure 8.8b
Cary Grant

Diana Vreeland (1903–1989)

Diana Vreeland was a British-American editor at *Harper's Bazaar* and *Vogue*. She brought a sense of fantasy to fashion magazines for the first time in history, and her outlandish fashion column "Why Don't You" is legendary. She was known for her bold, dramatic personality, her love for the color red, and her distinctive profile accented by a large nose and swept-back black hair. (See Figure 8.8a.)

Cary Grant (1904–1986)

Cary Grant was a famous actor known for films such as *An Affair to Remember* and *North by Northwest*. He was born in England and immigrated to the United States after a turbulent childhood. He moved to Hollywood in the 1930s and went on to have an illustrious film career. He was known for his masculine good looks. Classic suits, ties, and a timeless side-parted haircut were key points of his style. (See Figure 8.8b.)

Josephine Baker (1906–1975)

Josephine Baker was an American, but later French, stage performer in the 1920s and 1930s and a civil rights activist in the 1960s. She was known for her vaudeville performances in the United States and for her erotic stage performances during the Jazz Age. Baker's signature style includes her 1920s Eton haircut, flapper dresses, cloche hat, and a bikini-style costume with a skirt made of bananas. (See Figure 8.8c.)

Figure 8.8c
Josephine Baker

Katharine Hepburn (1907–2003)

Katharine Hepburn was an American movie actress best known for films such as *Bringing Up Baby* and *Guess Who's Coming to Dinner?* When it came to clothing choices, Katharine Hepburn was known for wearing trousers and for her seemingly effortless menswear-inspired looks that continue to influence the fashion world today.

Iris Apfel (1921–)

In 2005, the Costume Institute at the Met mounted an exhibition dedicated to Iris Apfel's couture, exotic ethnic jewelry, and the way she combined the two, which made her among the most stylish women in New York. Apfel wasn't technically a fashion person—she and her husband owned a successful textile firm—but the success of the show made the octogenarian a sudden style sensation. Since then, Apfel has designed a jewelry and fashion collection for Macy's, been the face of M.A.C. Cosmetics, and had a documentary made about her. She is known for her distinctive look: close-cropped white hair, enormous, owl-like black circular eyeglasses, and layers upon layers of amazing statement jewelry from all over the world.

Marilyn Monroe (1926–1962)

Marilyn Monroe was a world-famous yet tragic American actress known for movies such as *Gentlemen Prefer Blondes* and *Some Like It Hot*. She was also known for having enormous sex appeal but being very fragile at the same time. Her signature style was platinum blond full-styled hair, red lipstick, and form-fitting dresses. Perhaps her most famous look is from a scene in *The Seven Year Itch*, when she stood on top of a subway grate that blew up her white dress.

Audrey Hepburn (1929–1993)

Audrey Hepburn was a Belgian-British actress and fashion legend best known for her roles in *Roman Holiday*, *Sabrina*, *Funny Face*, *Breakfast at Tiffany's*, and *My Fair Lady*. She collaborated with and wore many designs by Hubert de Givenchy, and among her many oft-referenced looks are her little black dress with diamonds and sunglasses from *Breakfast at Tiffany's* and her beat movement black trousers and turtleneck from the dance sequence in *Funny Face*.

Jacqueline Kennedy Onassis (1929–1994)

The former First Lady fascinated a generation during the early 1960s when her husband was in office. Her style and parties breathed life into the White House. Her husband, John F. Kennedy, was assassinated in 1963. She married wealthy Greek shipping tycoon Aristotle Onassis in 1968. He died in 1975, and she started working in publishing in New York City later that same year. She was known for the pink Chanel suit and pill box hat she was wearing when JFK was shot, and later for her love of giant sunglasses and a Hermès scarf tied around her head.

Grace Kelly (1929–1982)

Grace Kelly was an American actress and later princess of Monaco who was known for her classic, all-American beauty and sophisticated style. She was a muse to famous horror film director Alfred Hitchcock, and her movies include *Rear Window* and *To Catch a Thief*. She left Hollywood in 1956 to marry Prince Rainier of Monaco. The Hermès Kelly bag was named after her because she often used it to hide her pregnancy from the press. She most often wore sheath dresses, but her long-sleeved lace wedding gown also has become iconic. (See Figure 8.8d.)

Figure 8.8d
Grace Kelly

James Dean (1931–1955)

James Dean was an American actor known for movies such as *East of Eden* and *Rebel Without a Cause*. His style and films were representative of the disenfranchised 1950s youth movement. Key aspects of the style were rolled-up denim jeans, white T-shirts, black leather jackets, and slicked-back hair. There is also an oft-imitated photo of James Dean where his hair is unkempt and his face is partially obscured by a turtleneck sweater.

Elizabeth Taylor (1932–2011)

Elizabeth Taylor was a British-American actress best known for movies such as *Cat on a Hot Tin Roof* and *Cleopatra*. Her style was over-the-top glamorous. Her signature look was her full, styled black hair that contrasted with her violet eyes. She had a great figure that she showcased in form-fitting dresses. Her fine jewelry collection, largely accumulated through multiple marriages, is world famous. Her huge contributions to AIDS charities are also world renowned. She is known for her Cleopatra look, which includes heavily made-up eyes and golden Egyptian jewelry, and in later years, for her giant hair and for wearing diamond necklaces with caftans.

Talitha Getty (1940–1971)

The socialite Talitha Getty died in 1971 from a heroin overdose, but not before she made her mark on fashion generations to come as an icon of bohemian style. An international beauty married to the heir of an American banking dynasty, she lived in a castle in Morocco and threw fabulous parties filled with rock stars, fashion designers, and lots of drugs. Getty is known for her flowing caftans, for her exotic style, and for an oft-referenced photograph taken at the castle where she is crouching against a wall wearing boots and a caftan.

Jimi Hendrix (1942–1970)

James Marshall "Jimi" Hendrix is considered one of the greatest rock guitarists who ever lived. His albums topped the charts, he headlined Woodstock, and was at one point the highest paid musician in the world. Although he died of complications from a drug overdose at the age of twenty-seven, he made an impression on the fashion world that is still heavily referenced today. Hendrix understood the power of image and created a look based on his love of vintage fashion, mixing it with the psychedelic

Figure 8.8e
Jimi Hendrix

styles popular at the time. Classic Hendrix style includes velvet, lots of gauzy scarves wrapped around the neck, Native American jewelry, low-slung bell bottom pants, and the pièce de resistance, a gilded vintage Hussars Military jacket. (See Figure 8.8e.)

Grace Jones (1948–)
Revered for her fierce, powerful, and sexy androgynous style, the Jamaican-born Grace Jones has been a fashion inspiration to top designers and a provocative muse for photographs for decades. Jones is a singer, model, actress, and author. Her signature look is a close-cropped square afro with wraparound sunglasses, but anytime a model is seen stomping down the runway in a power suit, or is photographed with a cigarette dangling from her mouth or wearing only colorful, geometric body paint, chances are it's a nod to Jones.

Madonna (1958–)
Born Madonna Louise Ciccone, this American actress, singer, author, and philanthropist is so famous she only needs one name. Although Madonna has inhabited numerous styles across her career, each one is so fully realized that each phase can be used as style shorthand. For example, "Lucky Star Madonna" refers to a rebellious, tulle-skirted girl with messy hair, layered crucifixes, and rows of rubber bracelets along her arms, while "Papa Don't Preach Madonna" means a bleach-blonde pixie cut in a striped sailor top and ballet flats.

The Rat Pack
The Rat Pack of the 1960s was comprised of five actors and entertainers: Frank Sinatra (1915–1998), Dean Martin (1917–1995), Joey Bishop (1918–2007), Peter Lawford (1923–1984), and Sammy Davis Jr. (1925–1990). Collectively, their style was slim-fitting custom-made suits each with their individual flair. They were known as much for their talents as they were for their style.

> "It's a new era in fashion—there are no rules. It's all about the individual and personal style, wearing high-end, low-end, classic labels, and up-and-coming designers all together."
> —Alexander McQueen, fashion designer

INDUSTRY INTERVIEW

Interview with Ise White

After styling Michelle Obama in 2011 and being featured by Italian *Vanity Fair* for her work, Ise White joined Italian *Conde Nast* for eight years as a contributing fashion editor before moving to *Hearst International* and freelance-styling for U.S. publications and celebrities. She has produced some of the most globally recognized iconic covers of the past few years and has also served as lead art director at Onassis, Saks, and Elie Tahari.

Website: *www.isewhite.com*
Instagram: *@Isewhitestylist*
Twitter: *@Isewhite*

What celebrities, companies, or high-profile clients have you worked with?
There's a celeb link on my site, but my top favs are Helen Mirren, Michelle Obama, Robert Redford, Ewan McGregor.

How did you get into the fashion industry? Did you have formal training, or is it something that evolved or you fell into?

My family is in fashion. My aunt is a pattern maker; my other aunt was a costume designer for the Danish Opera. And my mother was trained as a dressmaker. I was in the art world as a painter and a writer, and I kept getting pulled into fashion. I realized that was where I was meant to be.

Did you go straight into styling, or did you assist first?

I went straight into styling without assisting. I was very lucky.

Now that you are styling, what qualities do you look for in an assistant?

Organization, the ability to think on their feet. Loyalty, communication. I also have a strict zero drug policy during jobs.

What kinds of job duties did you do when you first started working?

I started off as a fashion editor.

What's something you wish someone had told you before you started? What advice would you give your younger self about styling?

Give yourself time; don't feel you have to have a style right away; this needs to evolve naturally. It takes five years to really have the skills to start, ten years to get over your own arrogance; by fifteen years you can start to have something to say.

What do you feel is a common mistake that many people make when they first start out in the industry? Or a common misconception about what you do?

Everyone is rushing to get to some undetermined finish line. This is a craft, and a craft takes time to develop. You must travel, gain experience, grow as a person to become a great artist.

What's your philosophy of styling or dressing a client?

I always try to dress them to not just look the best but to feel the best. Especially for red carpet and long events, I try to find them shoes that will work for the entire evening and outfits they can eat and breathe in without sacrificing style.

Where do you like to shop?

I don't have a lot of time or patience for shopping. So I will usually do sample sales: make a list of all the items I need to update my wardrobe for that season and usually [I add] an "It" bag.

Who are some of your favorite designers?

I personally own a lot of Alexander McQueen and Dolce. But I also love Saint Laurent, Givenchy, and for casual wear, Rag and Bone.

What are some hidden gems or offbeat places where you pick up stuff for jobs?
There are a few consignment boutiques and stores that are stylist owned. I love Pilgrim in NYC, Reciproque in Paris. I missed out on this Kenzo jacket and years later on a job in Paris I found a mint condition one at Reciproque. In NYC I also love Opening ceremony, Assembly, Carolina Sarria, Odd. In Paris, where would we be without Colette?!

How much of your own personal style can be influenced on a job?
An ad job should only be influenced by my sensibilities, not my personal taste; an editorial has to be influenced by my personal taste, like a thumbprint.

Who are your muses? How or where do you find inspiration?
I look up to Polly Mellon. She's everything I think an editor should be.

What's something that you don't like about being a stylist? If you could change something about the industry, what would it be?
I really love my job. There's a lot of politics in the job, negotiations on a level that would make a treaty negotiator proud. Your skills in this arena to be a successful editor must grow with the job, and I always jokingly have said that if I ever want to quit fashion I'd go work for the CIA as a fixer; it's the same skill set. If I could change anything, it would be to encourage healthy body images and weights. Sometimes people are quite cruel to each other, especially the talent; I never allow such behavior on my sets.

It can be difficult keeping track of so many items on a big job or when juggling a multitude of shoots. How do you keep organized? Do you have a special system, so to speak, that you like to use?
I have my own system, but with every first assistant and new team, there has to be an evolution, a compromise in working styles. The best assistants trained with Conde, Hearst, or Interview. They like me and are OCD about details. We take photos of everything, and lists upon lists.

Name a styling tip.
Never dress for a trend; always dress for your body and for your personality. Dress to give yourself and your audience a feeling. Sometimes for fun, dress way outside your comfort zone and stretch those fashion muscles.

How do you present your work (e.g., website, portfolio, comp cards)? How did you establish your aesthetic or brand?
I have a website, a comp card of that year's covers I use for thank-you notes, and a business card which is more of a calling card. My agents and I work together to tailor the work presentation for each agency, and I have my own site which is branded with its typeface and simple presentation to reflect my personality: straightforward, elegant, and forthcoming.

How have technology and social media changed the styling profession and fashion industry?
It has mostly in this: When I started in the biz, when we worked with a celebrity or client, we were to keep it in the strictest confidence. Now you see the artists as much in front of the camera as their clients. With social media everyone wants to be a star. I believe it's still about the work first.

Summary and Review

Stylists and all members of a photo shoot team rely on fashion terminology throughout every phase of a job. This terminology is especially applicable when discussing inspirations and reference points for the styling, lighting, and poses that will be used. Being able to talk about film influences, specific style icons, and other design icons is invaluable.

Clothing terminology is critical knowledge for fashion stylists. They use it to communicate verbally and in writing. Being fluent in clothing terminology is especially important when writing editorial credits. Knowing key designers, eras, and influences is crucial to communicating in the styling industry. Editorials are constantly referencing the past. Now more than ever, the fashion world is drawing from a wide variety of influences. Our era is unlike any other simply because of the wide variety of clothing available in the marketplace.

Key Terms

- clothing-construction terminology
- design terminology
- fashion icon
- hand
- iconic style
- knit fabrics
- natural fibers
- shapewear
- synthetic fibers
- woven fabrics

Review Questions

1. List three reasons why a stylist must keep up with what's going on in the fashion world.

2. List an example of a type of garment typically made from a hand-woven weave, a twill weave, and a satin weave.

3. Why should a personal stylist be familiar with different types of tops? List two examples of shapewear for men.

4. What information should a stylist include when writing an editorial credit for a gold and diamond necklace?

5. What is design terminology, and why is it important for stylists to understand its principles?

6. What makes a garment iconic?

7. How do historical eras inspire designers?

8. List three popular items of clothing or accessories that are associated with a fashion icon.

9. Who do you think is missing from the list of fashion icons and why?

Learning Activities

Learning Activity 8.1: Create a collaged look based on an iconic movie. Use one of the movies listed under "Must-See Movies." Research the movie and create a complete outfit based on the looks of one or more of the characters. The outfit should have shoes and be fully accessorized. Include a description, price, and brand or designer name next to each outfit piece. Create the collage on 8.5- × 11-inch paper.

Learning Activity 8.2: Choose three designers from the following list. Write a paragraph for each of the three explaining how they have been influenced by art, music, movies, subcultures, or fashion icons. Cite specific examples of collections that show this connection.

Raf Simons
Rodarte (Kate Mulleavy, Laura Mulleavy)
Lisa Perry
John Varvatos
Alexander McQueen
Jeremy Scott
Public School (Maxwell Osborne and Dao-Yi Chow)

Learning Activity 8.3: Choose five fashion icons from the list in this chapter. Be sure to choose a mix of men and women, living and dead. For each icon, find and print out a photo of one of his or her signature looks. Then, research current fashion collections. For each example of an icon's look, match that with a photo of a look from a recent collection that was inspired by the icon's look.

RESOURCES

Abling, Bina. *Fashion Sketchbook*. New York: Fairchild Books, 2008.

"About Diane." DVF.com. http://www.dvf.com/about-diane-von-furstenberg.html.

"Biography." Josephine Baker. http://www.cmgww.com/stars/baker/about/index.php.

Cohen, Allen C., and Ingrid Johnson. *J. J. Pizzuto's Fabric Science*. New York: Fairchild Books, 2010.

"Different Types of Watches." Gevril Group. http://gevrilgroup.com/watch-types/.

Doonan, Simon. "What Is a Fashion Icon?" *Slate*. November 18, 2011. http://www.slate.com/articles/life /doonan/2011/11/fashion_icons_the_seven_kinds_.html.

Dwight, Eleanor. "The Divine Mrs. V." *New York Stores*. November 4, 2002. http://nymag.com/nymetro/shopping /fashion/features/n_7930.

"Elizabeth Taylor Biography." https://en.wikipedia.org/wiki/Elizabeth_Taylor.

Fox, Adam. "Cary Grant: Style Icon." AskMen. https://www.askmen.com/fashion/style_icon/58_style-icon-cary -grant.html.

Fox, Adam. "Style Icon: Jimi Hendrix." AskMen. http://www.askmen.com/fashion/style_icon_100/126_style-icon -jimi-hendrix.html.

Gaga Fashionland. http://gagafashionland.com.

"Gemstone Cuts." Jewels for Me. https://www.jewelsforme.com/gem_and_jewelry_library/gemstone_cuts.

"Grace Kelly Biography." The Biography Channel. http://www.thebiographychannel.co.uk/biographies/grace-kelly.html.

"IMDb Charts: Top Movies: Votes by Decade." IMDb. http://www.imdb.com/chart.

"Iris Apfel." Wikipedia. https://en.wikipedia.org/wiki/Iris_Apfel.

"James Dean Biography." The Biography Channel. http://www.thebiographychannel.co.uk/biographies/james-dean.html.

"Jewelry Education—Rings, Earrings, Necklaces, Clasps." JTV Blog. May 2011. http://www.jtv.com/library/jewelry -education.html.

"Katharine Hepburn." IMDb. http://www.imdb.com/name/nm0000031.

"Lady Gaga." IMDb. http://www.imdb.com/name/nm3078932.

Lebland, Romuald, and Jessica Vaillat. "Muses: Talitha Getty." The Red List. http://theredlist.com/wiki-2-24-525-770 -771-view-1960s-4-profile-talitha-getty.html.

Lester, Tracey Lomrantz. "A Brief, Chic History of the Motorcycle Jacket (AKA Fall's Must-Have Item). *Glamour*. August 25, 2009. http://www.glamour.com/story/a-brief-chic-history-of-the-mo.

"Madonna." *Wikipedia*. https://en.wikipedia.org/wiki/Madonna_%28entertainer%29.

"Marilyn Monroe." IMDb. http://www.imdb.com/name/nm0000054.

"Marvin Gaye Biography." The Biography Channel. http://www.thebiographychannel.co.uk/biographies/marvin -gaye.html.

McFadden, Robert D. "Death of a First Lady; Jacqueline Kennedy Onassis Dies of Cancer at 64." *The New York Times*. May 20, 1994. http://www.nytimes.com/learning/general/onthisday/bday/0728.html.

McRobie, Linda Rodriguez. "The Classy Rise of the Trench Coat." *Smithsonian*. May 27, 2015. http://www .smithsonianmag.com/history/trench-coat-made-its-mark-world-war-i-180955397/.

"The Most Iconic Designs of All Time." Elite Traveler. http://www.elitetraveler.com/features/most-iconic-designs-of-all-time.

"Movies." IMDb. http://www.imdb.com.

Nemy, Enid. "C. Z. Guest, Society Royalty, Dies at 83." *The New York Times*. November 9, 2003. http://www .nytimes.com/2003/11/09/nyregion/c-z-guest-society-royalty-dies-at-83.html.

Okwodu, Janelle. "Why Grace Jones, at 68, Remains the Ultimate Fashion Muse." *Vogue*. May 20, 2016. http://www.vogue.com/article/grace-jones-fashion-icon-turns-68.

"Our Earring Styles." Shane Co. http://www.shaneco.com/Jewelry-Education/Earring-Styles/.

"The Rat Pack." The Biography Channel. www.biography.com.

Rigg, Natalie. "How Audrey Hepburn Became a Style Icon: Her 8 Chicest Screen Moments." https://www.vogue .com/article/audrey-hepburn-chicest-moments-on-film.

"The Top Ten Fashion Icons." Style.com. http://www.style.com/trendsshopping/stylenotes/090710_Top_Ten _Fashion_Icons.

Vreeland, Lisa Immordino. "Diana Vreeland." *Harper's Bazaar*. August 26, 2011. http://www.harpersbazaar.com /magazine/feature-articles/diana-vreeland-bazaar-years-0911.

Wang, Connie. "The Weird, True History of the Wrap Dress." Refinery29.com. October 22, 2013. http://www .refinery29.com/2013/10/55868/dvf-wrap-dress-anniversary.

9 Preparing for a Test Shoot

CHAPTER TOPICS CALL SHEET

In this chapter you will learn:
- The benefits of testing and assisting
- How to prepare for a test shoot
- Pulling and prepping for the shoot
- How to assemble a killer styling kit
- What happens after the shoot

TESTING AND ASSISTING: HOW TO BUILD A PORTFOLIO AND GAIN EXPERIENCE

As introduced previously, testing is an essential part of building and maintaining a styling portfolio. It provides essential experience with shoot preparations, on-set etiquette, and the ins and outs of creating a visually successful photograph. Another term for testing is "TFP," which is short for "Trade for Print" (also "Time for Print" or "Test for Print"), meaning everyone is donating time in exchange for photos. Testing gives the aspiring stylist total creative control of the clothing used in a shoot, as well as heavy input on the concept or story. (See Figure 9.1.) Testing contrasts with paid shoots in that on a paid shoot the art director or client tends to have more, if not all, of the creative control, so the stylist has to make compromises.

Testing isn't the only way to build a portfolio. Assisting a lead stylist can also provide valuable experience. Assisting can be unpaid or sometimes pay a small fee, but there are other benefits. Lead stylists have a wealth of knowledge to share. They may also pass along paying job offers that they can't fit into their schedules, so it's worthwhile to cultivate those contacts with other stylists. It is best to think of other local stylists as professional peers rather than cutthroat competitors. Most beginning stylists build their portfolios with pictures from both test shoots and assisting shoots, if the lead stylist agrees to it. Some lead stylists are

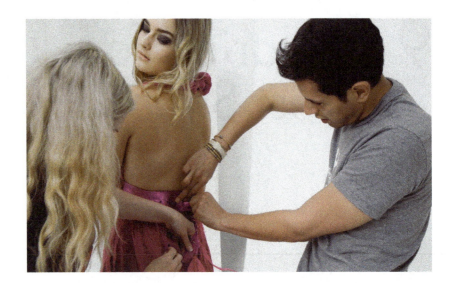

Figure 9.1
Testing gives the aspiring stylist total creative control of the clothing used in a shoot, as well as heavy input on the concept or story.

fine with their assistants using photos from past work, as long as it's noted in the editorial credits that the assistant was not the lead stylist. Beginning stylists use these portfolios to get hired for jobs, and as they start getting paying work they swap out the older photos with new tear sheets from paid jobs.

Testing for Portfolio Photos

Both beginning and experienced professional stylists participate in test shoots, but for different reasons. For aspiring stylists, testing is usually a way to build a portfolio. For professionals it is a way to add to existing portfolios. A test shoot allows the participants to have total creative control without answering to a client. (See Figure 9.2.) It is also a good way for all participants to get portfolio photos for very little cost. Testing allows the photographer and stylist to experiment with different ideas and themes that they may not get to try otherwise. In the end, the photographer, stylist, model, hair stylist, and makeup artist all get pictures for their portfolios.

"I had tried a lot of different things, and I just had heard about this job and I thought, 'I'm going to be a stylist!' . . . I literally started testing, and I put this book together and the next thing I know, I was working with great photographers and doing this job."
—Lori Goldstein, fashion editor-at-large. Elle Magazine, *http://www.thedailybeast.com /articles/2013/11/07/meet-the-stylist-behind-some-of-fashions-most-iconic-images.*

Figure 9.2
For professionals a test shoot is a way to add to existing portfolios. A test shoot allows the participants to have total creative control without answering to a client.

> "You have to intern and learn. You have to put that time in. No one makes it overnight; the industry requires a lot of hard work and you have to sacrifice a lot."
> —Meghan Blalock, associate editor, StyleCaster, http://stylecaster.com/how-to-break-into-fashion/.

HOW TO PREPARE FOR A TEST SHOOT

In a test shoot, an inexperienced stylist gets the opportunity to be the lead stylist. If a stylist has never been to a shoot or participated in one, it can be a daunting prospect. After all, there is a lot to organize, a lot to plan, and a lot that can go wrong. That is why careful preparation and organization are crucial before testing. Preparing for a test shoot includes finding a group of people who want to test, discussing story ideas in preliminary meetings, assembling a storyboard, orchestrating clothing and props, assembling a styling kit, writing up cheat sheets, and performing final wardrobe prep.

Assembling the Test Team

Anyone can look for people who want to test. Sometimes it is the stylist who organizes it; other times it might be a photographer or a modeling agency. The roles that need to be filled for a test shoot are fashion stylist, photographer, model, hair stylist, and makeup artist. Sometimes the hair stylist and makeup artist are one and the same person. Other times, in a pinch, a model can do his or her own hair and makeup. A stylist's initial goal for a test shoot should be to find people to fill all of the roles so that he or she can focus on fashion styling.

Finding a Photographer

Finding a good photographer who wants to test is a great stroke of luck for any stylist. Many stylists have a favorite photographer who they work with, and many photographers have a favorite stylist. A good photographer–stylist relationship inspires beautiful images. For a stylist, there is nothing like the feeling of helping to capture an image at exactly the right moment. The best styling takes place when the photographer and stylist understand each other and have a symbiotic relationship. Ideally they should bring out the best in each other.

Good places to start looking for photographers who want to test are local colleges and art schools with photography departments. Usually student photographers are also building portfolios and would love the opportunity to work with a budding stylist. A department chair or instructors can often pair stylists with good student photographers.

Professional photographers sometimes test too. Aspiring stylists who have an opportunity to test with one are lucky. Professional photographers are usually skilled, and they charge highly for their services.

Finding the Talent and Hair and Makeup Stylists

Once a stylist finds a photographer, they agree on the story or theme for the photo shoot and discuss what types of clothing and props will be necessary. They also start talking right away about where to find models, hair stylists, and makeup artists. Trendy beauty boutiques like M.A.C. and Sephora are good places to find hair and makeup artists who are trying to build side businesses or practice their skills and might want to donate their time to a test shoot. Upscale salons and beauty schools also can be options. It's important to find a hair stylist who can create on-trend looks that are much different from a prom updo and a makeup artist who knows what's new and also how to create a look that photographs well, which is different from what looks good in person.

Models who want to test often can be found through local modeling agencies. Agencies usually have a list of models who are just starting out and need to build their book, too, in order to book jobs. (See Figure 9.3.) They need photos that showcase the range of looks they can achieve.

It can sometimes be intimidating to find and work with a model on a first test shoot. It is tempting for people to ask a

Figure 9.3
A **book** is a model's portfolio that showcases the range of looks he or she can achieve. New models often haven't had many paying jobs. However, they need photographs for their books in order to get hired professionally, so they need to test.

relative or friend to model, out of convenience. It might be more comfortable to approach someone familiar who is tall and attractive, but this is a terrible idea. An experienced model knows which poses work best for his or her body and adjusts accordingly. A good model allows the photographer to simply shoot and doesn't have to be directed as much as a novice. (See Figure 9.4.) In the end, what is the point of putting all of the effort and work into organizing a test shoot if the model isn't right? A bad model can ruin a shoot and become a major distraction when viewers see the final product.

Planning the Theme in Preliminary Meetings

When it comes to the story or concept of a shoot, the stylist, photographer, and art director will be the main decision makers. (See Figure 9.5.) Great places to look for test-shoot inspiration are magazines, vintage photographs, movies, art, and pop culture. This is why it is essential for stylists to stay informed. When it comes time to think of concepts for a shoot, an informed stylist has more material to draw from.

Figure 9.4
An experienced model knows which poses work best for his or her body and adjusts accordingly.

Figure 9.5
When it comes to the story or concept of a shoot, the stylist and photographer will be the main decision makers.

Budgeting for Expenses

Everyone working on a test shoot is working for free, but that doesn't mean testing is free. A stylist must be prepared for the expenses associated with a test shoot. Generally, team members absorb the expenses associated with their part in the test. For example, a makeup artist covers the cost of cosmetics, and hair stylists will buy any products, wigs, and extensions needed to achieve the desired look of the test. If there are additional expenses like location fees, however, it is up to the team to decide how to divvy them up.

Having the Preliminary Meeting

It is best, if possible, to have at least one face-to-face meeting among all participants before a test shoot, even if this ends up being over Skype or Facetime. This is especially true for a stylist who is testing for the first time. The preliminary meeting should cover the game plan for the shoot. This includes agreeing upon a time, place, and theme. It's also important to talk with the photographer about his or her schedule following the test to determine a ballpark time when everyone on the team should expect to receive the photos from the test. It can be helpful to ask for both high-resolution versions, for print or portfolio use, and low-resolution versions, for posting on social media. Be sure to exchange email addresses in case everyone has been communicating via text only.

Another discussion point should involve marketing and social media goals. For example, the makeup artist might want a few "action shots" while he's painting the model to post his website and Instagram feed, so the photographer should be given a heads-up in case this requires that she needs to bring a different lens.

Because the fashion stylist is often orchestrating the test shoot, he or she might have to meet with other participants individually when people can't agree on a meeting time. At the very least, the other participants' reliability can be gauged by how they treat the meeting and whether they are late or no-shows.

Inspiration and Ideas for Test Shoots

When an aspiring stylist starts to think about testing, it can be difficult to know where to begin. A good place to start looking for ideas is fashion magazines, where different editorials can jump-start inspiration. Stylists are always making note of locations that might be good for shoots. Once the brainstorming process begins, the possibilities become endless. Here are some inspiration and location ideas.

- Glamorous gowns worn in front of old buildings
- Futuristic clothing worn in a junkyard
- Swimwear on a deserted beach
- Funky clothing and accessories in an art gallery
- Minimalist clothing in a modern architectural setting
- Bold statement accessories worn only with a white T-shirt in a studio setting

There is also a lot to be said for a very simple test shoot that revolves around a classic garment, such as a trench coat or white button-down shirt. Keeping a narrow focus can free up the stylist to hone technical skills, such as creating a good sharp crease, or clipping the garment in the back to create the perfect fit. The photographer can create drama with lighting, and the model can work the clothes with his or her poses and expressions.

OTHER CONSIDERATIONS FOR THE TEST SHOOT

Using a Storyboard to Communicate Visually

The only way for a photographer, hair stylist, makeup artist, and model to understand a fashion stylist's vision is to see it. Describing the same look in an email can yield four completely different perceptions, so ideas need to be shown in pictures so that there is less room for interpretation. The fashion stylist creates a storyboard beforehand so that everyone has a visual touchstone on the day of the shoot.

As introduced in Chapter 2, a storyboard is a collection of magazine clippings attached to a piece of poster board that show the fashion story, lighting, hair, and makeup that the stylist has in mind. Storyboard clippings usually come from a stylist's **clip file**, a collection of pictures torn from fashion magazines. (See Figure 9.6.) Most designers and stylists maintain these collections. A clip file includes pictures of fashion, makeup, and hair ideas that appeal to the stylist, and it is a great source of inspiration for future projects.

If possible, it is best to email all shoot participants a few storyboard clips before the shoot so that they have an idea of what to expect. The stylist can also bring storyboards to preliminary meetings.

Sourcing Clothing

Testing is not like a professional shoot, where the stylist can borrow clothing for free in exchange for editorial credits. This can make pulling merchandise more difficult, and the temptation exists to simply buy everything and return it after the shoot. While this is certainly easy, it is not the best option. It can be

Figure 9.6
A clip file includes pictures of fashion, makeup, and hair ideas that appeal to the stylist. It is a great source of inspiration for future projects.

cost-prohibitive, especially for a beginning stylist, and if something is damaged, the stylist will be stuck with the item and the bill. Also, if a stylist does this too many times, he or she could jeopardize a relationship with a smaller store and get "flagged" at a larger store, making returns more difficult in the future. Instead, a stylist should approach a test shoot as a chance to experiment with a variety of different sources that are not always available on a commissioned shoot. Here are six creative ways to source clothes, accessories, and shoes for test shoots:

1. Shop closets: Most stylists love fashion, and they usually have collected a fair share of fabulous pieces that they'd love to use on a shoot. Also, stylists tend to have fashionable friends who might be willing to loan an item or two. This also works for product-styling shoots. It doesn't matter if the stylist or the stylist's friend is a different size than the model or even a different gender; there can be plenty of items that would work, from motorcycle jackets and men's shirts to belts, jewelry, and bags. Be creative!

2. Shop the stylist's own studio: This is a great opportunity to repurpose items purchased for a shoot in the past that have been collecting dust on a rolling rack. The stylist can also use shoes and accessory staples that have been purchased for his or her kit (see the section "Prepping the Styling Kit" for more information).

3. Discount stores, consignment shops, and thrift stores: These sources are often off-limits on an editorial shoot when it's imperative to use in-season items, but sometimes the most dramatic merchandise can be found on a discounter's damaged clothing rack or in a consignment shop. (See Figure 9.7.) Vintage items also can work for some shoots. Websites like eBay, Tradesy.com, and TheRealReal.com are great place to find good deals on pre-owned designer clothing from recent seasons, and a stylist can always turn around and sell the items again once the shoot is over.

4. Boutiques and designers: This is the time to call in favors and reach out to friends in the fashion industry. While test photos aren't often published, a stylist sometimes can offer photos to a boutique to use for promotion in exchange for pulling merchandise. Most professional photographers have their own **copyright release form** that they are accustomed to using. (See Figure 9.8.) If the photographer gives the boutique owner rights to reproduce an image, then he or she signs a release form that states which images the boutique owner can use and the ways in which they can be used. An easier and faster alternative is to offer the retailer some camera phone photos and videos instead. After all, there's nothing like "behind-the-scenes" images to spice up any social media feed and spread some hashtag love. If a stylist has a strong connection to someone in fashion PR or at a showroom, this also might result in a pull. Everyone understands the importance of testing, and even older PR reps, designers, and showroom managers were beginners once.

5. Clothing rental services: In larger cities like Los Angeles and New York, a department store or showroom might offer this service for a fee (often a percentage of the total amount of the merchandise pulled), or if this option is not available to a stylist, check out clothing rental websites like RentTheRunway.com. While neither option is necessarily inexpensive, both allow a stylist to access on-trend, designer styles, and even one or two pieces can elevate the taste level of a shoot.

6. Bonus resource: Never shy away from asking the model if he or she happens to own a desired item that he or she can bring to the shoot to use. Models love fashion, too, and often they have fabulous pieces they'd love to show off, and they're guaranteed to fit!

Figure 9.7
A good way to find a shoot concept is to visit a local thrift store or a friend's closet before deciding on a shoot theme.

Flashpoint Photography Studios

234 Oak Avenue
Mytown, USA 54321
(555) 555-5555
www.flashpointphoto.com
info@flashpointphoto.com

Copyright Release

Photographer name: _____

Photographer e-mail / phone #: _____

Copyright requestor name: _____

Copyright requestor e-mail / phone #: _____

I (*photographer name*) grant permission to (*copyright requestor name*) to reproduce the following images for personal portfolio use only. These images may not be used for commercial promotional purposes.

Image description(s):
1. _____
2. _____
3. _____
4. _____
5. _____

Photographer signature: _____ Date: _____

Copyright requestor signature: _____ Date: _____

Figure 9.8
Most professional photographers have their own copyright release form that they are accustomed to using.

Sourcing Props

Props can be great when used selectively in a photo shoot. Sometimes they can be a distraction from the subject, so they need to be chosen carefully. (See Figure 9.9.) Start noticing the props that are shown in published editorials. They tend to be very simple and often go unnoticed because they don't take away from the model and clothing. Some great props are a simple chair, a giant painting, pillows set on a sofa, or solid-color low platforms for sitting or lying down.

Props to Avoid

- Silk flowers: Difficult to find ones that look good for the camera. Stick with real flowers instead.
- Wicker furniture: Can snag clothing and take away from the styling because it is too busy visually.
- Playing cards, poker tables, or other gambling props: Tend to be overused. These props work great for a lifestyle shoot for advertising, but not for an editorial shoot. They would be great in an ad for Las Vegas or for a casino.
- Any car manufactured after 1980: Classic cars can add great panache to an image, but a newer car doesn't necessarily have a "cool vintage" feel.
- Lollipops or other candy that the model eats while posing: Hard to make work and can easily become overly provocative and trite. There are many pictures of scantily clad models eating lollipops, and a marketable styling portfolio needs to be more imaginative.
- Sofas or other furniture that is overstuffed: Use furniture with clean lines, which tend to have a more classic and timeless look.
- Seasonal or holiday items such as Santa hats or jack-o'-lanterns: These items are great in lifestyle shoots for advertisements. Props like these would be appropriate in an advertisement for a party store, for example. They are not the best props for editorial shoots.
- Fabrics or home accessories with abundant tassels or fringe: Props with a lot of design details tend to detract from the actual fashion styling of a shoot.
- Televisions or other large electronic devices: Hard to make work in a shoot because they don't photograph well and are so quickly obsolete. Exceptions are electronic devices that are more than thirty years old, because they might have retro charm.

Figure 9.9
Props can be great when used selectively in a photo shoot. Sometimes they can be a distraction from the subject, so they need to be chosen carefully.

PREPPING THE STYLING KIT

A styling kit is a collection of tools that enables stylists to do their jobs properly and efficiently. It often includes a portable garment rack, a garment steamer, a lint brush, and myriad other clothing-care items. These kits should be assembled at least a day or two before the first test shoot, and stylists must always double-check and replenish their kits before every shoot.

If possible, it is best to invest in top-quality items when building a kit. In the end, it is more expensive to buy a cheap garment steamer and have to replace it when it breaks or does not work well.

It is essential for stylists to be prepared with proper tools for a shoot. Being unprepared is unprofessional. If you aren't prepared, it's possible that the art director or photographer will remember and pass you up for the next job. Another reason is that being unprepared can cost money in postproduction (all of the work that goes into a photograph after that shoot is over). Usually that work entails retouching using computer-graphics software, and imperfections like price tags sticking out of a collar or a watch face that's upside-down can cost the client money to fix.

The following is a basic list of indispensable professional tools. Many fashion stylists have their own must-haves that go beyond this list. (See Table 9.1, "The Styling Kit.")

Online Sources for Styling-Kit Supplies

Supplies for styling kits can often be purchased at fabric stores, art-supply stores, and office-supply stores. Some websites are also good sources for necessary tools. Following are some styling-kit sources for industry-specific and specialty items:

- Manhattan Wardrobe Supply (wardrobesupplies.com)
- Western Costume Company Supply Store (lawardrobesupplies.com)
- American Hanger and Fixture Corporation (americanhanger.com)
- The Container Store (containerstore.com)

The Styling Kit

Toolbox

Tool belt

Rolling rack

Rack dividers

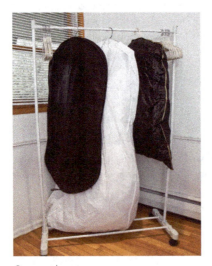

Garment bags

Hanging mesh bags

Ziploc bags

Plastic hangers with cotton hanger covers

Tagging gun with refills

Iron

Garment steamer

Ironing surface

Plastic clothespins

Hem tape

Chicken cutlets

Breast petals

Mesh hair and makeup
protector hood

Garment guards

Static-cling removal tools

Clothing shaver

Wet wipes

Hand sanitizer

Laundry stain-removal tools

Lint remover

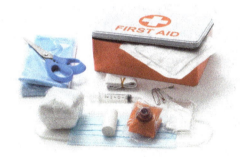

First-aid kit

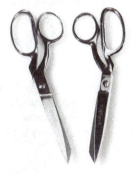

Scissors

Clipboard with paper

Permanent marker and pen

Components of the Styling Kit

Toolbox

A **toolbox** holds kit materials. Sometimes, it can literally be a toolkit; many stylists favor large rolling hardware organizers like those available from major home improvement stores because they have multiple drawers and sectioned compartments, and they have wheels and a handle, which makes them ultraportable. Other stylists are able to fit their kit essentials into a tote bag or a large cross-body bag.

Tool Belt

Fashion stylists, hair stylists, and makeup artists often wear **tool belts** while shooting. For fashion stylists, they hold some smaller items such as clothing clips or a lint roller. For makeup artists, tool belts hold items such as pressed powder and makeup sponges. Because stylists usually stand on the periphery of a shot during shooting, they need easy access to these quick-fix items so that they can jump into the shot to make adjustments. One thing to keep in mind when purchasing a tool belt is that it's best to buy one made for stylists. They are more compact, stylish, and streamlined than those purchased at home improvement stores.

Rolling Rack

A **rolling rack** is a portable folding rack with wheels that is used for hanging clothing. It should fold flat and be lightweight for easy transport and storage. A stylist uses the rack at home to organize clothing before a shoot, putting clothing into garment bags to be transported to the shoot. Once on location, the rack is unfolded, and the clothing is hung to be steamed and prepped to be shot.

Rack Dividers

Rack dividers are plastic plates that fit on a rolling rack between hangers. Dividers are especially useful for larger shoots or shoots with multiple models. They help to keep the clothing organized and to keep track of which garments go together. They are sold as blank plastic plates, and labels can be affixed to them if the stylist desires.

Garment Bags

Often when a professional stylist borrows clothing from a store, the retailer puts it in a disposable plastic garment bag for protection. A stylist's goal with borrowed merchandise is to return it in perfect condition. Sometimes if an item is damaged, the cost comes out of the stylist's pocket, not the client's. This means that careful transporting is vital, and it's good to get in the habit of protecting garments from the beginning. Purchasing durable garment bags with zippers helps to ensure that clothing has another layer of protection. Clothing might be transported to a shoot in a car, where it is difficult to avoid errant smudges and stains. Any type of good-quality garment bag is sufficient, but clear ones are easier to use because it is possible to see what is inside without having to unzip the entire bag.

Hanging Mesh Bags or Ziploc Bags

Hanging mesh bags with divided sections are a great way to organize small items such as jewelry. The bag can be hung on a rolling rack or a hanger along with garments and used to store any number of small items. Also, Ziploc bags are great organizers and can be attached to hangers to help match garments with their coordinating accessories.

Quality Hangers

A garment may hang from a wooden or cushioned hanger in a boutique, but when the manager loans it to a stylist, chances are he or she will change out that expensive hanger for a plastic one. Plastic and wire hangers are not good for clothes, and they are not durable enough for transportation or for holding extra weight from plastic bags full of accessories. Wooden hangers can snag clothing and also are heavy and add weight to a stylist's already heavy merchandise load. A good alternative is the velvet flocked hanger. These are widely available and can even be found at Target and Walmart. A stylist should invest in several sets of these hangers and transfer clothing to these hangers once they arrive in the studio.

Assorted Shoes

It can be handy to have a few pairs of women's and men's shoes in a few larger different sizes. These sizes can be difficult to find, especially at the last minute. Make sure to have a few different styles like a wingtip style for men and a high heel pump and sandal for women. While these shoes can't be used for styling editorial fashion shoots, they can come in handy for commercial shoots and test shoots or when styling fashion shows where shoes are not provided.

Tagging Gun with Refills

A **tagging gun** is used in retail stores to attach hangtags and price tags to clothing. When a stylist borrows clothing for a shoot, the tags might be able to be left on the clothing if they don't interfere with the photographer's shot. Sometimes tags can be discreetly tucked into clothing and hidden while shooting. Other times it is necessary to remove tags. Tags can be reattached to garments right after the model changes out of them. If a stylist is removing several tags, it is best to reattach them as soon as possible. Losing track of which garments match each tag can spell trouble. If tags are incorrectly reattached to garments, it can cause problems for retailers when they try to sell them at a later date. There are several different types of tagging guns for different weights of fabric, but a beginning stylist need only have a standard tag gun.

Garment Steamer

Garment steamers are a must for stylist kits. They are the safest way to remove wrinkles on delicate fabrics like chiffon and for taking out creases on garments that often come folded, like men's dress shirts. Most stylists have a garment steamer with a larger water tank that sits on the floor. These devices are also good for freshening borrowed clothes after a shoot before returning them to the retailer. On set, however, a stylist usually brings a travel-sized steamer because it's more portable. For all steamers, it's best to fill the water tank with distilled water only because sometimes tap water has a high mineral content, which can damage fabric or the machine itself. Hard water can cause metal components inside a machine to rust. In addition, when the steam comes out, iron stains can splatter onto fabric.

Iron and Ironing Surface

Unlike steamers that remove wrinkles, irons flatten fibers and create creases in fabric. Irons are necessary to create crisp collars, cuffs, and creases. It is important that a stylist know which fabrics and items need to be steamed and which are more responsive to an iron. A stylist's iron must allow for temperature control depending on fabric types. If it is not possible to bring an ironing board onset, an ironing blanket is a handy thing to have, allowing ironing to be done on any surface. A pro tip for collars, laces, pussy bows, and other thin fabric strips is to use a ceramic flat iron from a beauty-supply store.

Clips and Clamps

Often a model's clothing looks like it fits perfectly from the front, but it is a different story from the back. If the model is turned around, a network of clips and pins sometimes is revealed. These are necessary for adjusting the fit of clothing from behind. A stylist needs to own a variety of clips and clamps, including small plastic clothespins, metal bulldog clips, and spring clamps in a variety of different sizes. This will ensure the stylist can adjust anything, from a sleeve to the corset of a bridal gown.

Straight Pins and Safety Pins

Sometimes it's the small things that make the biggest difference, and sometimes there's no substitute for a simple straight pin or safety pin. Be sure to keep these in their own boxes and also to have a variety of different sizes of safety pins. These come in handy in hundreds of ways, from lengthening a necklace to keeping hang tags together.

Strong Double-Sided Tape

Ultra-strong double-sided tape is perfect for keeping hems in place and necklines from moving, and it can be removed in a jiffy from fabric or skin. Many stylists swear by Topstick hairpiece adhesive strips.

Chicken Cutlets and Silicone Covers

It is essential to have these two items on set when styling women. **Chicken cutlets** are gel inserts that are used to fill out the bust and can be especially helpful when shooting swimwear and evening wear.

Silicone covers smooth over and obscure nipples, which can eliminate the need to retouch when the model is wearing sheer fabric or an open knit without a bra underneath. Petals do the same thing, but because they have decorative edges, they can create visible lines under fabric. Both items can be reused, but a stylist should clean them after every use.

Mesh Hair and Makeup Protector Hoods
Made from washable nylon chiffon, these zippered hoods cover models' heads and protect their hair and faces, as well as the stylist's clothing, while they are dressing and changing.

Undergarments and Socks
Models have kits, too, that they are supposed to bring on set, and included in these are different styles of neutral-colored bras and camisoles and a seamless thong underwear. In the event that a model forgets to bring these, it's important to be prepared.

Garment Guards
Garment guards are underarm shields that protect borrowed garments from models' perspiration stains. They can also save the stylist from costly dry-cleaning bills before returning borrowed clothing to the retailer. They are especially useful on warm sets or shoot locations in hot climates.

Static-Cling Removal Tools
Static cling can be a problem during a shoot, especially with thinner fabrics. There are a few options for fixing this problem. The first option is sprays. Static removal spray and aerosol hair spray remove static cling in clothing. Another option is lotion, applied lightly to the model so that fabric doesn't stick to him or her. Use discretion if clothing is borrowed for the shoot because it must be returned in perfect condition. Fabric-softener sheets can be rubbed onto the model's skin to remove cling as well, but unscented ones are best for borrowed clothing.

Clothing Shaver or Sweater Stone
Pills are small balls of fibers on a fabric's surface. They come from repeated friction that dislodges the individual fibers and causes them to cling together in a ball. Common areas for pilling are under arms and on sides of clothing. A clothing shaver or a sweater stone can solve the problem in a pinch and keep fabric pills from ruining a shot.

Wet Wipes and Hand Sanitizer
Wet wipes can be used to clean a variety of things so that clothing stays clean. Hand sanitizer is also a good thing to carry, just in case.

Stain-Removal Tools

A stylist is a master of stain removal. Most stylists have multiple types of solvents to tackle stains caused by makeup, grease, and dirt as well as to remove adhesive or residue left from price tags, masking tape fails, and anything else that can and does happen on set. An aspiring stylist should start with a bottle of Goo Gone, a liquid solvent to dissolve makeup stains, a general stain-remover pen, and a deodorant removal sponge.

Sewing Kit

A stylist must have a basic sewing kit to attend to small details like reattaching clothing labels or reattaching buttons or snaps.

Lint Remover

Lint on clothing can ruin a shot and require retouching afterward. A lint roller covered in disposable adhesive paper, a lint brush, and washable, reusable lint rollers are options for a kit.

Tape

A stylist must mask shoes to make sure they are not damaged. Ideally, the stylist would do this the day before in his or her studio, but it's important to be prepared for anything, so it can be helpful to bring along a roll of masking tape, along with regular clear tape and double-sided tape.

Cotton Balls and Cotton Makeup Remover Pads

These are inexpensive items that can come in handy, especially when using stain-remover solvents.

First-Aid Kit

This is good to have in case someone gets hurt. Bandages are especially important so that no one gets blood on the clothing.

Scissors, Clipboard with Paper, Permanent Marker, and Pen

These are handy for clipping threads, labeling, and jotting down notes.

Helpful Extras

It's a stylist's responsibility to anticipate anything and to be prepared for anything. Experience is the best teacher as to what extras to add to a kit, but here are ten items that can be handy to have on set:

1. Phone charger cable and plug
2. Roll of quarters

3. White tank top
4. Hard candy like Lifesavers or lemon drops
5. Over-the-counter allergy pills and a pain reliever like Advil
6. AA batteries
7. Twisty ties
8. Hair elastics
9. Tampons
10. Nail polish remover

WRITING UP CHEAT SHEETS

As introduced in Chapter 2, cheat sheets are typed summaries of outfits and accessories for each scene or shot. A stylist should be taking notes while he or she prepares for a test shoot and plans how clothing will coordinate. The notes summarize the outfits for each shot. They should read like editorial credits and include accurate clothing descriptions and designer names. Prices and retailer information are also included on cheat sheets for paying jobs, but not for test shoots. In paying jobs, cheat sheets help stylists to keep track of editorial credits that appear in the magazine. In a test shoot, cheat sheets are simply used for organization.

["I started working as a fashion assistant when I was 20. I mostly worked for free. That is how it is in fashion—nobody gets paid at the beginning. I always knew that it would be difficult, but I was motivated to succeed."
—"Alice," fashion assistant, https://www.vice.com/en_us/article/fashion-assistants-paris -fashion-week-876?utm_source=vicetwitterus.]

THE DAY OF THE SHOOT

A test shoot can be wonderful or not so wonderful. Testing can be especially difficult when there are students involved. It is common to have people commit but then not show up on the day of the shoot. The best-case scenario for a test shoot is when a professional or student photographer wants to build a fashion-photography portfolio. At the same time, a talented and reliable hair stylist, makeup artist, and model all want to build their portfolios. Everyone comes together and has a great time working together. Everyone thinks highly of the job everyone else is doing, so much so that they plan to test together again in the future.

However, the reality is that everyone is working for free, and if something better comes along to fill their schedules, they may be no-shows who could ruin the shoot for everyone else. It isn't uncommon to have to scramble for a model for a test shoot, or for the student fashion stylist to have to do hair and makeup. For this reason, a basic working knowledge of photography, hair and makeup styling, and modeling poses can help a fashion stylist save a test shoot that's headed toward disaster. It is always advisable to be prepared for disaster so that the shoot can go on, especially if the test shoot is a class project and a grade hangs in the balance.

A great way to salvage a shoot if the photographer doesn't show up is to know some photography basics and carry a digital camera. A cell phone is never ideal, but some of the lenses on newer models can produce some amazing results. Hopefully the stylist won't have to take his or her camera or phone out, but if the photographer is a no-show, at least the shoot can still go on. Lighting, composition, and background need to be taken into consideration to get a decent picture.

Hair and Makeup Basics

If the no-show to the test shoot is the person in charge of hair and makeup, it is best to stick to a simple, clean look. Often a model will know how to do his or her own hair and makeup, but in the event a stylist must pitch in, here are some helpful items to bring along:

BASIC ITEMS

- [ ] Translucent pressed powder and disposable sponge applicator
- [ ] Bronzer and a clean powder brush
- [ ] Mascara and disposable wands
- [ ] Black and blond eyebrow pencils (flatter all brows) plus sharpener
- [ ] Clear lip gloss applied with finger or clean lip brush
- [ ] Hair spray and dry shampoo
- [ ] Fine- and wide-tooth combs
- [ ] Blond and black bobby pins and clear hair elastics
- [ ] Flatiron and wide-barrel curling iron
- [ ] Light moisturizer for face and body

INVESTMENT ITEMS

The following "investment items" add up to a bigger expense. However, if a stylist is testing a lot, they might come in handy.

- [ ] Pressed powder palette with disposable sponge applicators
- [ ] Bronzer and blush palette with brushes in two sizes
- [ ] Eyelash curler
- [ ] Neutral eye-shadow palette
- [ ] Lip-color palette
- [ ] Styling balm, serum, and/or texturizing spray
- [ ] Paddle brush and round brush
- [ ] Assorted headbands
- [ ] Blow dryer and water in spray bottle
- [ ] Body spray

Posing a Model

Models can sometimes be as unreliable as the other participants in a test shoot, and a last-minute stand-in sometimes is required. If the model was booked through an agency, the agent often can help to find a new model at the last minute. If this is the case, try to make sure the new model has the same shoe size as the model who couldn't come. While most models wear clothing that's between sizes 0 and 4, a model can have a shoe size anywhere from a 7 to a 12.

If the only option is to work with a nonmodel, understanding how to help pose and light a nonprofessional model can sometimes salvage the shoot and yield at least a few good pictures. In the end, the model's appearance should gel with the feel or theme of the shoot.

Certain tricks flatter and trim the model for the camera lens. As noted in the previous chapter, professional models know these tricks and pose accordingly. Nonprofessional models might need coaching during the shoot, so the stylist should know how to direct in case the photographer doesn't. The model should be elongated as much as possible from head to toe. For example, the model should stand at an angle to minimize hip width or hold the head up to avoid a double chin.

Before the stylist jumps in to direct, he or she always needs to run it by the photographer first. This is good professional etiquette, so it is good to get into this habit from the start.

[
"To establish yourself as a stylist, start testing as soon as possible . . . Building a portfolio, getting experience, and making contacts are the first steps in a styling career."
—"Alexandra," blogger. Alexandra, "Fashion 101: What Does a Stylist Do?" http:// searchingforstyle.com.
]

AFTER THE SHOOT

Once the shoot wraps, a stylist on a test shoot does what he or she does on any shoot: returns merchandise. Now, the responsibility shifts to the photographer to provide photos to everyone on the team from the shoot. Be patient. Retouching takes time, and a photographer may be balancing school or other paying jobs that must come first, which is why it is important to discuss timing expectations in the initial meeting. If it seems like the photographer is taking an inordinate amount of time in sending out photos, it is fine to send a short, polite reminder email.

Interview with Cynthia Altoriso

Cynthia was born in Brooklyn, New York, and attended college at Tyler School of Art at Temple University in Philadelphia. Tyler had a program in Rome, and when Cynthia first went to Rome as a student of nineteen years, she loved it so much that she stayed there. She dropped out of school and lived life in "la dolce vita."

Website: *www.cynthiaaltoriso.com*
Instagram: *@altorisonyc*

What celebrities, companies, or high-profile clients have you worked with?
Alan Cumming, Alec Baldwin, Joey Pantoliano, Simon Doonan, Nicholas Vreeland, Deepak Chopra, Alexander Vreeland, Sukey Forbes, Princess Keisha Omilana, Lizzy Jagger, Charlotte Kemp Muhl, Stella Schnabel, Lisa Vreeland, Katheryn Winnick, The Zombies, Jonny Cota/Skingraft, Jordan Eagles, Theodora Richards.

How did you get into the fashion industry? Did you have formal training, or is it something that evolved or you fell into?
My training was in fine art. I was always friends with artists and later, photographers.

I was used to being a muse to artists. I evolved into styling. I was, am, married to a noted backdrop artist who works with set stylists. I found myself styling shoots over the phone to his clients. If I knew that finding a prop would seal the deal, I became resourceful at finding it no matter how obscure. From there the styling developed. As an artist, I always had an eye and a knack for making people and things look "pretty."

Did you go straight into styling, or did you assist first?
In my youth, I assisted a stylist twice. Once we dressed Patti Hansen and the other time it was actor Rick Schroeder.

Now that you are styling, what qualities do you look for in an assistant?
PUNCTUALITY, dependability, respect and care for the garments and accessories, pleasant personality but no chatter on set, resourcefulness . . . don't wait to be told what to do, be observant and see what needs to be done, and no drama! Capable hands with steaming, ironing, pinning, and taping.

What kinds of job duties did you do when you first started working?
Sourcing clothes, arranging pickup and return of clothes, caring for the clothes as far as steaming, ironing, etc. Dressing models in preparation for camera.

Do you have any funny or horror stories of when you first started?
I had a model dressed in a very expensive white ermine coat; she got her period while standing there.

I had an actor walk into the bathroom while talking to me and he left the door wide open while peeing so as to continue talking.

Thankfully, no horror stories! I knock wood when I say I have never lost or damaged an item.

The downside of this is that my extreme focus renders me a bit detached from socializing. I call it being "in the zone." I may appear unfriendly, but it's about being in deep concentration.

What's something you wish someone had told you before you started? What advice would you give your younger self about styling?
Study problem-solving as far as potential clothing damage. Learn how to remove stains and perspiration odor.

Take pics of all hang tags with the garments so you know on which garments they belong for returns. This is especially helpful for high-volume wardrobe shoots.

Get used to folding and packing clothes quickly.

What do you feel is a common mistake that many people make when they first start out in the industry? Or a common misconception about what you do?
Don't assume you can purchase clothes for a photo shoot and be able to return. Some stores have strict return policies. Check before buying.

Styling might seem glamorous, but it is hard work. A lot of time goes into prepping; getting the clothes, fitting the models, and steaming the clothes is arduous and physical, and you're on your feet a lot. Even with assistants and messengers, it's a lot of "schlepping," as we say here in NYC.

Be on top of your emotions; as the saying goes, "Leave your ego at the door." Practice diplomacy and learn patience with needy or bratty models.

What's your philosophy of styling or dressing a client?
No matter who they are, man or woman, old or young, slender or plump, I seek to discover their beauty and celebrate it. I want my subjects to feel attractive so they feel good on set and perform accordingly before the camera. If they look good, I look good.

Tell us a little about your job role working with *Spirit and Flesh* magazine (also please include a magazine weblink).
www.spiritandflesh.com

I style, produce, art-direct, and write. I develop and provide story content.

Where do you like to shop?
Bergdorfs, abc home, Bloomingdale's, H & M, J Crew, Barneys, hardware stores and drugstores.

What are some of your favorite designers?
Maggie Norris Couture, Gabrielle Carlson, Etro, Maison Martin Margiela, Yohji Yamamoto, Commes des Garcons, Rag & Bone, Rodarte, Dries Van Noten, Dior, Balenciaga, Stella McCartney, Jil Sander, John Varvatos, David Hart, Stephen F. Palmer Trading, Lilith, Valentina Kova, etc., etc. These are quick answers off the top of my head; I'm sure there's many more.

What are some hidden gems or offbeat places where you pick up stuff for jobs?
Thrift shops, sporting goods like Modell's, Carhartt, Manhattan Saddlery, MJ Trim, Pearl River Mart, Mood Fabrics, Jamali Floral, Capezio, and the above-mentioned hardware and drugstores.

How much of your own personal style can be influenced on a job?
It's 50-50. If I'm producing as well as styling, it's mostly my choices.

If I'm hired to do wardrobe, I'm working with the client or the agency's direction.

Who are your muses? How or where do you find inspiration?
As far as muses, do you mean other stylists?

Since I am a historian, much of my inspiration is from classical portraits, or early designers such as Paul Poiret, Callot Soeurs, Madame Grès, Fortuny, also, nature: flowers, mosses, beetles, feathers, shells.

What's something that you don't like about being a stylist? If you could change something about the industry, what would it be?
The worst challenge for me is not having enough room to lay out all of my accessories. If you don't readily see things, chances are you won't use them. It's always a disappointment after a shoot to realize that you forgot to use a beautiful item because it got "lost" in a pile.

My personal dislike is having to prep clothes in a crowded location van.

Alas, as a visionary, it often seems that more time is spent in soul-numbing prep than in artistic creation.

And then there is the limitation of lack of time to create; ideally one likes to ponder and try out different solutions for a look. We tend to pull more than we use, and then there is the stress of snap judgment.

It can be difficult keeping track of so many items on a big job or when juggling a multitude of shoots. How do you keep organized? Do you have a special system, so to speak, that you like to use?
I always try to have assistants precisely to not only keep track, but to guard particularly costly items such as jewels and furs, or fragile items such as vintage pieces or lingerie.

I try to keep a "library" of iPhone pics as quick visual referencing so that I don't forget a piece.

Even on a rack, items can get "lost" to the eye if there's a lot of wardrobe.

Name a styling tip.
Keep lists.

Write the order of the looks; write down the accessories for each look.

Write everything down: names, addresses, and contact numbers of designers and showrooms.

This info is important to have ready at your fingertips.

You need to make returns soon after the project.

SUMMARY AND REVIEW

Testing is an excellent way to build a styling portfolio. Testing allows the stylist to be more creative because he or she is collaborating with a photographer without the input of a lead stylist or a client. However, testing requires extensive preparation. Prep work includes meetings, communication, and schedule coordination. It also requires creativity in sourcing, pulling clothing, and assembling a styling kit. The styling kit is a toolbox that holds technical tools needed by the stylist for the job. Most of these tools relate to adjusting and caring for clothing, but a stylist must try to be prepared for any situation that could affect a shoot, from a headache to a ripped-out hem.

KEY TERMS

- chicken cutlets
- clip file
- copyright release form
- garment guards
- rack dividers
- rolling rack
- tagging gun
- tool belt
- toolbox

REVIEW QUESTIONS

1. List three reasons why a stylist should always be testing.
2. Where should a stylist look to find models for a test shoot?
3. Why is it important to have a face-to-face discussion with the creative team when planning a test shoot?
4. List three things that a creative team must discuss when planning a test shoot.
5. How do stylists use storyboards in preparation for a test shoot?
6. List and discuss three alternative resources for sourcing merchandise for a test shoot.
7. List three props that should be avoided in a test shoot and explain why.
8. What do you think are the three most important items in a styling kit and why?
9. Name one item not listed in this book that a stylist could put in his or her kit that could come in handy on set.
10. What happens to photos taken on a test shoot?

LEARNING ACTIVITIES

Learning Activity 9.1: This activity has two options: one for people who want to do a test shoot and the other for those who don't.

Option 1: If you want to do a test shoot, assemble what you think are the ten most essential items for your styling kit. Find an organized way to carry them, such as a tackle box or bag with compartments. Bring your kit to class to share for feedback.

Option 2: If you don't want to do a test shoot, create a collage of what you think are the ten most essential items for a styling kit. Copy and paste them on a standard-size piece of paper. Source the kit items from online retailers and note the price of each. Add up the total cost on the page to give you an idea of the financial investment required to create a kit.

Learning Activity 9.2: Conduct an internet search for test shoots. Find one photographer or stylist who has posted some test shoots on his or her website. Look through all of the tests and write at least a half-page summary and critique of what you might have done differently.

Learning Activity 9.3: You are a stylist creating a plan for a test shoot. Decide on a theme for the shoot, and describe the look you are trying to create. Make a list of ten sources where you can find merchandise to style the shoot. These sources must be a mix of online resources, brick-and-mortar businesses, and people that you know. Next to each source, write a sentence or two summarizing what merchandise is to be sourced and how much it will cost.

RESOURCES

Cox, Susan Linnet. *Photo Styling: How to Build Your Career and Succeed*. New York: Allworth Press, 2006.

Dingemans, Jo. *Mastering Fashion Styling*. Philadelphia: Trans-Atlantic Publications, 1999.

"Lessons with Luke: Test Shoots." YouTube. May 26, 2016. https://www.youtube.com/watch?v=yvrQN-mtRks.

"Looking Inside a Wardrobe Kit." Manhattan Wardrobe Supply. http://blog.wardrobesupplies.com/2011/01/19/looking-inside-a-wardrobe-kit/.

Matthews, Erica. "Fashion Stylist Tutorials | The Stylist Tools Kit—The Essentials a Stylist Carries Everywhere!" YouTube. January 26, 2016. https://www.youtube.com/watch?v=1GCc_Agc124.

"Photographers Copyright Form." Templatesample.com. March 6, 2012. http://www.templatesample.net/2012/03/photographers-copyright-form.html.

Sasso, Ben. "Test Shoot with Models: Why & How." http://bensasso.com/blog/shoot-tips-test-shoots/.

Serrano, Amy. "Wardrobe Kit Styling Essentials." YouTube. October 10, 2016. https://www.youtube.com/watch?v=fqw97LvvNU0.

"Stylists' Wardrobe Kit and Survival Tips." The Fashion Spot. July 23, 2004. http://forums.thefashionspot.com/f90/stylists-wardrobe-kit-survival-tips-26929.html.

"Time for Print." *Wikipedia*. https://en.wikipedia.org/wiki/Time_for_print.

10 At the Shoot

CHAPTER TOPICS CALL SHEET

In this chapter you will learn:
- Winning behavior and etiquette tips for the stylist on a shoot
- Photography and composition basics
- Essential tasks to perform on the day after the shoot

WHAT TO DO ON A SET

A shoot can take anywhere from a few hours to several days. A standard day on set can last up to 12 hours, so everyone needs to be prepared to be very busy for the entire time. (See Figure 10.1.) There are a few key points to remember that will take some stress off the stylist: dress for comfort, know when to arrive at the shoot, and use proper shoot etiquette.

Dress for Function, Not for Fashion

The stylist usually doesn't get to sit down much at a shoot, so it is best to dress for comfort. A shoot is not the time to wear high heels or show off a trendy but impractical outfit. A stylist should be dressed to work. That said, there are some style tips that a stylist should follow when shooting in a studio and on location.

In a Studio

1. Dress neatly and professionally. Comfortable clothing does not mean a ratty flannel shirt and sweat pants (unless they are Alexander Wang!). Jeans and a T-shirt are fine if they are neat, clean,

and fashionably accessorized. Any pants must be flexible enough for the stylist to bend and move, and any top must allow the stylist to move his or her arms to steam, hang, and reach.

2. For women, be wary of wearing a dress or skirt. There are many times on set when a stylist, and especially an assistant stylist, will be on his or her hands and knees. For example, a stylist must help models into their shoes on set, and a stylist must tape hems once the garments are on the models.

3. Dress in layers. No matter the weather outside, inside can be a different story. The air conditioning might be broken, or the building might be an ice box. Dressing in layers will help a stylist feel comfortable regardless of the situation. One thing a stylist must never do, however, is complain about being hot or cold.

4. Have an edge. Many stylists find it helpful to attach clamps and clips to the edge of a pocket or shirt tail or to the side of a cardigan so that he or she can fix a garment in a pinch without having to go back and forth to his or her styling kit or wear a tool belt.

5. Bring socks. Comfortable shoes are a necessity, and wearing fashion sneakers or flat slides without socks is perfectly acceptable. It is, however, important to bring a pair of socks that can be worn in the studio. When a stylist is working on a model in the space where the model is being photographed, the photographer might prohibit shoes so that the floor area can be kept clean. A stylist must be able to move quickly back and forth from his or her staging area to the shooting space without having to stop and put on or take off shoes. Socks solve this problem.

On Location

1. A location shoot can be anywhere from a deserted island to a busy city street. It is imperative to dress for the location. Talk to others on the team or other stylists and ask for their suggestions on what to wear.

2. When packing a kit for a location shoot, be sure to add sunscreen, bug spray, and any other item that might be helpful on set.
3. Dress in layers to account for temperature changes from morning to daytime to evening. Remember, the key to staying cool isn't always wearing fewer clothes; it's dressing smartly in light-colored clothing in breathable fabrics like linen and cotton.
4. Wear sensible footwear. Think about the type of terrain involved on the shoot. If it's in the city and involves lots of walking, wear comfortable shoes with good arch support. If it's in a field, be sure to wear closed-toe shoes that can get dirty. If it's on a beach, choose waterproof sandals that strap securely to the foot, because if the model has to get in the water, you do, too.

Respect the Call Time and Place

A call time is the time that everyone is expected to be on set and ready to start the shoot. A stylist should aim to be early in order to have all merchandise, rolling racks, and other items ready on set by the call time. As explained in Chapter 2, it's a good idea to map the directions before the day of the shoot and to check traffic conditions on a real-time navigation app in advance of departure time to account for any problems. Also, be sure that the call sheet includes information about arrival procedure. For example, if the studio is in a building, know where to park during and after unloading. If there is a lobby, know whether to check in with a receptionist first.

Even the most organized and prepared stylists can encounter problems on the way to a shoot. Do not assume the client will figure out that there was an accident on the freeway or a flight was delayed. The minute a problem arises that looks as if it could be serious, let the client know what is going on. Also, if a stylist has an agent, it might be wise to give the agent a heads-up, too.

When a stylist arrives on set following a delay, the stylist cannot walk around explaining or complaining. He or she has a job to do and time is money, so the best strategy is to apologize quickly and sincerely, and then get to work as soon as possible.

Use Proper Professional Etiquette

As just described, being punctual is the first thing that a stylist can do to make a good impression. Being prepared and organized with all necessary supplies is just as important. Always ask the client where to set up before unpacking; if the studio space is shared between shoots or publications, it may be very important to stay within a designated area. Usually a studio will provide a stylist with a table and chair at the very least, but you cannot make any assumptions as to the size or quality of the setup area. Consider bringing a blanket to set items on; garment bags also can be used, and you should be prepared to share space, power outlets, and tabletops. (See Figure 10.2.)

A stylist is responsible for all the merchandise he or she brings onto the set. Organization and neatness at all times are key, but it also is important to safeguard the merchandise. This means that if there's any monkey business or selfies being staged by creative team members, it's the stylist's responsibility to make sure it doesn't involve the merchandise. If any merchandise is damaged, it impacts the stylist's reputation, and if any selfies are posted to social media that involve horsing around with merchandise, this also could affect the stylist's reputation.

Safeguarding the merchandise is especially important at mealtimes and if the model wants a snack or a drink. If the team breaks for lunch, it is perfectly acceptable for a stylist to gently remind a model to

Figure 10.2
Studio or indoor shoot locations should be able to provide the stylist with a table and chair for the work area. However, this shouldn't be expected, and if no table is available, it might be advisable to bring a sheet or blanket to set things on.

change out of the merchandise he or she is wearing and return to his or her street clothes. Similarly, if a model would like to snack on set while wearing merchandise, it is acceptable for the stylist to make sure the snack won't put the clothing at risk. For example, never let a model eat berries, chocolate, or anything with a greasy or powdered residue like donuts or Cheetos unless he or she has changed back into street clothes. When it comes to drinks, be very careful about allowing a model to drink coffee or juice when wearing merchandise. Water is always best, and using a straw is preferable.

While the photographer is shooting, everyone else should be standing on the periphery of the shot, ready to step in and make adjustments when necessary. When a stylist needs to make adjustments, he or she must notify the photographer first. It can be intimidating for a stylist who is working with a professional photographer for the first time, but it is important, and the photographer wants the shot to be perfect, too. Just say calmly and politely, "May I jump in? I need to jump in to fix the model's shirt. The collar isn't lying flat." Giving a reason before jumping into a shot allows the photographer to have more control, plus have the ability to refuse if he or she likes the shot the way it is. A makeup artist should always be ready to ask to jump in as well, for example, with powder for shiny areas on the face.

Creative input from the stylist is often welcome. However, the stylist doesn't have the ultimate say, and teamwork is more important. Creative input might come in the form of pose suggestions for the model or makeup suggestions for the makeup artist. Teamwork means showing consideration for other ideas and making compromises.

> "For me, the most important aspects of my work is to give people something to dream about, just as I used to dream all those years ago as a child looking at beautiful photographs. I still weave dreams, finding inspiration wherever I can and looking for romance in the real, not the digital, world."
> —Grace Coddington, creative director at large, *Vogue. Grace Coddington,* Grace: A Memoir, *(New York: Random House, 2012), 332–333.*

Etiquette Example: Makeup Changes

On a paid shoot, the photographer and art director give final say about makeup, not the stylist. If they all work together regularly, then the stylist might be able to give suggestions, depending on comfort level. If this is their first time working together or they are not very familiar with one another, then the stylist should focus on the clothing only, and not other aspects of the shoot.

That said, the makeup and the clothes must work together, so if creative decisions are being made on set, it is important for everyone to communicate. The stylist also must notify the team if there is merchandise involved in a look that will affect a model's hair or face. For example, a hat or sunglasses affect not only the hair and makeup artist's plan but also can change the shoot order, and that affects the photographer and the art director. It might be easier to shoot a look with a hat last because the hair doesn't have to be fluffed back again for another look.

[
"Let the mua [makeup artist] know if there will be any exposed body parts like legs, so they can give some body makeup to make sure the skin looks flawless and matches the face."
—Rachel Toledo, celebrity makeup artist. www.rachelmakeup73.com
]

Etiquette Example: Dressing a Model

A stylist who cannot behave with respect and decorum around a naked person should rethink his or her career path. Photo shoot styling involves helping models in and out of clothing and adjusting garments in ways that sometimes requires touching or adjusting in areas that are usually off-limits. Sometimes such contact cannot be avoided, but it always must be professional, and the model must never, ever be made to feel uncomfortable. Regardless of the amount of clothing a model is wearing, the focus must always be on the task at hand, whether that is helping to take a top off without having it touch the model's red lips or adjusting the way a shirt is tucked into a model's pants. Do not stare, look away when it seems appropriate, and always give a model a quick heads-up if you need to pull, tug, adjust, or clamp in a sensitive area.

Etiquette Example: Fit Issues

It is a model's job to fit into clothing, and a model and his or her agency must make every effort to ensure that when the model arrives on set, he or she matches the measurements that were sent to the stylist in advance. If the stylist has not been able to have a fitting before the shoot, he or she must be ready for anything, and even a fraction of an inch can make the difference between an evening gown or a suit fitting or not. Sometimes, a model does not match his or her measurements because of weight gain. Other times, a showroom may have sent the wrong size, a sample could have been mislabeled, or a sample arrives that is damaged or stained. If any of this happens, a stylist must adapt and move forward. Luckily, clothing doesn't actually have to fit perfectly or even look good from all sides; it just has to look perfect within the frame of a photo.

The easiest rule of thumb for avoiding such issues is to always bring options, alternatives, and several different sizes of everything. If there is a serious fit issue that could affect the photos, the stylist must notify the photographer and art director. It is their call whether to try to work with the look or to move on to the next look, not the stylist's. If they decide to photograph the look, everyone can work together to adjust angles, lighting, and poses to mask any imperfections. A photographer also knows the extent to which a pulled or stretched seam can be fixed in postproduction. Above all, the stylist must not be rude to the model or complain about the situation.

Here are five ways to help make ill-fitting items look good in photographs:

1. If shoes don't fit, suggest the model hold them instead.
2. If pants won't zip up, experiment with leaving a shirt hem untucked or having the model pose at an angle.
3. If a back zipper can't be zipped or a back button cannot be fastened, use safety pins (or many safety pins connected together) to bridge a gap. Alternatively, the sides of a garment can be taped to a model's body with double-sided tape.
4. If shirt sleeves are too long, roll them up or put the model's arm through a hair elastic, bring it up to the elbow area, and manipulate the fabric over the elastic to create a natural blousing effect.
5. If a jacket doesn't fit, ask the model to pose holding it over the shoulder or position it across the shoulders without using the arm holes.

"When working with a hairstylist, you need to mind the model's hair. For example—clothing going over the head especially a turtleneck. Make sure you communicate with the hair person that clothing might be tricky to get over the head."
—Carmel Bianco, hairstylist. @raybrownpro-

FROM SUNRISE TO SUNSET: ON THE JOB

A photo shoot can be a very long day. Rarely are there complete breaks for the entire crew, except for perhaps a short meal break. However, each person gets the chance to have some downtime at different times. For example, while the makeup artist is working on the model, the fashion stylist might be able to use the restroom or run out to the car to fetch something. While the model is being prepped by hair and makeup, the photographer might have time to sit and have some coffee while scrolling through previously captured images and uploading them to a laptop. Slower periods when a stylist is not working with the model or photographer are still productive; for a stylist it might mean retagging or steaming a piece of clothing, making notes on the cheat sheet, organizing the kit, and making sure that everything gets put back. Every shoot, no matter if it's for print or film, has to fit into a certain time frame and requires rigorous work from the crew in order to meet deadlines.

Before packing up and leaving for the day, a stylist should make sure the cheat sheet has been correctly notated to reflect all of the outfits and the order in which they were shot. This should be done during shooting or directly after. On paid shoots, retailers and designers are counting on seeing their products correctly listed in editorial credits. Also, borrowed merchandise needs to be accounted for prior to leaving a shoot so nothing turns up missing. Be wary of throwing anything away, even empty boxes or crumpled bits of tissue that may look like trash. This way, if something is missing like an earring or an important garment tag, there is less of a chance that it was accidentally thrown away if it happened to fall into that empty box or tissue ball.

Photography Basics

Sometimes a stylist will be working one-on-one with a photographer. For example, a shoot may not use a model or a hair and makeup artist if it is shooting products or doing an off-figure fashion story. In these situations, there is more room for artistic collaboration. Knowing the basic skills of photography is helpful, as is understanding the art of photography. A great way to gain awareness of what makes a great shot is to study the best of the best. This can be done through formal education, but also by simply developing an interest in the greatest artists of photography. (See Figure 10.3.). Stylists also need to know these names and their work as a point of reference when working with photographers and clients.

Twenty Famous Fashion Photographers, Past and Present

These fashion photographers have produced iconic images and worked with the biggest names in modeling and fashion. Stylists need to know them as a point of reference when working with photographers and clients. This is by no means a comprehensive list. However, it is a good starting point in coming to understand the past and present world of fashion photography. Photographers are listed in alphabetical order by last name.

1. **Richard Avedon** (1923–2004)
2. **Cecil Beaton** (1904–1980)
3. **Corinne Day** (1965–2010)
4. **Patrick Demarchelier** (1943–present)
5. **Steven Klein** (1961–present)
6. **Nick Knight** (1958–present)
7. **David LaChapelle** (1963–present)
8. **Inez Van Lamsweede** (1961–present)
9. **Annie Leibovitz** (1949–present)
10. **Peter Lindbergh** (1944–present)
11. **Vinoodh Matadin** (1961–present)
12. **Craig McDean** (1964–present)
13. **Steven Meisel** (1954–present)
14. **Helmut Newton** (1920–2004)
15. **Irving Penn** (1917–2009)
16. **Terry Richardson** (1965–present)
17. **Herb Ritts** (1952–2002)
18. **Mario Testino** (1954–present)
19. **Ellen von Unwerth** (1954–present)
20. **Bruce Weber** (1946–present)

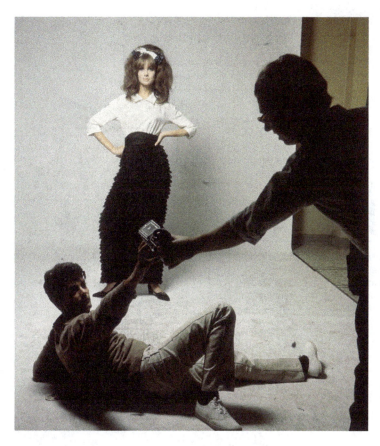

Figure 10.3
Richard Avedon at work on a shoot, preferably with a stylist at his side.

Focus on Lighting

The two main types of lighting are **natural** and **artificial**. Photographers make decisions about which type to use and then figure out how to obtain it. Planning a shoot to be outdoors in the early morning or late-afternoon hours is a good way to ensure nice lighting. The natural, more even golden light at those times makes beautiful pictures. If the shoot is planned for midday outdoors, the natural light won't be as good, and the colors might appear washed out. Using a flash outdoors during cloudy weather will illuminate the subject and compensate for flat lighting.

An indoor or studio shoot involves artificial lighting. The photographer typically works with a camera, a strobe, a light, and a collection of modifiers that change the light levels and how the light looks on camera to create the right mood for the shoot. For examples, a soft box or a translucent umbrella creates a softer, more diffused light by reducing the amount of light that reaches a model. A reflector can increase the amount of light landing on a model, resulting in a harder and more defined look. (See Figure 10.4.)

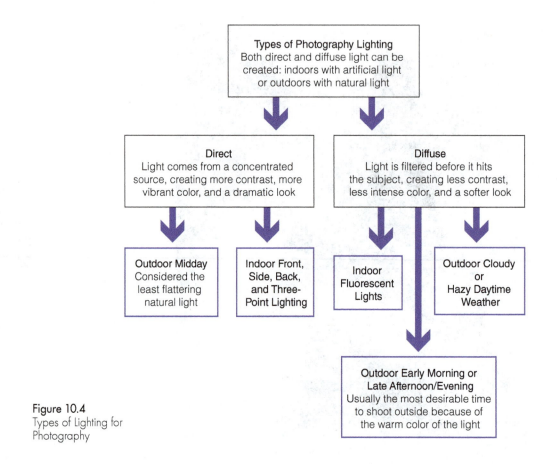

Figure 10.4
Types of Lighting for
Photography

Focus on Composition

Composition is the decision on how objects should appear within the frame. Generally, it is better to place the subject slightly off-center in the frame. (See "Composition Rules for Photography.") Getting down at the subject's eye level or slightly lower is the most flattering angle. People rarely look good when someone slightly taller photographs them. Their heads look disproportionately large to their bodies.

Focus on Background

A simple monochromatic background leaves the least room for error. A busy background can interfere with a good picture. It is best to treat the background like the props, meaning be selective when choosing. Posing the subject in front of a wall is a great alternative to using a backdrop.

Composition Rules for Photography

There are two composition rules that many photographers use as guidelines when shooting pictures or when cropping them after they are shot. Both rules can be helpful to stylists collaborating with photographers and to stylists who are cropping photos for their portfolios.

RULE OF THIRDS

The rule of thirds states that the focal point(s) of the photo should be placed on the four intersecting points or on the four horizontal or vertical lines. In this composition the frame is simply divided into thirds horizontally and vertically. The focal points might fall on one, some, or all four lines.

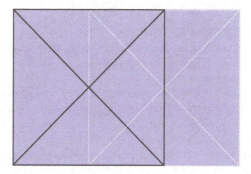

THE DIAGONAL RULE

The diagonal rule states that the focal point(s) of the photo should be placed on the four diagonal lines. In this composition two squares are drawn overlapping in the middle of the frame. Each square takes up two-thirds of the frame. Diagonal lines are drawn to connect the corners of each square.

THE DAY AFTER

The day after a paid shoot is different from the day after a test shoot. The test shoot doesn't require the stylist to bill a client or submit editorial credits. Like a test shoot, however, the day after a paid shoot is a good time to tie up all loose ends related to the job. This includes returning clothing, billing the client, restocking the kit, removing tear sheets from the storyboard, and filing the tear sheets for later use. Shoot days can often be long and exhausting, and it is tempting to procrastinate when it comes to the wrap work that needs to be done. It is best to schedule an open day on the day after a shoot so that all of these tasks can be completed efficiently and while the details of the shoot are still fresh in the stylist's mind. Often, for the paid shoot, time spent on wrap work can be billed to the client.

Invoicing

Invoicing for billable hours should be done soon after a job is complete. The quicker the client is billed, the faster the client will reimburse for the stylist's hard work.

Dealing with Merchandise Problems

If there was any damage to merchandise during a shoot, a stylist must deal with this after the shoot. Most important, don't panic. Most things can be fixed with focus and patience. If an item was stained, it may be easier to try removing the stain at home or in the studio rather during the hustle-bustle of the set. Research the stain and make sure to use the correct solvent in the right way. If there is time, it might be helpful to consult a professional drycleaner. If an item is ripped, it may be possible to make a quick repair or call in a tailor for a small fix. If an item is lost, it can be helpful to go back through everything brought back from the shoot, including items that look like trash. Be meticulous: check the bottoms of garment bags, look through all boxes, delve into and under the seats of the car, and then do it all again. It also may be helpful to call the art director and return to the studio to look around the set, especially in the dressing room, where the model may have left it by accident instead of returning it to the stylist after changing.

If the damage is major or an item truly is lost, a stylist must notify the PR representative, the retailer, or the designer immediately. Honesty is always the best policy. While damage is always regrettable, things happen, and people understand. That said, it is up to the stylist and the client to work with the merchandise owner to resolve the situation.

Returning Pulls

As noted in Chapter 2, pulls are merchandise borrowed for a shoot. All merchandise should be returned as soon as possible. This can mean doing in-person returns or mailing items back to a designer, showroom, or PR representative. Items pulled from retailers must be returned as soon as possible so that they can go back onto the sales floor. When the stylist returns items in person, the stylist must make sure that the person handling the return verifies that every pulled item has been included in the return. If there is paperwork to sign, be sure to get a copy or take a quick photo of the form. If there is no paperwork, a smart stylist makes a note of the date and time of the return and the name and title of the person processing the return.

For items mailed back, a stylist must be sure to pack the items carefully, preferably using the same packing materials that came with the merchandise. If there is paperwork to return, be sure to include it in the box and save a copy for your files. The stylist also must make sure to return the items to the correct contact. If it is unclear who that is, the stylist should make a quick call or send an email to find out exactly where to ship the items. This can make a big difference if the merchandise is expected in another city for a trunk show or if the merchandise must be returned to a brand's fulfillment center, not to its PR representative.

It is very important that a stylist use a shipping service that provides a tracking number and, when needed, the ability to purchase additional insurance. If the shipper did not include a prepaid mailing label, the stylist either must pay for the cost of shipping or use the client's account number. If the client is to reimburse the stylist for shipping expenses, that should have been negotiated at the time of booking, and the stylist will need a receipt to submit when invoicing. If the stylist is paying for shipping, a receipt must be kept so that the stylist can record it as a business expense at tax time.

The stylist should obtain an email, printout, or some other type of confirmation that shows the address the package was shipped to, along with the expected delivery date and the tracking information. A con-scientious stylist always sends an email to the contact that arranged for the pull with a heads-up that the package is in the mail and tracking information. Later, a stylist can use the tracking number to confirm that the package has been delivered to the intended recipient. Even if the package appears to have been delivered, a stylist should still save tracking information until he or she is certain that the package reached its intended recipient and the merchandise definitely has been returned safely.

Writing and Submitting Editorial Credits

Editorial credits should be submitted in their final-ized form as soon as possible after a shoot. These should be written while they are still fresh in the stylist's mind. If the cheat sheet was saved on a computer, often it can be opened, edited, and then submitted as editorial credits. (See Figure 10.5.)

Restocking the Kit and Tidying the Work Space

The day after either a paid or a test shoot is a good time to make sure that supplies are stocked, that papers are filed, and that the work space is ready for upcoming jobs. If supplies are running low in a kit, a stylist should make a point to replenish them.

Figure 10.5
Editorial credits should be submitted in their finalized form as soon as possible after a shoot. These should be written while they are still fresh in the stylist's mind.

When the Pictures Publish

It may be weeks or months before the stylist gets to see the result of his or her labor. Once the editorial or the commercial shoot has published, the stylist should save the images to import into his or her portfolio and to post on social media (making sure to tag everyone involved in the shoot, including designers and retailers). The agency also needs a copy of the link, if the stylist has agency representation. If the client restricted social media posts from the shoot until publication, this is a good time to look through casual snaps and videos and schedule posts. These posts are great marketing for the stylist, showing that he or she is busy with fabulous jobs and getting paid. A stylist also should reach out to the contacts that helped with pulls for the shoot with a quick email. The email should begin with a thank-you and include links to the photos. This is always appreciated, and it will go a long way toward building and maintaining relationships that help the stylist get the job done, beautifully, each and every time.

INDUSTRY INTERVIEW

Interview with Melissa Rodwell

Melissa Rodwell has been a fashion photographer for over thirty years. She is the owner of Breed Networks, LLC, which is the largest online educational website for fashion photography. She also owns and runs *Alice Magazine*, a rock 'n' roll/fashion magazine based in New York City.

Website: *www.melissarodwell.com/www.jointhebreed.com/www.alicemagazine.nyc*
Instagram: *@melissarodwell*
Twitter: *@MelissaRodwell*

What celebrities, companies, or high-profile clients have you worked with?
Nike, NBC Television, Coca Cola China, Rolls Royce, Honda, Ralph Lauren, Dell Computers, Chiat/Day, Innerscope Records, Virgin/EMI Records, Warner Brothers Music.

Cameron Diaz, Sam Elliot, Perry Farrell, Monet Mazur, Tom Jones, David Lee Roth.

How did you get into the industry? Did you have formal training, or is it something that evolved or you fell into?
I attended the Art Center College of Design and graduated in 1987. Back then, photography was a more difficult medium because of film. So I felt I needed an education to learn how to expose, develop, and print film. Nowadays, I don't think college is that important.

How important is it that the stylists you work with understand the style of your magazine?
For my magazine, it is very important for the stylist to understand the aesthetic. *Alice Magazine* is a rock 'n' roll fashion magazine, so everything HAS to be representative of this genre, and the stylist has to implicitly understand this.

What's your opinion or ethos when it comes to the photographer-stylist relationship on a job?
The relationship with the stylist is the most important relationship on an editorial. We have to share the same vision or at the least understand each other's vision. The stylist for a shoot must understand the mood and direction for each shoot. There is a lot of communication before we even arrive on set.

Did you have any funny or horror stories of working with stylists?
I once saw a stylist have a complete meltdown over a lack of hangers in a studio, which at the time was a horror story, but looking back I actually can laugh at it. I also worked on a shoot once for a magazine, which I will not mention, that hired two stylists for the same job, and these two stylists did not get along. They fought the entire shoot.

What do you feel is a common mistake that many stylists make when working with photographers?
A stylist has to work with the photographer. If they don't follow the direction of the photographer or try to take over and take control, it can make for a very complicated and difficult shoot.

Who are some of your favorite stylists, muses, or icons that have great style?
Sally Matthews from Harper's Bazaar Arabia was one of the best stylists I've worked with. She has an impeccable eye and an exquisite attention to detail. Diana Vreeland and Grace Coddington are huge icons for me. Their work is unsurpassed.

You also run an industry learning and networking website, The Breed. Please list the website information and tell us a little about what you do for photographers and stylists, the workshops, etc., and why you thought there was a need for this in the market.
www.jointhebreed.com

Breed started in 2013 after The Fashion Photography Blog, which was started in 2008. Many people in the fashion and fashion photography industry guard ideas, and my goal was to expose the method and process of fashion photography. It was always my vision to "expose" the inside world of fashion photography to those who were interested in it.

Anything else you would like to add?
Thank you for this opportunity! My thirty years in the industry has afforded me wonderful opportunities. I've traveled the world, met amazing people, and photographed beautiful people on incredible locations! It's been a dream life!

How do you network? Why is it important to build relationships in this industry?
I established my career pre-internet, so I learned how to cold-call people and meet people face to face. Now we have Facebook and Instagram, but I still believe in face-to-face meetings, and I'm one of the few people that prefers a phone call to a text message or email.

How do you present your work (e.g., website, portfolio, comp cards)? How did you establish your aesthetic or brand?
I used to use print portfolios and promo cards, but today I just have a website that I keep updated frequently, and I do use Facebook and Instagram.

How have technology and social media changed the styling profession and fashion industry?
In my opinion, social media sources have opened up the industry to a lot of people who really need to learn more about the medium of photography and the understanding of fashion and fashion design before calling themselves a fashion photographer.

Do you have any tips for working as a freelance or independent contractor (anything from tax tips to professional practice, like contracts and insurance, getting paid, setting rates)?
Please make sure you love this, that you love what you do! It's a tough industry; passion is a necessity! There are a lot of ups and down, lots of rejection; you have to develop a thick skin so you can get back up and keep on going!

Summary and Review

Shoot days are long, grueling, and incredibly rewarding. Safeguarding merchandise on set and making sure it looks beautiful in every frame is a big job, and one a stylist needs to do with kindness and courtesy. Every shoot requires teamwork, and understanding the basics of photography and composition can make it easier to work with a photographer. After a shoot, stylists have myriad responsibilities, like restocking their styling kits, returning merchandise, and writing editorial credits. Once the photos are published, stylists can send out links to their contacts and use the links and related social media pictures and videos for marketing and promotion.

Key Terms

- artificial light
- the diagonal rule
- invoicing
- natural light
- the rule of thirds

Review Questions

1. A stylist is booked for a two-day shoot. The first day is in a studio, and the second is on the beach. How should the stylist dress for both days' shoot?

2. What should a stylist do if he or she is running late to a shoot?

3. List three wardrobe problems that can occur and how a stylist can solve them.

4. Why is it necessary for a stylist to know about photography?

5. Which type of lighting is easier to control, indoor or outdoor lighting, and why?

6. How should the camera shoot a subject in order to get the most flattering picture?

7. What are three things a stylist must do before leaving the set?

8. How can a stylist safeguard merchandise when shipping it back to a retailer, designer, or PR representative?

9. What should a stylist do once the photos from a shoot are published?

10. List two ways a stylist can use behind-the-scenes photos and videos for marketing.

Learning Activities

Learning Activity 10.1: Create a photo shoot timeline. Choose a theme and begin the timeline a week before the shoot. Include pulling, prepping for the shoot, responsibilities on set, and tasks that lie ahead once a shoot wraps.

Learning Activity 10.2: Choose five photographers from the list of "Twenty Famous Fashion Photographers, Past and Present" on page 244.

Be sure the list contains a mix of living and dead photographers along with both men and women. Print out two examples of work from each photographer, and label each photo with the photographer's name, the year the photo was taken, and where it was published. For each photographer, write a paragraph-long biography, describe his or her signature style, and explain why that style does or does not appeal to you.

Learning Activity 10.3: Today's shoot has been your worst nightmare. Everything has gone wrong, and now that the shoot has wrapped, you must work to set things right. For each scenario of the following three scenarios, set out the steps you would take to remedy the situation, and if that did not work, explain in detail what you would do next.

1. While unpacking from the shoot in your studio, you realize that you are missing an earring that you pulled from a local retailer.
2. While packing up a garment that a PR representative sent to you, you realize that you do not know where to return the item, and you do not know who will pay for return shipping.
3. During the shoot, you notice a ring of makeup on a shirt collar that you bought from a department store and were hoping to return. You quickly brush it with solvent, but it does not come out.

RESOURCES

Barrows, Daniel. "Basic Types of Lighting in Photography." eHow. http://www.ehow.com/about_4740753_basic -types-lighting-photography.html.

Campbell, Naomi. "Naomi Campbell: 15 Favourite Fashion Photographers." *British Vogue*. http://inteveo.com /demos/fashion/vogue/www.vogue.co.uk/spy/15th-anniversary/naomi-campbell-.html.

Diagonal Method. http://www.diagonalmethod.info.

Grundberg, Andy. "Richard Avedon." *The New York Times*. http://topics.nytimes.com/topics/reference/timestopics /people/a/richard_avedon/index.html.

Kodak. "Top 10 Tips for Great Pictures." http://foundation.rch.org.au/library/b5_69/documents/7404.pdf.

McIntire, John. "Learn How to Set Up Studio Lighting in 15 Minutes." Digital Photography School. https://digital -photography-school.com/learn-how-to-setup-studio-lighting-in-15-minutes/.

"My Top 10 Favorite Fashion Photographers." Fashion Photography Blog. http://www.fashionphotographyblog .com/2008/12/my-top-10-favorite-fashion-photographers.

"Nigel Barker." IMDb. http://www.imdb.com/name/nm1521007.

"Top Fashion Photographers of All Times." Design Float Blog. March 9, 2011. http://www.designfloat.com/blog /2011/03/09/top-fashion-photographers-all-times.

Rutter, Chris. "Color Theory Fundamentals for Digital Photography." http://www.graphics.com/article-old/color -theory-fundamentals-digital-photography.

Glossary

APPLE-SHAPED BODY TYPE A body type that gains more weight in the stomach, chest, back, and sides.

ART DIRECTOR A member of a production team who provides creative vision, oversees a shoot, and communicates the client's wishes.

ARTIFICIAL LIGHT Light from an indoor source.

ASSETS Money, property, and other items of value that belong to a business.

ASSISTING The process of helping a lead stylist before, during, and after a photo shoot.

ASSOCIATION OF IMAGE CONSULTANTS INTERNATIONAL (AICI) An influential professional association for personal stylists.

BATTING Polyester fiberfill that is used to fill out an off-model-styled garment.

BLEEDS Printed photos where the image extends all the way to the edges of the page.

BOHEMIAN A clothing style for men and women that is sixties- and seventies-inspired.

BOOK Another word for a model's portfolio.

BOOKING AGREEMENT *See definition for* confirmation.

BOOKING A committed job on a stylist's calendar.

BRAND A stylist's unique professional image.

BREAKDOWN SHEETS Documents in which each scene from a script breakdown gets compartmentalized into sections.

BUSINESS PLAN A plan that spells out the important details of a business, such as marketing and funding.

CALL TIME The scheduled time to meet on a set or on location of a photo shoot.

CELEBRITY STYLISTS Personal stylists who work with celebrities.

CHEAT SHEETS Typed summaries of outfits and accessories for each scene or shot that help a stylist plan how clothing will coordinate.

CHICKEN CUTLETS Gel-insert breast pads that enlarge bustlines when placed in bras.

CLASSIC *See definition for* Modern Classic.

CLIENT The person or company that hires the stylist.

CLIP FILE A collection of inspirational pictures torn from fashion magazines.

CLOTHING-CONSTRUCTION TERMINOLOGY A general term that describes the vocabulary of garment details.

CONFIRMED JOB *See definition for* booking.

CONFIRMATION The initial form that a stylist drafts and submits to the client. It spells out the terms of the job, such as dates, job description, and rate of pay.

CONTINUITY Keeping film or television characters' appearances the same throughout; for the wardrobe stylist, it means that costumes look consistent if they are worn throughout multiple scenes.

CONTINUITY BIBLE *See definition for* costume bible.

CONTRACT *See definition for* confirmation.

COPYRIGHT RELEASE FORM A photographer's release form, which states which images can be reproduced for personal use.

COSTUME ATTENDANT *See definition for* costumer.

COSTUME BIBLE A binder that holds all of the information pertaining to a film production's wardrobe.

COSTUME DESIGNER A member of the production team who designs and constructs costumes for film or television production.

COSTUME SUPERVISOR A member of the production team who oversees fabric sourcing, cutting, and sewing for television and film costumes.

COSTUMER A member of the production team who works under the costume supervisor to help talent dress for each scene and to ensure that the costume department stays organized.

COUTURE Clothing that is made to order for specific clients using highly skilled construction techniques.

CREATIVE BRIEF A document that summarizes pertinent information about the client, the product being advertised, the target market, the purpose and main message of the ad, and the production schedule.

CREATIVE EDGY This personal style for men and women is characterized by interesting silhouettes or clothing construction techniques.

CRUISE *See definition for* Resort/Cruise.

CURVED LINES Lines such as ruffles that tend to soften a look and can sometimes add bulk.

DAY RATE The rate for a standard day's worth of professional service.

DESIGN TERMINOLOGY The general term for vocabulary that describes line, form, shape, space, texture, and pattern, as well as balance, emphasis, rhythm, proportion, and unity.

DESIGNER SHOWROOMS Places where designers keep samples. Sales representatives show the samples to buyers, who place orders.

DIAGONAL LINES Lines, such as asymmetrical hemlines, that direct the eye to a point on the body.

THE DIAGONAL RULE The focal point(s) of the photo should be placed on the four diagonal lines.

DRESS FORM A headless mannequin.

DRESSERS People who work behind the scenes at a fashion show to clothe models as quickly as possible.

DUPLICATE COSTUMES Kept in television and film wardrobe departments in case costumes go missing or get damaged.

EDITING The technique of rearranging raw film or television footage and changing the length of scenes.

EDITORIAL CREDITS A list found on fashion editorials that describes the clothing, explains where to buy it, indicates how much it costs, and tells who participated in the shoot.

EDITORIAL LOOK A description of a look that is more fashion-forward than an everyday look.

EDITORIAL STYLING The high-fashion styling seen in fashion magazines.

EFFECTIVE IMAGE A photo that fulfills the goals of the client and the creative team.

ENTERTAINMENT INDUSTRY STYLING Styling for professional performers who are being filmed or watched by the public, such as actors and musicians.

EXPENSES The operating costs incurred by a business.

FASHION EDITORIAL Published photographic fashion stories that are centered on a central idea or theme.

FASHION ICON A person with high-profile social presence, memorable personal style, and memorable personality/demeanor.

FASHION STYLING The process of orchestrating clothing and other fashion products for photo shoots, film shoots, fashion shows, and special events.

FASHION STYLIST The person responsible for coordinating the clothing, accessories, and other fashion merchandise necessary to create a specific outfit, image, or look.

FASHION TERMINOLOGY The wording used to describe the details and construction of clothing.

FASHION WEEK The week in a particular city during which designers debut their collections for either the spring/summer or the fall/winter season.

FLATLAY A style of arranging items in a photograph to be posted on social media.

FOOD STYLING Styling food to be photographed or filmed.

GARMENT GUARDS Underarm shields that protect borrowed garments from models' perspiration stains.

GLAMAZON A personal clothing style for women that is about sex appeal and not being afraid to be noticed.

GREEN LIGHT A term that means that the television or film producer and screenwriter have pitched their idea to a studio and the studio has agreed to provide funding.

GREEN ROOM A place for television or film talent to unwind before or after shooting.

GROSS RECEIPTS A record of any income made. These can include bank deposit slips and invoices.

HAND How fabric feels.

HOLD When a stylist is tentatively booked for a shoot, but a confirmation has not yet been signed.

HORIZONTAL LINES These lines tend to widen the areas of the body where they are worn.

HOURGLASS-SHAPED BODY TYPE A body type that has a defined waist with a full chest and full legs.

ICONIC STYLES Classic clothing pieces that are wardrobe building blocks and can add modernity and style to even the most envelope-pushing editorial piece.

IMAGE CONSULTANT A professional who works with clients to cultivate and refine a personal image.

IMAGE CONSULTING An area of the styling industry in which stylists help clients to refine their appearances and improve the way they are perceived.

IMAGE MANAGEMENT *See definition for* image consulting.

INTERNATIONAL ASSOCIATION OF CULINARY PROFESSIONALS (IACP) A professional association open to food stylists.

INVOICE A document submitted to the client after a job is completed. It summarizes all charges that are being billed to the client.

INVOICING The process of charging a client for billable hours.

KEY COSTUMER A member of the production department who assists the costume designer, helps ensure wardrobe stays within budget, and oversees fittings.

KNIT FABRICS Fabrics made of continuous strands of yarn that are looped together row by row.

LETTER OF RESPONSIBILITY (LOR) A letter (or a PDF of one) written on the client's letterhead that confirms the stylist has been hired for the specific job and that the client and/or the stylist will assume responsibility for the items borrowed.

LIFESTYLE STYLING A type of styling focused on a more overtly commercial goal, like a department store advertisement or website.

LINE DIRECTIONS The most basic elements of design; they serve as great examples of the kind of detail that every fashion stylist must work with. The four main line directions are horizontal, vertical, diagonal, and curved.

MARKET WEEK Held the week after Fashion Week when buyers place their orders for upcoming seasons.

MASKING The process of covering the soles of shoes with masking tape to prevent scuffing or other damage caused by contact with the ground.

MINIMALIST MODERN A clothing style for men and women that is about a very simple neutral color palette.

MOCK-UPS Food styling test runs that are set up to check composition and lighting. Mock-ups feature food that is similar to what will be shot.

MODERN CLASSIC The most timeless style category for men and women, defined by items such as white button-down shirts and loafers.

NATURAL FIBERS Fibers from natural plant, animal, or mineral sources.

NATURAL LIGHT Light from an outdoor source.

OFF-FIGURE STYLING Involves showing clothing folded, draped, or tacked to a board.

ON-FIGURE STYLING Styling clothing on dress forms.

PEAR-SHAPED BODY TYPE A body type that gains weight in the thighs, hips, bottom, and legs.

PERSONAL SHOPPERS Hired to shop for wardrobe pieces, gifts, or whatever else the client needs.

PERSONAL STYLISTS *See definition for* image consultant.

PHOTOGRAPHER The person who takes the photos on a set; the photographer may also be responsible for hiring the creative team and editing the photos.

PHOTO SHOOT STYLIST *See definition for* fashion stylist.

PORTFOLIO A collection of the stylist's work, either digital or in a hardcopy format, that conveys to the client that the stylist has the experience, the talent, and the work ethic to accomplish a client's goals.

POSTPRODUCTION (FOR FILM AND TELEVISION) The phase of editing and reshoots after a television or film production ends.

POSTPRODUCTION (FOR PRINT STYLISTS) Entails digitally editing photographs after the shoot is finished. Sometimes it involves fixing a shiny nose, erasing lint or wrinkles on clothing, or eliminating a blemish or two.

PREP WORK Preshoot responsibilities such as borrowing merchandise, organizing the styling kit, and typing a cheat sheet.

PREPRODUCTION Also known as the planning (prep) phase before a television or film production begins.

PRINCIPAL PHOTOGRAPHY Another word for the television or film production phase. There are no sound effects added yet, and the scenes aren't necessarily shot in chronological order. *See definition for* production.

PRINT STYLING Styling for a variety of print media. *See definition for* print stylists.

PRINT STYLISTS Stylists who work on photo shoots for different publications, including fashion magazines, nonfashion magazines, brochures, clothing catalogues, printed advertisements, and stock photography.

PRODUCER *See definition for* production manager.

PRODUCTION Also known as the set-work phase during a television or film production.

PRODUCTION MANAGER A member of the production team who provides creative vision, oversees a shoot, and communicates the client's wishes. *See definitions for* art director and producer.

PROP STYLING Styling props and background objects on the sets of television shows, films, commercials, home-catalogue shoots, and magazine shoots.

PULL Pulling is the process of borrowing clothing from retailers, PR agencies, or designer showrooms for a shoot.

PULL LETTER A letter that is issued or endorsed by the client. A stylist takes it to a retailer when pulling (borrowing) clothes. It assures the retailer that the stylist is not solely liable for any damaged merchandise.

RACK DIVIDERS Plastic plates that fit on a rolling rack between hangers. They help to keep the clothing organized and keep track of which garments go together.

READY-TO-WEAR Referring to clothing that is manufactured according to standard sizes and is sold in a store.

RESHOOTS When certain scenes of a film or television show are shot again after some changes have been made.

RESORT/CRUISE One of the three main ready-to-wear seasons/markets, along with Spring and Fall.

RISERS Pedestals used by visual merchandisers to showcase retail goods.

ROCK 'N' ROLL A men's and women's personal clothing style known for embellishment, combination of different elements, and mix of clothing from different places.

ROLLING RACK A portable folding rack with wheels that is used for hanging clothing.

ROMANTIC VINTAGE A very feminine personal style defined by delicate fabrics, lace, and vintage-inspired clothing.

THE RULE OF THIRDS The focal point(s) of the photo should be placed on the four intersecting points or on the four horizontal or vertical lines.

RUN OF SHOW A list of looks presented in a fashion show.

RUNWAY STYLING Involves coordinating accessories with clothing before they hit the runway.

SAMPLE Clothing created during the design process that is meant to show what a finished garment might look like when it is produced for sale.

SAMPLE SIZES The clothing sizes that correspond to American sizes 0 and 2.

SCRIPT BREAKDOWN Entails color-coding each television or film scene's cast members, extras, costumes, and hair/makeup.

SEE-NOW, BUY-NOW A system in which a collection is available for purchase immediately after a fashion show.

SET DESIGNING *See definition for* prop styling.

SET STYLING *See definition for* prop styling.

SHAPEWEAR Undergarments that smooth and trim body lines.

SITTING Another word for an editorial photo shoot.

SOURCING The process of finding clothing and other items for a shoot or job.

SPORTY *See definition for* Urban Sporty.

STORY The central inspirational theme of a photo shoot.

STORYBOARD (FOR FILM AND TELEVISION) Visual layouts of the script that are created in the preproduction phase.

STORYBOARD (FOR PHOTO SHOOT) Tear sheets and inspirational pictures from magazines or the internet collaged together onto a board. A storyboard is a visual communication tool.

STUDIO SERVICES A department of a major retailer where clothing can be borrowed for a film or television production.

STYLE CATEGORIES Different types of styles and tastes that define someone's wardrobe.

STYLE CONSULTANT *See definition for* image consultant.

STYLING Styling is arranging things in a visually pleasing way. It can mean working in varied areas, including fashion styling, hair styling, makeup styling, food styling, or prop styling.

STYLING KIT A collection of tools that enables stylists to do their jobs properly and efficiently.

SYNTHETIC FIBERS Fibers that are derived from liquid chemical mixtures that are extruded through small holes in showerhead-like devices called spinnerettes to form fibers and then hardened to maintain their shape.

TAGGING GUN Used by stylists and in retail stores to attach hangtags and price tags to clothing.

TALENT Usually known as the model, but can include anyone in front of the camera lens.

TALENT AGENCY Represents stylists, books jobs, and takes care of paperwork for a cut of the stylist's fee.

TEAR SHEETS Published print styling that has appeared in fashion magazines, printed advertisements, or catalogues.

TEST KITCHENS Kitchens independently owned, owned by publications, or owned by food companies. Sometimes photographers set up shoots involving food in test kitchens.

TEST SHOOTS Unpaid photo shoot collaboration between people who want to build or add to their portfolios.

TESTING The process of organizing and executing a test shoot.

THEMES Occur when multiple designers are showing the same trend, or when a trend can be seen frequently on the street.

TOOL BELT Stylists wear them during a shoot to hold small styling tools that they might need.

TOOLBOX Holds styling kit contents.

TRENDING The process of popular themes emerging in fashion.

URBAN SPORTY A clothing style characterized by traditional roomy cuts and athletic-inspired apparel.

VANITY SIZING A designer or manufacturer's practice of attributing a smaller size to a garment that may be larger than the measurements most commonly corresponding to that size in order to appease the customer.

VERTICAL LINES Lines that tend to elongate the areas of the body where they are worn.

VISUAL MERCHANDISING Involves using a wide variety of props to create retail displays.

VOUCHER A certificate issued by a stylist for free or discounted styling services or an agency receipt used to document a stylist's time on a set.

WARDROBE ASSISTANT A person who helps source and organize costumes and runs the wardrobe department of a film or television production.

WARDROBE CONSULTANT *See definition for* image consultant.

WARDROBE MISTRESS *See definition for* wardrobe assistant.

WARDROBE STYLING The process of finding and altering clothing and dressing talent for a film or television shoot.

WARDROBE SUPERVISOR A member of the production team who oversees the entire film or television cast's costumes and works closely with the director to execute the correct vision for the production.

WOVEN FABRICS Fabrics made of two different sets of yarns that intersect and interlace.

WRAP The end of the principal photography phase of a film or television production.

WRAP WORK Everything that is done after shooting ends. It is often done the day after the shoot. Wrap work includes invoicing, returning the borrowed clothing, and writing and submitting editorial credits taken from the cheat sheet.

Credits

Figure 2.12: Courtesy of Fairchild Archives
Figure 2.13: Courtesy of Fairchild Archives
Figure 2.14: Cyrus McCrimmon/
Getty Images
Feature 2.1: Adam Walker and Jen Drawas
Feature 2.2: Brandy Joy Smith

Chapter 3
Figure 3.0: Jamie McCarthy/Getty Images
Figure 3.1: ValeStock/Shutterstock.com
Figure 3.2a: BRENDAN SMIALOWSKI/
Getty Images
Figure 3.2b: Suhaimi Abdullah/
Getty Images
Figure 3.3: GP Images/Getty Images
Figure 3.4: Rob Kim/Getty Images
Figure 3.5: Colin McPherson/
Getty Images
Figure 3.6: Student project, designed by:
Amy Pospiech
Figure 3.7: Fairchild Books
Figure 3.8: EZIO PETERSEN/UPI Photo
Service/Newscom
Figure 3.9: Africa Studio/Shutterstock.com
Figure 3.10: © Hulton Archive/
Getty Images
Figure 3.11: Jenny B. Davis
Feature 3: Victoria Barban

Chapter 4
Figure 4.0: Mindy Small/FilmMagic/
Getty Images
Figure 4.1: Rodin Eckenroth/Getty Images
Figure 4.2: Todd Williamson/
Getty Images
Figure 4.3a: Courtesy of Fairchild Archives
Figure 4.3b: Courtesy of Fairchild Archives
Figure 4.3c: Karl Prouse/Catwalking/
Getty Images

Figure 4.3d: Catwalking/
Getty Images
Figure 4.4: Courtesy of Fairchild Archives
Figure 4.5a: Courtesy of Fairchild Archives
Figure 4.5b: Courtesy of WWD/
Steve Eichner
Figure 4.5c: Courtesy of WWD/
Steve Eichner
Figure 4.5d: Courtesy of Fairchild
Archives
Figure 4.5e: Catwalking/Getty Images
Figure 4.5f: Karwai Tang/Getty Images
Figure 4.5g: Courtesy of WWD/
George Chinsee
Figure 4.6: © Avital Aronowitz
Figure 4.7: Estrop/Getty Images
Feature 4: Preston Konrad

Chapter 5
Figure 5.0: Archard/WWD/
© Conde Nast
Figure 5.1: Astrid Stawiarz/Getty Images
Figure 5.2: Courtesy of WWD/
Steve Eichner
Figure 5.3: Courtesy of Fairchild Archives
Figure 5.4: Courtesy of CN Digital Studio
Figure 5.5: Fashion Snoops
Figure 5.6: LEON NEAL/AFP/
Getty Images
Figure 5.7: Emma Tuccillo
Figure 5.8a: Krzysztof Dydynski/
Getty Images
Figure 5.8b: VCG/Getty Images
Feature 5: Rebekkah Roy

Part 2
Part 2 Opener: Arun Nevader/
Getty Images

Chapter 6
Figure 6.0: Dabrowski/WWD/
© Conde Nast
Figure 6.1: Courtesy of WWD
Figure 6.2: © Superstock
Figure 6.3: Thos Robinson/Getty Images
Figure 6.4: HECTOR MATA/AFP/
Getty Images
Figure 6.5: Courtesy of misterleestyle.com
Feature 6: Alexandra Lipps

Chapter 7
Figure 7.0: ED JONES/AFP/Getty Images
Figure 7.1: Lisa Lake/Getty Images
Figure 7.2: Fairchild Books
Figure 7.3: Fairchild Books
Figure 7.4: Fairchild Books
Figure 7.5: Wallflower Management (SM)
Figure 7.6: Dabrowski/WWD/
© Conde Nast
Figure 7.7: Fairchild Books
Figure 7.8: Charley Gallay/Getty Images
Figure 7.9: Courtesy of WWD/
Kyle Ericksen
Feature 7: Joseph A. Delate

Chapter 8
Figure 8.0: Frank Povolny/Twentieth Century
Fox/Sunset Boulevard/Corbis via
Getty Images
Figure 8.1: Courtesy of WWD/
Thomas Iannaccone
Figure 8.2: Courtesy of CN Digital Studio
Figure 8.3: Michael Buckner/
Getty Images
Figure 8.4: Vasilina Popova/Getty Images
Figure 8.5: Courtesy of WWD
Figure 8.6: Paramount Pictures/
Getty Images

Figure 8.7: PBS/Photofest
Figure 8.8a: Courtesy of WWD
Figure 8.8b: Herbert Dorfman/Image
Works/Getty Images
Figure 8.8c: George Hoyningen-Huene/
Getty Images
Figure 8.8d: Archive Photos/Getty Images
Figure 8.8e: Petra Niemeier—K & K/
Redferns/Getty Images
Feature 8: Ise White

Chapter 9
Figure 9.0: Jenny B. Davis
Figure 9.1: moodboard Photography/Veer
Figure 9.2: Tasia Wells/Getty Images
Figure 9.3: Kzenon/Shutterstock.com
Figure 9.4: Courtesy of WWD/
Thomas Iannaccone
Figure 9.5: Fancy Photography/Veer
Figure 9.6: Ericksen/WWD/
© Conde Nast
Figure 9.7: RyanJLane/Getty Images
Figure 9.8: Fairchild Books
Figure 9.9: Matthias Nareyek/Getty Images
for Kilian Kerner
Figure 9T1: © Avital Aronowitz
Figure 9T2: mihalec/Shutterstock.com
Figure 9T3: © Avital Aronowitz
Figure 9T4: Courtesy of The Clutter Diet
www.clutterdiet.com
Figure 9T5: Avital Aronowitz
Figure 9T6: Avital Aronowitz
Figure 9T7: Avital Aronowitz
Figure 9T8: © Stockbyte
Figure 9T9: Courtesy of University Products,
Inc.
Figure 9T10: Avital Aronowitz
Figure 9T11: Avital Aronowitz

Figure 9T12: Avital Aronowitz
Figure 9T13: Avital Aronowitz
Figure 9T14: Avital Aronowitz
Figure 9T15: Avital Aronowitz
Figure 9T16: Avital Aronowitz
Figure 9T17: Courtesy of Betty Dain
          Creations, LLC
Figure 9T18: Courtesy of http://
          solutionsthatstick.com/
Figure 9T19: Avital Aronowitz
Figure 9T20: © Lusoimages—Objects/Alamy
Figure 9T21: Avital Aronowitz
Figure 9T22: © LAMB/Alamy
Figure 9T23: Avital Aronowitz
Figure 9T24: Avital Aronowitz
Figure 9T25: omphoto/Shutterstock.com
Figure 9T26: Avital Aronowitz

Figure 9T27: Billion Photos/Shutterstock.com
Figure 9T28: Avital Aronowitz
Feature 9: Cynthia Altoriso

Chapter 10
Figure 10.0: Rochelle Brodin Photography/
          Getty Images
Figure 10.1: Courtesy of WWD/
          Steve Eichner
Figure 10.2: Courtesy of WWD/
          Kyle Ericksen
Figure 10.3: Hulton Archive/Getty Images
Figure 10.4: Fairchild Books
Figure 10.5: Avital Aronowitz
Box 10 ab: Fairchild Books
Feature 10: Melissa Rodwell

Index

CPSIA information can be obtained
at www.ICGtesting.com
Printed in the USA
BVHW051207231121
622110BV00001B/1